MANAGEMENT
AND
CREATIVITY

Dedicated to Tony Wright (1934–2002), creative businessman.

MANAGEMENT AND CREATIVITY

FROM CREATIVE INDUSTRIES TO CREATIVE MANAGEMENT

CHRIS BILTON

BLACKWELL PUBLISHING
350 Main Street, Malden, MA 02148-5020, USA
9600 Garsington Road, Oxford OX4 2DQ, UK
550 Swanston Street, Carlton, Victoria 3053, Australia

First published 2007 by Blackwell Publishing Ltd

1   2007

Library of Congress Cataloging-in-Publication Data

Bilton, Chris.
　Management and creativity : from creative industries to creative management / Chris Bilton.
　　p. cm.
　Includes bibliographical references and index.
　ISBN-13: 978-1-4051-1995-5 (hardback : alk. paper)
　ISBN-10: 1-4051-1995-0 (hardback : alk. paper)
　ISBN-13: 978-1-4051-1996-2 (pbk. : alk. paper)
　ISBN-10: 1-4051-1996-9 (pbk. : alk. paper)   1. Management.   2. Creative ability in business.
　I. Title.

　HD31.B4965 2007
　658.4′063–dc22

2006002731

A catalogue record for this title is available from the British Library.

Set in 11/13pt Dante
by Graphicraft Limited, Hong Kong
Printed and bound in Singapore
by C.O.S. Printers Pte Ltd

For further information on
Blackwell Publishing, visit our website:
www.blackwellpublishing.com

CONTENTS

Foreword viii

Acknowledgements xi

Introduction: Creativity and the Creative Industries xiii

1 Defining Creativity 1

A Tale of Two Corridors 1

What Is Creativity? 2

What Creativity Is Not 7

Case Study: A Vision in a Dream? 10

Mapping the Great Divide: From Education to the Workplace 12

The Mythology of Genius 14

Case Study: The Genius and the Water-carrier 18

False Profits: The Creative Industries 19

2 From Individuals to Processes: Creative Teams and Innovation 23

From Individuals to Teams 23

Innovation and Teams 24

Beyond Specialization: Creative Work in the Creative Industries 26

Playing Many Parts: Creative Roles in the Creative Industries 28

Case Study: Repositioning Creativity in Advertising 30

Growing the Creative Team: Familiarization or Specialization? 33

Managing the Creative Team 34

Creative Tension and the Need for Trust 39

Creative Teams Need Uncreative People 42

**3 Creative Systems: Implications for Management and
    Policy in the Creative Industries**   **45**
    The Cultural Geography of the Creative Industries   46
    The Strength of Weak Ties   47
    Case Study: Theatre as a Creative System   50
    Implications for Management   52
    Managing Creative Systems by 'Brokering' Knowledge   56
    Implications for Policy   59
    Systems and Sustainability   62

**4 Managing Creative Work through Release and Control:
    The Myth of the Self-motivated Creative Worker**   **66**
    The World Turned Upside Down   66
    Case Study: Changing Management Styles at the BBC   67
    Whistle While You Work: Changing Theories of Employee Motivation 70
    Out of Control: The Myth of the Self-motivated Creative Worker   72
    The Isolation of Creative Work   74
    Bounded Creativity: Creativity through Control and Constraint   76
    Case Study: Musician for Hire – Boundaries for Musical Composition 78
    False Freedom: The New Management Style in Practice   80
    Case Study: Management in the Movies – Wise Children and Men
      in Suits   81
    Beginnings and Endings   85
    The Rules of the Game   87

5 Seeing the Pattern: Strategy, Leadership and Adhocracy   **91**
    The Strategy Wars: Orientation versus Animation   91
    Strategy and Creativity   92
    Strategy in an Open System   96
    Case Study: Emergent Patterns in Film Marketing   97
    Strategy as Continuity in Change   102
    Case Study: Are You Paying Attention? Jazz, Improvisation and
      Creative Listening in Strategy Formation   106
    Strategy and Posthocracy: Being Decisive   108
    Strategy as Process   111

6 Business Development and Organizational Change   **116**
    What Is Organizational Change?   116
    The Change Cycle   118
    Incremental Change   121
    Case Study: Creativity and Change at Marks and Spencer   122
    The Aesthetics of Organizational Change: Organizational Integrity 126

Aligning Individual and Collective Change   129
Evolutionary Change   132
Creativity and Change   135

7 From Creative Marketing to Creative Consumption   138
Symbolic Goods   138
Postmodern Marketing   139
Case Study: Arts Marketing – From Products to Experiences 142
From Segments to Sub-cultures: Bringing the Audience Back in 145
The New Value Chain   147
Case Study: In Search of Oldton   149
Towards the Social Product   151
Letting Go   153
The Aesthetics of Marketing   155

8 The Politics of Creativity   159
Promoting the Creative Economy   159
Case Study: Creative New Zealand – The Branding of Creativity 163
From 'Cultural' to 'Creative' Industries   164
Creative Industries and Cultural Policy: Assumptions and Models 166
The Politics of Management   171
Creativity Is Difficult   172

Bibliography   176
Index   186

FOREWORD

The concept of the creative industries as a key driver of post-industrial public policy only really emerged in the wake of the Labour party's election victory in the spring of 1997. Under the leadership of Chris Smith, Secretary of State at the newly renamed Department for Culture, Media and Sport, the importance of the creative industries was quickly enshrined as an article of faith.

The centuries-old orthodoxy that culture mattered only to the extent that it was 'good for you' was jettisoned in favour of a belief that creativity and innovation not only contributed to the cultural richness of the nation but also, and increasingly, to its economic well-being.

The creative industries, it was argued – industries like film, music, design and fashion – generated intellectual property in the form of copyrights, patents and trademarks which, at their core, had substantial economic value. They created highly skilled jobs. They gave rise to the dissemination of innovative ideas and knowledge with applications in a number other spheres – many of which, such as computing or engineering, had historically seemed totally divorced from creativity. Among other things, the rise of the concept of the creative industries challenged C. P. Snow's long accepted shibboleths about the Two Cultures.

These developments were extremely welcome to those of us who had spent some twenty dismal years arguing with a seemingly endless succession of Conservative ministers that creativity and culture mattered, not only because they offered pleasure and enlightenment, but also because their seemingly intangible products generated something of real value to the underlying economy.

In the rush to embrace refreshing and invigorating new ideas, some policy wonks and commentators became hopelessly seduced by the gloss and the hyperbole, by the belief that the creative industries would, in fairly short order, replace much of the manufacturing economy as we had known it. At their most extreme, they even encouraged us to include 'Call Centres' (which have unquestionably formed an integral – if temporary – part of the economy of some regions of the UK) as part of this new 'knowledge economy'.

It was, of course, pretty unarguable that traditional manufacturing was in decline, but the notion that these creative industries would supplant long-established and well-entrenched manufacturing sectors was advanced with far too little serious thought.

Conversely, there were those who refused to buy into the concept of the creative industries at all, somehow seeing these industries as a soft and easy option to the challenge of developing a 'real and sustainable' industrial strategy. They preferred to look to a renewal based on a much lamented industrial heritage typified by thousands of well-ordered men, and even a few women, happily marching through factory gates with lunchboxes under their arms, as the 7 o'clock 'hooter' blew on what was invariably a cold, damp and misty morning.

Whilst these differing visions of the future jostled for attention, globalization continued its inexorable march, and the Internet began to really make itself felt as a crucial instrument of economic, cultural and societal change. It became increasingly difficult to credibly argue that the creative industries agenda was merely a passing fad, soon to be replaced by a return to some improved form of metal bashing. The term 'creative economy' began in a very helpful way to reduce hostility to the notion of the creative industries as it became increasingly obvious that these two visions of our industrial future were in fact, at heart, entirely complementary.

The prominence given to the concept of a genuinely 'creative' economy reinvigorated 'industrial' and cultural policy in the UK around a few very specific forms of intellectual property. It also helped to ensure that the disciplines that underpinned creativity and innovation became part of the policy landscape across a far wider range of disciplines. This was true not only in Britain but far beyond. The European Union's Lisbon Agenda was constructed upon the idea of promoting a knowledge economy which, in turn, owed much to the early thinking that lay behind the development of the UK's creative economy.

In the midst of these developments, the concept of creativity, always nebulous at best, became ever more difficult to pin down. It was unquestionably an advance to ensure that creativity was not exclusively defined by its association with individual inspiration or genius – that traditional Romantic model had remained dominant for far too long. Needless-to-say there was also a danger that the very notion of creativity could become so generalized as to allow *any* activity, such as parking a car, to be redefined as a creative act!

Unfortunately, in the headlong rush towards transformation, many of the issues around the management of creativity became marginalized. Managing creativity can be a difficult and demanding process. Without effective management, it is very unlikely that the optimum value of creativity and innovation will ever be unlocked. Therefore, this failure to engage with issues around management was a serious one.

In the pages that follow Chris Bilton admirably addresses many of the issues that surround the management of creativity in an environment increasingly reliant on innovation and intellectual property. Chris persuasively argues that our concept of creativity cannot simply be reduced to innovation, any more than it can be passed off as an act of individual genius. Creativity has to be understood as part of a complex cultural phenomenon, one in which the movement of different forces, one against another, shapes the final result.

He goes on to argue that the idea of a rigid distinction between creatives on the one hand, and 'uncreative' managers on the other is an illusion. As he puts it: 'The separation of creative individuals from their . . . managers, and the splitting of innovation and novelty from questions of value and judgement reflects a partial, incomplete view of the creative process.'

As a former film producer, I believe that Chris's notion that creativity is distributed across teams and organizations, and does not simply attach to the 'genius' of a single individual, is profoundly right. This is, for example, where those who developed the 'auteur' theory of film making went badly astray – they argued that the director of a film, to the virtual exclusion of all other creative inputs, including those of the scriptwriter, was the sole source of creative inspiration behind a film. Experience has shown me time and time again that the film making process is primarily a highly collaborative process in which creativity engages the talents of a great number of people, albeit that the director's vision is invariably the most influential.

Chris subjects the current and wildly over-simplified notions of creativity and innovation to rigorous interrogation. He is right that 'definitions of creativity and the creative industries have been deliberately extended and manipulated', sometimes to a point at which they cease to be meaningful, becoming instead synonyms for just about any form of activity that involves 'novelty'. Conversely, as he argues, we have been too quick to adopt a 'management by the numbers' approach to what are sometimes very complex issues. What is clear is that, in the end, the process that we have come to call 'creativity' rests on a series of extremely complex interactions between very different kinds of people. This important book demonstrates exactly why a full understanding of creativity really matters – not only in the context of developing more vibrant and personally satisfying areas of economic activity, but even more importantly, in its ability to help us develop a better understanding of the value of creative individuals in the twenty-first century.

David Puttnam, May 2006

ACKNOWLEDGEMENTS

This book has developed out of my teaching at Warwick and my experience of working in the cultural sector. Ideas have been assembled from books, seminars, parties, arguments, conversations, offices, pubs and rehearsal rooms featuring a cast too numerous to mention. What follows is a list of the main protagonists.

First I would like to thank all my students and colleagues at the University of Warwick. The content of this book is a direct product of running the MA in Creative and Media Enterprises at the Centre for Cultural Policy Studies since 1999 – proof that 'teaching-based research' can be a more enriching collaborative process than research-based teaching. Special thanks to my colleague Ruth Leary for helping to develop my ideas about creativity, and to Dave Wilson and Steve Cummings at Warwick Business School for helping develop my ideas about management – and for introducing me to the creative side of business schools. Thanks also to Steve for advice on an early draft of the book.

Thank you to Lord Puttnam for writing the foreword. As somebody who has successfully combined the roles of artist, entrepreneur, manager and educator, he was one of the inspirations for this book.

Other direct and indirect contributors include: Jerry Ahearne, Balloonatics Theatre Company, Jeremy Bennett, Roger Bolton, Paul Brindley, Bill Cashmore, Hannah Charlton, Mike Crossman, Paul Dornan, Gonzalo Enriquez-Soltero, Susan Fenichell, Frank Ferrie, Simon Goldberg, John Goudie, Matt Hardisty, Nick Hornby (for performance-related pay), Geraint Howells, Chris Johnston, Peter Jukes, Sylvia King, Anne Leer, Ben Lockwood, Heather Maitland, Debbie Manners, Jim McGuigan, Mark McGuinness, Sam Mendes, Neil Mullarkey, Steve Perrin, Richard Perkins (librarian, researcher, midfield dynamo), Eileen Quinn, Alan Rivett, Mike Sims, Nigel Sykes, Tim Walker, Alison Wenham and Tim Wright.

One of the themes of this book is that ideas are cheap – it is what you do with them that counts. I must accordingly pay tribute to a small group of people who helped to turn my ideas into realities. Thanks to Oliver Bennett not only for encouraging and cajoling me to write this book (Theory X and Theory Y), but for getting me started on all this in the first place. Thanks to Rosemary Nixon at Blackwell

Publishing for recognizing what I was trying to do with the book and for her enthusiasm and expertise. Thanks to the rest of the team at Blackwell Publishing for making sure everything ran smoothly and for answering all my questions. A special thank you to Elaine Bingham for her patient and thorough work as my copy editor.

Finally, the biggest thanks of all go to my wife, Anna Wright, not only for creating the space for me to write this book but also for her invaluable editorial comments on the final draft. And for managing me.

INTRODUCTION: CREATIVITY AND THE CREATIVE INDUSTRIES

'Creative', 'creation', 'creativity' are some of the most overused and ultimately debased words in the language. Stripped of any special significance by a generation of bureaucrats, civil servants, managers and politicians, lazily used as political margarine to spread approvingly and inclusively over any activity with a non-material element to it, the word 'creative' has become almost unusable.

(Tusa 2003: 5–6)

[The creative industries are] those industries which have their origin in individual creativity, skill and talent and which have a potential for wealth and job creation through the generation and exploitation of intellectual property.

(Department for Culture,
Media and Sport 1998)[1]

Creativity Is Difficult

Creativity and the creative industries are the success stories of the new century. Creativity, once considered to be the work of God, or latterly the work of the god-like artist-genius, has been democratized. Today, politicians, business leaders, footballers and schoolchildren aspire to be 'creative'. In business, creativity has become the key to unlocking competitive advantage in crowded markets. In almost every field of human endeavour, the word 'creative' is a promiscuous prefix, used to signal generalized approval – so not only do we have creative industries, a creative economy, creative thinking, creative accountancy, but also a host of registered businesses and domain names which have incorporated 'creativity' or 'creative' into their titles. Creativity is everywhere and nowhere – paradoxically, while it is accessible to all, it is nevertheless marketed as a rare commodity.

As a result of this ubiquity, creativity has been devalued through over-use, emptied out of any real meaning. One of the difficulties with defining creativity is its mystical, quasi-spiritual quality. In the Western philosophical tradition, creativity is associated with a kind of irrationality or divine madness, opposed to the rules and boundaries of common sense and reason. This mystical quality has allowed creativity to be claimed by everybody. We all have our moments of madness, and according to this discourse of irrational creativity, we all possess the potential to be creative. Our only problem is that we do not seem able to unlock our potential. Accordingly training courses, self-help books, 'inspirational' literature and management gurus promise to give us the key. We are all frustrated novelists, unfulfilled creative geniuses, prize-winning artists in waiting. The lucky few who make it are simultaneously envied and patronized – they may be successful, but we could have done it too, if only we had really let ourselves go, if only we had the time, resources and techniques to exploit our own undoubted talents. Privately, we might comfort ourselves with the thought that these creative types are not to be taken too seriously – they have embraced the irrational impulses we all have, but are too sensible to express, they are the holy fools and office jokers, possessed of luck and a lack of inhibitions rather than any real talent or propensity for hard work.

One of the arguments of this book is that 'creativity' is actually a much more complex, demanding process than simply coming up with bright ideas, being 'inspired' or indulging in moments of spontaneous invention. Accordingly, while 'creativity' is not the possession of a precious handful of geniuses, nor is it something we all have within us, if only we dared follow our impulses. Rather it depends upon a combination of processes and personalities which might appear contradictory. Creativity requires that we think irrationally *and* rationally, that we cross boundaries between different ways of thinking, that we not only have the ideas but the resources and inclinations to do something with them. Creative individuals have the ability to hold these different, often contradictory impulses in equilibrium. But the ability to combine different thinking styles and processes is not the sole possession of creative individuals – it is, if anything, more likely to be found in groups of people working together, in teams, networks and systems, bringing together complementary competences and personalities.

The focus of this book is on creativity in systems and organizations rather than creative individuals. This is not to deny that creative individuals do exist, but they certainly do not fit the stereotype of the spontaneous, natural genius. Creativity is difficult. Even Mozart had to learn to play the piano, even Coleridge started with a first draft. Creative people know how to deploy and manipulate their own talents and those of other people, crossing and recrossing different perspectives and different stages in a process. Shakespeare's genius depended not only on his own invention but on his ability to draw out and develop his own ideas and the ideas of other people, from the actors he worked with to the historians and storytellers of the past.

Definitions of creativity are riddled with ideas of duality and paradox, the combination of different ideas into new and unexpected patterns, combinations of innovation and value, of different thinking styles, rationality and irrationality. While these combinations might be sustained by exceptional individuals, they are more likely to be achieved through networks and systems. This leads us into a consideration of the possibilities of creativity in management and the creative industries.

Creativity in Management: Tolerating Difference

Creativity in management discourse has suffered the same fate as creativity in general. A complex, multifaceted process has been reduced down to a stereotype. When managers talk about creativity, they are often referring to the capacity to innovate or to 'think different'. But the capacity to come up with new ideas and challenge conventional ways of thinking is not in itself always very useful. Individual innovation and non-conformity is ultimately destructive and pointless unless linked into the needs of the organization as a whole. Individual creativity needs to be integrated with organizational resources, capacities and systems if new ideas are ever to bear fruit.

More broadly, creativity in management is used to describe alternative approaches to business processes, such as strategy formation and organizational change, and at the operational level to refer to new product development and technological innovation. Again, there is a danger of romanticizing or over-selling the purely innovative aspects of creativity and ignoring more incremental, less dramatic aspects of changing organizations and products. The desire to think outside the box and challenge conventional wisdom is all very well, but can also lead to rash decisions and a fetishization of novelty at the expense of continuity. Innovations need to be applied and integrated. Behind much of the rhetoric of creativity in management is a binary opposition between 'business as usual' and 'challenge everything', with the assumption that creativity requires a radical break with tradition and convention, while any more pragmatic, grounded approaches to management are to be derided as 'uncreative'. In fact the challenge of creativity in management is to overcome these stereotypes of novelty and continuity, and to find ways of stitching together or tolerating the paradoxes and contradictions between them. This acceptance of eclecticism and paradox is to be found in the work of many management theorists, notably Charles Handy and Henry Mintzberg.

Once we define creativity in terms of duality and contradiction, the implications for management extend beyond the obvious applications of creativity in product development and innovation. This book will consider creativity in relation to organizational structure and strategy, attempting to get beyond the stereotypical opposition of 'creative' and 'uncreative' approaches. If creativity is seen in terms of complex systems and developing relationships between apparently contradictory elements, then management becomes in itself a creative process. One of the arguments of this book is that just as creative artists are far better managers than they are prepared to admit, so too managers are required to be creative, especially as they confront increasingly complex organizations and unpredictable markets.

Creativity in the Creative Industries: All Our Futures?

The third strand in this book is a re-evaluation of the meaning and significance of the so-called 'creative industries'. What began as an opportunistic yoking together of art and industry in cultural policy for purposes of advocacy and investment has now been enthusiastically adopted by politicians, analysts and educators around the world as an umbrella term covering all or some of the arts, media and entertainment industries and associated branches of the knowledge economy. Today's creative industries are said to represent some of the fastest growing sectors of the global economy. Because they deal in intangibles, there is apparently no limit to their potential.

The value of these industries is measured not only in export earnings and GDP. Politicians and artists have claimed a plethora of economic and non-economic benefits flowing from the creative industries, with very little evidence to support them. Through employment, the creative industries are said to offer a key to social inclusion, a means for physical and spiritual regeneration, a source of identity and self-esteem, a solution to crime and delinquency, an alternative religion and a new moral and spiritual basis for our society. The political promises made on behalf of art and culture multiplied in the 1980s when advocates in Europe and the United States attempted to convince sceptical and fiscally conservative governments that the arts were worth investing in and represented 'value for money'. Research into the economic benefits and social impacts of the creative industries has subsequently been driven by political expediency and a pragmatic desire to justify public expenditure; policy has defined the research agenda rather than the other way round. Now these claims are being taken seriously, and the creative industries are seen to represent the cutting edge of a new creative economy.

As with creativity itself and creativity in management, the term 'creative industries' succeeds in being both over-simplified and vague. The UK government's 1998 definition, based on 'individual creativity, skill and talent' and 'the generation of intellectual property' is typical of the questionable assumptions made by politicians about the meaning and purpose of creativity. It is also so broadly framed as to be virtually meaningless – very few industries, businesses or workers are not to some extent implicated here and surely no self-respecting business could admit to lacking individual creativity, skill or talent. Very few contemporary businesses do not generate some form of intellectual property, in the form of copyright, trademarks or patents. The average family car is an amalgam from patents and trademarks no less than it is a physical construct of metal, glass and oil. Yet variations on this definition have been adopted by several governments including Taiwan, Singapore, Korea, Hong Kong, Canada, Australia and New Zealand. The effect has been to change the status of arts and culture from a matter for cultural policy into an issue of economic development and wealth creation.

What is interesting here is the attempt to redefine what used to be called the 'cultural' industries in terms of inputs (individual creativity, skill and talent) and outputs (intellectual property, profits). This definition frames the creative industries in terms of a conventional value chain, with products passing down the production line from producer to consumer. The definition also highlights the 'innovative', product-development aspects of the sector, over the cultural context which gives these products value and meaning. In this definition, questions of value are deferred and new ideas are de facto creative (provided they have the potential to generate wealth, of course). By equating creativity with novelty (and value with profit), the more complex production and distribution processes of the creative industries, frequently as much concerned with the reconfiguring and repackaging of existing ideas as with the generation of new ones, is reduced to a stream of new products. The difficulty of predicting and assigning value as a philosophical and economic problem and a managerial necessity is neatly sidestepped.

By emphasizing novelty over value and by focusing on individual talent over the contexts and collective processes through which talented individuals thrive, the creative industries concept perpetuates a singular notion of creativity and presents a simplified version of the cultural production process. As any film producer knows, there is no correlation between inputs and outputs in the creative industries. Processes are unpredictable and discontinuous. Creative industries are primarily in the business of communicating to audiences ideas, images and experiences, identified by Bourdieu as 'symbolic goods'.[2] The economic value of these goods is dependent on subjective interpretations of meaning. The creative industries are driven by value networks and relationships between producers, consumers and intermediaries, but these rarely proceed in a linear fashion. The assumption of profitability and merito-cracy contained in the metaphor of the supply chain ignores the messy, unpredictable and asymmetric relationship between production and distribution.

This complexity is, of course, one of the elements which makes the creative industries an important area of investigation for students of management and organization – but it does not make a comforting story for politicians and investors. Ironically, by attempting to describe the creative industries in terms of a conventional industry supply chain, today's cultural policy makers have reversed an emerging con-sensus among analysts and observers. Far from mimicking mainstream commodity production, the creative industries are being seen as a new model for others to fol-low. As noted by Scott Lash and John Urry, instead of creative industries becoming more like ordinary industries, ordinary manufacturing industry is becoming more and more like the creative industries (Lash and Urry 1994: 123).

In particular, the complex, contradictory nature of the creative industries has neces-sitated new approaches to organizational structure and strategy. These new ways of doing business in the creative sector may well be far more significant in the long run than the quantifiable benefits of the creative industries. By pitching the creative industries in terms of a string of (admittedly impressive) statistics, well-intentioned politicians have over-sold their economic significance and over-looked their under-lying structural capital. Instead of looking to the creative industries as the future base of a new global economy, we might instead consider their role as sources of new systems and structures. This book attempts to explore the creative industries not as a symptom of the creative economy, but as a process of organizing creativity and managing creatively.

The Creative Economy: Substitute or Prototype?

The creative industries are themselves only one aspect of a broader creative economy, whose currency is intellectual property. So in addition to the copyright industries, which broadly correspond to the creative industries, we have patent industries (science and innovation, research and development), trademark industries (brand-builders like Nike) and design-led industries (industries where form matters more than content). The influence of creativity on the economy is not restricted to discrete sectors. Intellectual property has now become a key ingredient in traditional industries like automobiles (patents, design) or agriculture (now perhaps seen as a sub-sector of the biotechnology industry).

At the same time as definitions of creativity and the creative economy have extended to encompass other forms of industry, the definition of culture has been broadened to include popular and commercial forms of entertainment. In order to compete for resources and prestige, the cultural sector has emphasized its economic outputs (measured in employment, export earnings, contribution to GDP) and economic significance (in relation to urban regeneration, civic marketing, tourism, quality of life). Consequently, the new creative economy has become pervasive and all-consuming. The creativity of industry (dynamic managers who 'thrive on chaos') and the industrialization of creativity (never mind the quality, measure the outputs) have in turn become allied with a neo-liberal celebration of the virtues of the new creative economy. According to its advocates in industry, politics and the arts, the creative economy stands at the threshold of a new industrial age, based on culture and creativity instead of material things.

The creative economy is likened to a paradigm shift from one industrial order to another, from Fordism to post-Fordism, from bricks to clicks, from atoms to bits. Here 'creativity' is thrown into the melting pot with an amalgam of economic, social and cultural transformations to suggest an emergent new world order. In reality, the transition towards new forms of production has been much more patchy. The creative industries continue to feed off and merge with traditional industries and vice versa. The 'weightless economy' of ideas and images still depends on manual labour for its logistics, hardware and transportation, even if some of this dirty work is kept discreetly hidden in the sweatshops and call centres of the developing world. What we have in fact seen is a reconfiguration of the old patterns of production and distribution on a global scale. The division of labour in the creative industries is based on a new economic geography. While the film industry has concentrated its capital and symbolic assets in Hollywood, its material production and labour costs have been exported to cheaper countries. The old economy continues as it always has done, providing the labour and the material components, while the glamorous world of creativity and culture takes the credit and the profit.

There is a moral dimension to the notion that the creative economy can provide a viable substitute for the old economy. As factories close and arts centres open, enthusiasm for the 'thriving' creative industries has encouraged politicians to abandon support for a 'dying' manufacturing industry. Yet manufacturing continues to be the main source of mass employment, while the creative economy is more likely to be characterized by self-employment and micro-businesses for an educated minority. Not all of us can afford to live on thin air. No matter how successful the creative economy becomes, it can never entirely replace or be independent of more traditional industries and skills. The new creative class relies on an army of skilled and unskilled workers to do its dirty work. While creative professionals congregate in metropolitan districts and bohemian communities, manufacturing, logistics and infrastructure have been exported to less fashionable areas or to other countries.

The danger of a 'digital divide' between information haves and have-nots was first highlighted by the American communications scholar Herb Schiller in the 1980s. His warning was repeated by Vice President Al Gore as the US government began to assemble the new global information infrastructure in the mid-1990s. The class divide between the creative class and the old working class is reproduced in the new cultural geography, linking up Indian call centres and Chinese manufacturing plants to global headquarters in Japan, the US and Europe. There may be a similar class divide within the creative economy itself, with the peaks of success disguising the large number of people who live in the creative economy but barely make a living. As will be discussed later in this book, the economics of the creative industries and the creative economy continue to favour those who exploit intellectual property rather than those who generate it. Living on one's wits – on 'creativity' – is appealing, but it may also carry a financial cost, borne disproportionately by the unpaid, aspirant and temporary workers at the bottom of the industry food chain.

Aside from the moral and political implications, there may be some more pragmatic reasons for questioning the creative economy as a substitute for the old economy. The statistical growth of the creative industries disguises the fact that many of those working there are either self-employed or dependent upon temporary project-based contracts, and the employment statistics are complicated by the complex definition of cultural work. Employment in the creative economy is tenuous and unpredictable, with little chance of career progression or job security. It has already been suggested that the tidy definition of the creative industries in terms of supply and demand, linear production processes and the generation of profit is a gross over-simplification. The capital assets of the creative economy are impressive, but depend primarily upon a valuation of intangible assets and future profits. This adds a volatile element to the creative economy, famously exposed in the collapse of the Internet-based dot.com companies in the late 1990s. The closest analogy here is the financial services industry, where profits depend upon the perceptions and good faith of the investors. In December 2001 the collapse of Enron, the utilities and financial services company, indicated the dangers of an economy built on thin air. While they would not recognize the imputations of fraud and corruption, many managers in the creative and media industries would perhaps empathize with the 'creative accountancy' of Enron, where future value is the basis for current valuation and where real assets are far less significant than intangibles and customer perceptions.

To reiterate the earlier comments about the creative industries, this volatility and complexity is precisely why the creative economy merits serious study – not because it represents a bright new future, but because it represents a future of uncertainty and risk. We should not pretend that the creative economy is going to provide a new era of unlimited profit and social integration. On the contrary, it may turn out to be no better or worse than what has gone before. What does seem clear is that certain elements of the creative economy, in particular the dependence on intangible assets and the reliance on customer perception as the basis of all economic value rather than any agreed 'gold standard', are likely to become more widespread for all of us. The management systems and structures which have evolved in the creative economy provide a case study in the management of risk and unpredictability. The social and organizational structures of the creative economy may turn out to be more significant than its profits and turnover. Many of the headline features of the new economy – decentralization, fragmentation, risk, uncertainty, intangibility, individualism – have been the historic reality of the creative and media industries. A study of the management and organization of the creative industries is therefore timely. The creative economy does not represent a 'substitute' for the old economy – on the other hand, in some of its constituent components, it may represent a laboratory for the future.

To summarize, creativity and the creative industries have been oversold. Definitions of creativity and the creative industries have been deliberately extended and manipulated, partly for self-serving reasons, partly to paint an inviting picture of our social and economic futures. In the process, the idea of creativity has been disconnected from the values which give it meaning and reduced to a banal pursuit of novelty. The creative industries have been similarly decontextualized, singled out for special mention as the cutting edge of a new economy. In reality the creative industries and the creative economy represent a shift in the way the economy as a whole is functioning, rather than a coherent category or industry sub-sector.

The aim of this book is first to rediscover a usable definition of creativity from the hype surrounding the creative industries and the creative economy. This definition of creativity will draw on psychological theories of creativity to emphasize the duality and complexity of creativity, rooted in innovation and the pursuit of meaning. At the same time, the book will attempt to reconnect the creative industries with a meaningful context, seeing the creative industries not as a substitute for ordinary manufacturing industry but as a set of business practices, patterns of work and organization where creativity in all its complexity and contradictions is being applied and tested. From the beginning, I wish to challenge the myth that managers are uncreative and artists are unmanageable. The book argues that creativity is a deliberately managed process and that management is necessarily and inherently creative. The corollary to this is an examination of the different forms creativity can take in business and of how its complex and contradictory qualities can be developed and sustained.

Research for this book has drawn on two related sources. First, I have focused on arts and media organizations, specifically smaller idea-generating enterprises, as a kind of laboratory where the inherent tensions and complexities of creative business management are being pioneered and tested. While these smaller enterprises are of course concerned with the realities of business survival, their lifeblood is their capacity to come up with new and marketable ideas. They are thus dealing with the everyday problems of management (cashflow, organizational change, suppliers and customers, etc.), but their major preoccupation is with managing their own creativity.

Secondly, I have drawn upon an existing literature on the creativity of management. The rhetoric of 'creativity' has permeated business management and business
schools over the past 20 years, not just in the special case of arts and media organizations, and not only under familiar headings such as 'product innovation' and 'risk
taking'. All managers are pursuing creative approaches to organizational change,
strategy formation and marketing. Yet some of these approaches rely upon a self-
regarding rhetoric of creativity which has little to do with the realities of the
creative process. I argue that creativity in business amounts to more than simply taking risks and thinking different.

Chapter 1 introduces a definition of creativity based on psychological theory as a
complex, multidimensional process. This complexity is contrasted with the rhetoric
of genius and the attempt to isolate creativity, creative people and the creative
industries themselves in terms of individual talent and novelty. Individualism and spontaneous inventiveness underpin Western popular and managerial attitudes to creativity.
According to this book, such attitudes are divisive both organizationally and socially,
and do little to nurture real creativity.

The next two chapters examine creative organizations, drawing especially on the
experience of managing creativity in the creative industries. Chapter 2 extends
the definition of creativity into an examination of creative people and creative teams.
Is there such a thing as a creative individual, and what can managers do to cultivate a
creative capacity in their organization? Much of the literature on innovation has centred on attempts to classify and arrange people into roles and teams. But given the
complexity of creative processes, attempting to isolate a single source or structure
for creativity seems unproductive. At the micro-level, I argue that the key to creative
teamwork is not so much the mix of creative individuals as the individual's capacity
to play multiple roles and to step in and out of character.

Chapter 3 places the creative team into a broader context, examining creative organizations and creative systems. Drawing on the experience of the creative industries
and the dependence of creative organizations on networks and the wider creative
ecology, this chapter argues that relationships outside and between firms may be more
significant for creativity than the firm's internal structure. This in turn leads to a
reassessment of the creative value chain. If production processes are outsourced and
spread across networks and chains outside the firm, managers and policy makers
need to focus less on creative individuals and new ideas, and more on the transactions and exchanges which precede and follow the point of innovation.

In chapters 4, 5 and 6, the book's attention shifts from the management of
creativity towards the creativity of management, considering how 'creativity' is
interpreted in management theory. Chapter 4 examines the relationship between
creativity, motivation and freedom. One of the prevailing myths of creativity is that
creative people work best when they are cut loose from all constraints. This assumption is part of an emergent orthodoxy in management books, represented by Tom
Peters' 'liberation management' and the attempt to recast management as funky,
creative and anarchic. According to this argument, perhaps the best thing a manager
can do for creativity is to put all the creative people in a room and wait outside with
the door closed. In this chapter I argue that creative processes and creative people
actually thrive on constraints and boundaries. Boundary-setting and targets need to

be seen as part of the creative process. This does not mean that managers need to be more or less strict with their deadlines and interventions; it suggests that creative and managerial processes are complementary rather than antagonistic.

Chapter 5 examines another area where management theory has embraced the rhetoric of creativity, in strategic planning and strategy formation. There is an analogy here between the creative process and the strategy process – both require moments of divergence and moments of synthesis. The most difficult part in the strategy process is perhaps the point where the pattern comes together and out of an apparently random sequence of decisions and events, a coherent direction and future intention emerges. Without this synthesis, strategy is arbitrary and chaotic. I argue that this process is analogous to the creative process. It is also connected to complexity theory and the emergence of order from chaos. But, at a more practical level, this alternation of randomness and purpose is typical of the planning process in creative organizations.

Chapter 6 compares the rhythm and structure of the creative process to the management of organizational change. Again, management theorists who apply creativity to organizational change tend to see creativity in terms of sudden leaps and breakthroughs. According to creativity theory, the process of change is more protracted and deliberate. Radical transformations and sudden discoveries rarely take place in isolation. A more considered, less flamboyant form of creativity underpins incremental change and implies a more deliberate, managed approach to both creativity and management.

Chapter 7 examines creativity in marketing. In the creative industries and in cultural theory, the audience or consumer has taken on a new importance. The audience-centred approach to value in the cultural sector is linked to postmodern theories of marketing; in both cases, the consumer takes centre-stage and the producer must learn to adapt and follow rather than attempting to lead. Marketing in the creative industries, because it deals in private interpretations of symbols and ideas and subjective definitions of value and beauty, has always had to deal with the unpredictable consumer. This chapter explores some of the implications of a creative approach to marketing.

Finally, in chapter 8 I return to the broader implications of a redefinition of creativity in terms of complexity and contradiction. What does this tell us about the future of the creative economy? Creative business management stands at the centre of a convergence between the creative, cultural sector and mainstream commerce which is prefigured in the creative industries. The creative economy is presented as the future not just of the creative industries, but also as the basis of a new knowledge-based capitalism. What are the political and cultural implications of this new economy and is the bright future it promises a real and sustainable one?

FURTHER READING

John Howkins gives an excellent overview of the 'creative economy' concept, basing his definition on the generation and exploitation of intellectual property (copyrights, patents, design rights) in *The Creative Economy: How People Make Money from Ideas* (2001). Howkins shares some of my criticisms of the 'specialization' of the creative industries concept in the UK, arguing that this rhetoric overlooks the creative function in other sectors, notably science, research and development and biotechnology.

Scott Lash and John Urry were among the first authors to articulate the convergence of 'creative' and 'ordinary' industries in their book *Economies of Signs and Space* (1994). Here they comment on the tendency for industry to become increasingly 'design-intensive' with the symbolic value and visual associations of products becoming more important and valuable than their material content and function. This leads them to conclude that the emerging economy will be based not on tangible products but on the encoding and decoding of 'signs' or, to follow Bourdieu's terminology, the production and consumption of symbolic goods and cultural capital. Lash and Urry's thesis has been criticized by Paul Du Gay and others in Du Gay and Pryke (2002).

For a critical discussion of the UK definition and concept of the 'creative industries' see Garnham (2005) and Heartfield (2000). Heartfield argues that the idea of the creative economy as a 'substitute' for traditional manufacturing industry is politically motivated wish fulfilment rather than commercial reality, and points to some of the ethical problems in investing resources (and hopes) in the creative industries at the expense of other forms of economic activity.

For a sophisticated and wide-ranging discussion of the creative industries from a non-UK perspective, see Caves (2000).

NOTES

1   The same definition is also used in the updated 2001 *Mapping Document*.
2   Bourdieu seems to have coined the phrase 'symbolic goods' in his book *Distinction* in 1979 (first translated into English in 1984). There is a more extensive discussion in the chapter entitled 'The Market for Symbolic Goods' in *The Rules of Art* (1996).

1 DEFINING CREATIVITY

The most fertile region [in the mind's inner land-scape] seems to be the marshy shore, the borderline between sleep and full awakening – where the matrices of disciplined thought are already oper-ating but have not yet sufficiently hardened to obstruct the dreamlike fluidity of imagination.

(Koestler 1976: 210)

Rather than setting out to paint something I begin painting and as I paint, the picture begins to assert itself . . . The first state is free, unconscious . . . the second stage is carefully calculated . . .

(Joan Miró in Sweeney 1948: 212)

A Tale of Two Corridors

Several years ago, a friend started working as a drama producer with one of Europe's largest commercial television companies. She shared her workspace with several other producers, mostly young, idealistic arts graduates who believed in the transforming power of art and literature. At the other end of a long corridor lay the commercial department, responsible for selling the programmes that she and her colleagues made to advertisers and other broadcasters. This room was full of older men, pragmatic and worldly-wise. The commercial and creative departments were divided not only by the corridor but by mutual suspicion, defensiveness and cultur-ally embedded assumptions and values. Nobody made the long walk from one office to the other, and the commercial and creative worlds remained separate. But she found herself drawn to the excitement of the business of television. She believed that understanding television commerce would make her a better television producer. And as an American woman who did not 'fit' into either of the predominantly male cultures which confronted each other in the organization, she found it easier to make the transition. So she began to walk the corridor. She startled her creative colleagues by pronouncing on the 'creativity of the deal' and surprised the commercial depart-ment with her interest and enthusiasm for making money. She has since become a leading film and television drama producer, as well as a successful entrepreneur, setting up her own company and selling it on to a larger media conglomerate, while continuing to forge creative partnerships with writers and directors.

What this story illustrates is the extraordinary polarization of 'creativity' and 'business' in Western culture, even within supposedly creative organizations. It also shows the extent to which the great divide is embedded in cultural assumptions which are in turn rooted in education and social class. Finally, it points to the possibility of crossing these barriers and suggests that real creativity does not lie in the self-contained and self-sufficient 'creative' team but in an ability to make connections between different ways of thinking and different types of people.

Roger Bolton is a prolific and respected composer of music for film and television. He tells the story of another corridor. This time it is an imaginary corridor, with a series of doors behind which different types of music are playing. He imagines himself walking along this corridor, half-opening the doors, allowing one piece of music to seep into another. In his own compositions, he works at great speed, using a computer to cut and paste themes and sounds, building the music in layers. As a composer of music for film and television, he is used to dealing with non-musicians and has trained himself not to talk about music to them; instead he uses emotions, visual metaphors, colours. His method of decoding a brief for a new composition is simple – ignore everything except the adjectives. He is a musical chameleon, adapting to conversations with media people, unsigned bands, software companies, pastiching musical styles and motifs in order to build musical pictures in the mind's eye of the listener. While he uses music technologies, what he does is not in any way mechanical or merely illustrative; he describes the need to surprise the listener, to subvert the expectations of the viewer and to exceed the expectations of the director. (For a more detailed discussion of Bolton's work, see the case study 'Musician for Hire' in chapter 4.)

This corridor, like the first, provides a metaphor for this book. In essence, the argument of this book is that creativity is not to be located in one state of mind, one room, one type of person, one individual. Rather it lies in the transition points between different ways of thinking. If we close the doors, we will never hear the full story. And above all we need to walk the corridor between creativity and the management of creativity. Creativity cannot exist in a 'pure' state, vacuum-packed. Creativity and business are not natural opponents – they have more in common than we may assume.

This book begins with an examination of the artificial distinctions and barriers which characterize contemporary definitions of 'creativity', and the origins of the great divide between 'creativity' and 'management' – the empty corridor. I will then argue that a richer, more complex definition of creativity already exists in the psychological literature. In the remainder of the book, by applying this multidimensional, dualistic definition of creativity to contemporary creative and management practices, we can perhaps begin to develop some more effective strategies for both.

What Is Creativity?

The easiest way to begin answering the age-old question, 'what is creativity?' is to consider what is missing from some of the current, popular definitions. In management literature, and in popular discourse, creativity has two principal aspects. First, creativity is all about novelty or difference – a deviation from conventional tools and perspectives. Secondly, and following on from this, it requires that creative individuals be given the freedom to express their individual talent or vision. These two themes, individualism and innovation, are rooted in a Western philosophical tradition which has reinforced a one-sided and destructive stereotype of creativity and creative people. What this conflation of creativity with individualism and innovation does is to disconnect creative thinking and creative people from the contexts and systems which give their innovations and individual talents meaning and value. It also perpetuates the idea that the creative industries can be separated out from 'ordinary' industries as a unique sphere of activity, as if creativity was the privilege of a few officially designated businesses and missing from everywhere else.

Psychological definitions of creativity generally contain two separate components. In the first place, creativity requires that we make or think something new, or a new combination of existing elements. This is the element of novelty or innovation already referred to. However, mere novelty is not enough. To be creative, the idea must also be useful, or valuable. This second part of the definition is reflected in the emphasis on 'problem-solving' in psychological creativity tests and in the argument that creative ideas must demonstrate 'fitness for purpose'.

Both these criteria are to some extent dependent upon context. Novelty is always relative. An idea might be new to the person who conceives of it, but as soon as this idea is expressed, it becomes clear that other people have got there first. After all, we have all had our temporary moments of brilliance. Margaret Boden distinguishes between these two levels of innovation as 'P-creativity' – that which is new to the individual – and 'H-creativity' – that which is new to the world (Boden 1994: 75–6). From a psychological perspective, the processes which lie behind these forms of innovation are essentially the same, but the outcomes have very different values. A personal breakthrough might impress our friends and families, but is of limited interest or value to anybody else. For an idea to be innovative in business or in art, it must deviate from the historically established norms and conventions, not just from our own personal history.

Once we introduce the notion of context, we introduce a second step in the creative process, beyond the original idea, and a second set of criteria. The idea or innovation must be tested against its external context. In order to meet the criteria required under patent law, innovation must represent a significant 'inventive step' beyond what is already known or done in the field, and it must make possible a new application or technique in practice. Similarly, for an idea to be protected under copyright law, it must be the deliberate result of individual skill, not accidental discovery, and the idea be expressed or 'fixed' in concrete, tangible form. Simply carrying an idea in one's head, and then claiming retrospectively that we had the idea before anybody else, is a form of intellectual sour grapes not defensible in law. So a writer might mail the idea for a new screenplay to an agent (or even to him/herself) in order to establish a paper trail which fixes the idea in a legally defensible form. The gap between having an idea and making it tangible or expressive is a painful one; the laborious development and application of the germinal idea is encompassed in the legal definition of intellectual property rights. It also recurs in creativity theory with the idea of creativity as a sequence encompassing different thinking styles.

The next stage or criterion in the creative process is that our idea has value or meaning. Our innovation must be not only novel, but useful; the phrase used in creativity testing is 'fitness for purpose'. Under US patent law, an innovative device or process must have 'utility'. This second half of the definition is more contentious than the first because value and usefulness are much more difficult to demonstrate. Again, context is all. Useful or valuable to whom, and for what? Some psychological studies resort to a definition of value as defined by a panel of experts within the appropriate field, so that Picasso's painting is 'creative' because art experts and art historians tell us so. In a business context, the value of an idea is likely to be measured against a specific set of criteria – did the innovation deliver on the brief? A brilliant advertisement which does not sell the product is not, according to this definition, creative, because it does not solve the client's problem. Of course the copywriter may argue that the client was asking the wrong question, so again the value of creativity in business, like the value of a work of art, becomes a matter for debate.

Other definitions of value centre on intention, not product. A child's drawings are random or incompetent, whereas Picasso's drawings are driven by a purpose or vision and executed by an experienced, trained artist with a historical knowledge of his field. This author-centred definition of value as 'innovation with a purpose' is accepted in psychological creativity tests but is less satisfactory when applied to the public sphere. Indeed, the childish drawings of a ten-year old may occasionally be valued as art, while many an artist (including Picasso perhaps) has found their own judgement out of step with that of the public. Good intentions alone do not make an innovation valuable; value, like originality, is dependent upon context, now or in the future. Before we can even begin to come up with a creative solution to a problem, we need to understand the context within which this problem has occurred and the values and assumptions that lie behind it. This is as true for an inventor like Thomas Edison as it is for painters and composers.

Finally, the assessment of value depends upon the circumstances surrounding the idea's reception as much as its production. An idea may strike a chord at a particular time, perhaps many years after its origin. So instead of fitness for purpose, we assess value according to fitness to the times. It is sometimes argued that the ideas and innovations which survive the test of time, and more especially of our times, have some absolute value which is not relative to the tastes and needs of the moment. Yet even here, value is relative to context. The 'Darwinian' paradigm of survival of the fittest, which has been applied to creativity theory, depends upon an element of chance, and the chance to survive into the future will depend upon a succession of temporary acceptances in the past.

According to this discussion, definitions of creativity depend upon two criteria. First, creativity must produce something new. Secondly, creativity must produce something valuable or useful. In practice these criteria might conceivably be opposed to each other and might in turn lead to contradictory assessments and personal conflicts. When Trevor Baylis invented his clockwork radio, his invention was initially rejected by the manufacturers, either because they did not believe it was commercially viable, or because they did not believe the market was ready for it. Inventors can describe a new idea, but they are not always best placed to communicate its value. Baylis was angered and frustrated by this experience, and went on to set up a new company to help other inventors evaluate the market potential of their products.

As the experience of Baylis and countless other inventors demonstrates, these judgements of novelty and value themselves depend upon some context, boundaries or reference points. By reconfiguring that context it is possible to shift the definition as to what is or is not 'innovative' or 'valuable'. When the Taiwanese-American film director Ang Lee made *Crouching Tiger Hidden Dragon*, its novelty and its box-office success depended on translating Hong Kong movie conventions into a Westernized idiom for Western audiences. On the other hand, Chinese audiences found the movie to be less innovative and were critical of certain inconsistencies and compromises designed to appeal to Western filmgoers (for example, the casting of a Malaysian actress, Michelle Yeoh, in one of the lead roles).

Translating these criteria into an analysis of the creative process, these concepts of duality and context become even more important. It is through the combination of different styles of thinking that the duality of creativity is likely to emerge. Similarly, creative work is more likely to meet our criteria if it takes place within certain boundaries, working within but also challenging expectations. If positioned too far 'outside the box', creative thinking is novel without being valuable and can no longer connect with an assessment of its value. If positioned too close to the centre, creative thinking follows the brief and fits its purpose, but ceases to be innovative. Positioned towards the edge of the conceptual space, the creative idea can build upon what is already known and understood while at the same time pushing those boundaries a little further. Margaret Boden calls this 'redefining the conceptual space' or 'boundary-tweaking' (Boden 1994: 79–84).

A further inference from the arguments in this chapter might be that the best recipe for creativity will depend upon assembling different components – different styles of thinking, different processes and ideas, different contexts – in unexpected combinations. It is the combination of innovation and value that in the end is both surprising and satisfying, achieved through a combination of spontaneous inventiveness and laborious preparation. It is also in relation to a specific, often unforeseen context that the creative idea manages to both acknowledge and subvert expectations. Creative thinking accordingly takes place on the borders between different parts of the brain or at the intersection between different styles of thinking and different realities. Successful creative thinkers are especially adept at exploring these boundaries, both internally in their own minds, and externally in the world around them (see table 1.1).

This process-based definition of creativity, an unexpected combination of elements which provides a surprising solution to a problem, forms the starting point for this book. Creativity, according to this analysis, takes place not in a zone of absolute freedom, characterized by chaos, irrationality and random innovation. Nor can it be located within a systematic pattern of carefully assembled and managed processes and people, characterized by order, logic and incremental progress. Rather, creativity is most likely

Table 1.1   Two theories of creative thinking

Divergent thinking	Convergent thinking
Think around or away from the problem	Think through or into the problem
Discontinuity / break	Continuity
'Dig another hole'	'Dig a deeper hole'
Spontaneous, informal, random	Systematic, formal, focused
Remove constraints	Work within constraints
Sub-conscious processes	Conscious processes

The 'myth of genius' suggests that creativity depends upon 'divergent' – or in De Bono's phrase 'lateral' – thinking. This fits with a Western tradition stretching back from Plato and Freud into today's management orthodoxies of 'brainstorming' and 'thinking outside the box'. In reality, creative thinkers need to switch between both divergent and convergent thinking if they are to achieve results.

to take place at the edge of chaos and order, on the mind's marshy shore. Creative people will succeed in traversing and negotiating this boundary between uncertainty and confidence, between irrationality and rationality, both in their own minds and in the art worlds they inhabit or construct around themselves. From this starting point, we can put forward a number of hypotheses:

- Creative organizations and individuals tolerate diversity, complexity and contradictions.
- Creative thinking is less likely to result from an individual 'act of genius' than from a combination of different types of thinking.
- The creativity of an idea depends not just on the content of the idea but the way in which that idea is developed, presented and interpreted.
- Creative thinking takes place neither inside the box nor outside the box, but at the edge of the box.
- Boundaries and constraints are a necessary part of the creative process.
- Diversity, compromise and collaboration are no more nor less important to creative work than singularity of vision and purpose.
- Creativity is embedded in a cultural context.

Taking these arguments forward, the remainder of this book will explore notions of management in creativity and creativity in management. Attempting to overcome the great divide between creatives and suits, I hope to show that these stereotypes bleed into each other. Instead of separating innovation and application, instead of treating 'creative thinking' and 'creative industries' as something distinct from ordinary experience and thinking in ordinary industries, I will focus on the duality and contradictions within creativity. Managing this complexity, whether as artists, as managers or as individuals, becomes the subject of this book. Before taking up these themes, I want to consider how and why our everyday definitions of creativity fail to reflect this complexity.

| What Creativity Is Not

What happens when we ignore the fundamental duality of creativity and start to reduce it down to 'mere innovation'? In the first place, we strip out the theories of value and purpose which give creativity meaning. Secondly, we lift 'talented individuals' out of the systems and processes which turn original ideas into creative acts. We start to simultaneously glamorize and patronize the creative individual as an alien species, exempt from normal rules of behaviour and possessed of a special 'gift' which they do not fully understand or control. Thirdly, we start to build around these assumptions systems of management and organization which are at odds with the real needs of creative people and processes.

The pursuit of innovation for its own sake is not the same thing as creativity. By focusing on this side of the equation, we undermine or defer value judgements. One of the assumptions of many so-called 'creative' processes is that we need to suspend our usual capacity for rational judgement and deliberately avoid any question of value or purpose, lest we damage the 'pure' creative impulse. An example of this is the practice of 'brainstorming', popularized by the advertising executive Alex Osborn (1957) in the late 1950s. The early advocates of brainstorming required that we open our imaginations to 'wild' ideas by deferring criticism and refusing to censor or self-censor any idea, no matter how unlikely. But most successful brainstorms today are preceded and followed by more rational processes in which problems are defined and solutions tested. Critics have argued that while brainstorming generates more ideas, quantity does not equate to quality, and a more deliberate, solitary effort is at least as likely to solve a problem as the spontaneous outpourings of self-consciously uncritical collectives (Weisberg 1993: 62–7). The point here is not that brainstorming is good or bad – its appropriateness would no doubt depend on the nature of the problem and the nature of the people involved – the old term 'fitness for purpose', used by creativity testers. The problem with too much brainstorming is that it isolates one particular aspect of the creative process and ignores the context in which the technique takes place.

At a broader organizational level, the exercise of pure innovation can be equally destructive. As Theodore Levitt noted in the 1960s, responding to a fashion for innovation in business, too often the innovators do not consider the competence and resources of the organization to absorb innovation, or questions of continuity and sustainability (Levitt 2002). Change is not always good. As will be discussed in chapter 6, creativity in business has come to be associated with radical change, rather than a more incremental, rigorous approach. In other words, innovation has been elevated above value. Those who dare to criticize innovation are portrayed as old-fashioned, stubborn or – worst of all – uncreative. Again, we are asked to withhold judgement. Yet for innovation and change to be effective in organizations, the same scepticism we apply to conventional habits of thought needs to be applied to the new scenarios. The value of the innovation – its 'fitness for purpose' – is as important as its novelty. True creative thinking thus requires a combination of thinking styles in order to reconcile a capacity for innovation with an ability to identify and develop its value.

The same isolation of one aspect of the creative process occurs with the designation of creative individuals. Here we find the so-called creative individual isolated from the commercial context in which his or her creativity is to be realized and delivered. This is equivalent to the long corridor referred to at the start of this chapter. Again there is an assumption here that creative people need to be protected from commercial realities, that budgets and deadlines might interfere with the eccentric, child-like world of pure inventiveness which these individuals are presumed to inhabit. Similarly, managers are warned from 'meddling' in the creative process because their rules and rationality have no validity in the world of art and innovation. As we will see later in this chapter, this stereotype of the creative individual has deep roots, but it still represents a very partial account of the creative process. The specialization of the creative process and its allocation to creative individuals and creative departments also reflects a growing specialization of tasks, especially in the creative industries, influenced by technologies, production processes and consumer demand. While such task specialization is to some extent inevitable, it is not always desirable. I will return to this theme in the next chapter.

The separation of creative individuals from their ('uncreative'?) managers and the splitting of innovation and novelty from questions of value and judgement reflects a partial, incomplete view of the creative process. In the late nineteenth century, the mathematician Henri Poincaré attempted to break down the creative process into four distinct phases: preparation, incubation, illumination, verification (see figure 1.1). During 'preparation', a problem is defined and analysed, and possible sources of information and inspiration are explored. This is followed by 'incubation', where the sub-conscious mind works upon the problem, while the conscious mind is resting or temporarily distracted. 'Illumination' describes the moment of creative breakthrough (also referred to as the 'aha' or Eureka moment) when the pieces in the puzzle suddenly fall into a new pattern and the solution presents itself. Finally comes 'verification', where the new solution is tested against the original problem. Poincaré's sequence resonates with the definition of creativity already introduced in this chapter; for Poincaré innovation comes at the moment of 'illumination', but usefulness and value must be tested at the point of 'verification'. Other commentators have described a similar duality in the creative thinking process, based on a combination of irrational and rational thought processes (e.g. Weisberg 1986; Sternberg 1988a; De Bono 1982). While these different commentators might choose to emphasize certain 'rational' or 'irrational' elements in the process, what they have in common is a sense of duality or dialectic.

Discussing this with artists and designers, they tend to respond particularly to the notion of 'incubation', taking place in that border country between sleep and waking identified by Koestler. This slipping between states of consciousness suggests that the creative process requires very different types of thinking. The sequence as a whole ranges across contrasting thinking styles, from sub-conscious inspiration to rational analysis. Creative solutions seem to emerge unexpectedly, from *not* thinking about the problem directly, but this period of relaxation in turn is the result and continuation of a longer period of preparation and reflection. When we hear of Archimedes solving the problem of mass and volume by observing the water level in the public

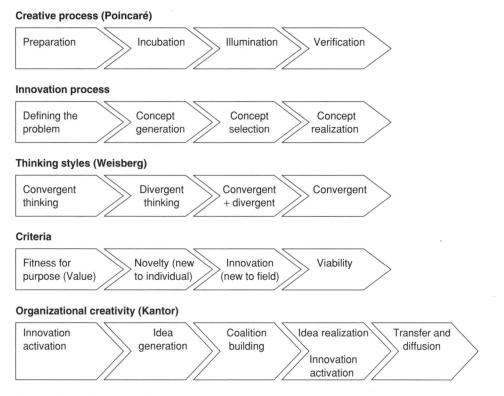

Figure 1.1 Steps in the creative process

baths, we tend to associate the creative moment with a period of meditative relaxation. But the visit to the baths only came after concerted analysis and reflection. It is the tension between conscious and sub-conscious thought in Poincaré's model that produces the new 'creative' ideas, not a reliance on one over the other. The argument here is not that creative thinkers need to release themselves into a meditative, trance-like state (the bath), any more than they need to lock themselves into an inexorable process of analysis (the workshop). Instead they need to find ways of changing gears mentally. They might achieve this, like Archimedes, through a change of location or activity. Artists are characterized not so much by a special type of thinking as by an ability to switch between different types of thinking (see the case study 'A Vision in a Dream?').

Artists and designers also recognize the unpredictable, non-linear progression of Poincaré's sequence; it is not clear how long each 'stage' will take, nor what precise relationship one 'stage' has with the next. One Dutch designer I spoke to thought that Poincaré's sequence might help him to explain to his clients why he had trouble meeting deadlines. His clients were impatient because they could not accept that creativity is not a linear process which follows a predictable timetable.

However, when we examine Poincaré's ideas from a more managerial perspective, we can find in his four-part sequence the beginnings of a rudimentary supply chain and an argument for task specialization. While Poincaré was describing how

Case Study: A Vision in a Dream?

In Xanadu did Kubla Khan
A stately pleasure-dome decree:
Where Alph, the sacred river, ran
Through caverns measureless to man
Down to a sunless sea.

In his 1816 manuscript, Coleridge famously claimed that his poem *Kubla Khan* had come to him in the form of an opium-induced dream or 'reverie'. The poem or 'fragment' has been cited as an example of the sub-conscious power of the imagination, acting without conscious direction. This account was challenged with the discovery in 1934 of an earlier manuscript featuring alternative drafts of the poem. There was other circumstantial evidence, from the literary influences of other works including sections of *Paradise Lost*, to the inconsistencies in Coleridge's account of the events and dates surrounding the poem's origins. This led some later critics to regard Coleridge's 1816 preface to the poem as a self-serving hoax.

These two responses to Coleridge's poem illustrate the polarization between rationalist and mystical accounts of creativity. When we discuss the creative process with our students, those with some practical experience of creative work usually acknowledge the importance of craft and technique alongside 'a vision in a dream'. On the other hand it is often the students from a business background who seem attracted to the more romantic, individualistic idea of spontaneous creativity.

In the arts and humanities, academic studies of cultural production have done much to demystify the creative process; in literature, art, film and media, poststructuralist and postmodernist academics have proclaimed the death of the author and introduced a quasi-scientific rationalism to textual analysis. The heroic tradition of great art and great artists has been democratized. Art is no longer seen as universal and artists are no longer regarded as prophets and visionaries.

The mythology of genius has fared better in the study of management. In the new information economy, writers like Kevin Kelly (1995; 1998) have adopted a quasi-religious rhetoric, describing the submergence of the individual in a collective Jungian consciousness emerging from the 'hive mind' of the Internet. In its advertising, Honda proclaims 'the power of dreams'. The transforming power of art has been replaced by a faith in the transforming power of technology. The visionary role of the artist has been usurped by the media mogul and the management guru.

Coleridge's own description of the creative process as 'synthesis' and his argument that the imagination 'dissolves, diffuses, dissipates, in order to recreate' suggest a way of reconciling conflicting accounts of his poem. If we accept the dualistic idea of creativity advanced in this chapter, Coleridge's poem was both consciously designed *and* subconsciously imagined. Indeed, even his drug-induced reverie was deliberately created. In support of this, the critic John Beer has suggested that Coleridge's half-dreaming state of mind allowed the continuation of intricate mental processes and that his 'reverie' was the resolution of 'a series of images which had been up till then the subject of intense thought on Coleridge's part' (Beer 1959: 206). In his *Biographia Literaria* Coleridge also emphasized the dualistic nature of the imagination. The primary imagination is a God-like act of creation, but the secondary function, while containing elements of the first, is nevertheless 'coexisting with the conscious will' and striving deliberately towards unity and synthesis. The dualistic concept of the imagination in *Biographia Literaria* seems at odds with the more one-sided account of his own poem given in the 1816 Preface.

The battle between 'mythical' and 'practical' interpretations of creativity prefigured in the debate over Coleridge's poem has been carried forward in unexpected directions. It may be that today's poets and artists are more likely than Coleridge to emphasize the laborious working out of successive drafts instead of the first flickerings of the idea, while our business leaders speak of visions and dreams. But Coleridge reminds us elsewhere that creativity is a synthesis of dreams and conscious effort. This hybrid, dualistic notion of creativity is what in the end we find manifest in the completed poem. This will be a more useful model for the management of creativity than a mythology based on dreaming poets and flashes of inspiration.

different types of thinking connect together, it is possible to read this as an argument for keeping them apart. This task specialization fits with Taylor's (1947) principles of scientific management and is perpetuated through contemporary theories of team roles at work. It also accords with cultural assumptions about the nature of creativity already alluded to in this chapter. Consequently, the creative individual is isolated and the processes of innovation and value creation are split down the middle.

This concentration on individual talent and the separation of innovation from the processes which precede and follow it are what creativity is not. Creativity is not the separation and specialization of creative work, nor is it the fetishization of novelty for its own sake. Creativity is not achieved through the pure rationality of preparation or the pure release of incubation. Creativity is not the simultaneous privileging and scapegoating of creative individuals as somehow exempt from conventional rules of behaviour, from rationality, and from managerial control. In the management literature on creativity, the duality, paradox and contradictions of creativity are frequently acknowledged and alluded to. But where I believe psychological theories of creativity, and Poincaré's model in particular, represent an argument for greater integration of different thinking styles and competences, the management literature tends to use these models to argue for greater specialization and separation.

The mythology of creativity as solitary, divine madness connects with the mythology of management as a machine bureaucracy. These two mythologies, while apparently opposite, actually feed off each other. The mad artist needs the calm bureaucrat and the dualism of uncreative manager / unmanageable creator allows both sides to retreat into their respective comfort zones. This book argues that these apparently opposite ways of thinking are actually intricately connected to the creative process. But having identified what creativity is not, we must now consider how these stereotypes of solitary genius and spontaneous inventiveness came to be so dominant in our culture.

Mapping the Great Divide: From Education to the Workplace

In an early draft of this book, one reviewer took issue with my use of the term 'creatives' and 'suits' as stereotypical and limiting. Of course this is true – yet such stereotypes are alive and well, not least in so-called creative industries such as advertising. The terms are used rather self-deprecatingly, even ironically. One former 'creative director' at a software company argues privately that anybody who includes 'creative' in their job title is unlikely to be creative in their job. Yet the terminology remains stubbornly ingrained in the psyche and in the employment ads. Here I want to argue that this mutual antipathy in the workplace is reinforced and institutionalized through education.

The separation which exists in Western cultures between the worlds of creativity and commerce has long historical and intellectual roots which I do not intend to trace here. But in terms of the individual career, the origins of the great divide can often be traced back to education. In many European countries, notably the UK and Germany, young people are forced to specialize at a relatively early stage in secondary education and begin on a trajectory which is likely to determine their future career. Actually the labelling of 'creative' and 'uncreative' individuals can start even earlier, at primary or even pre-school level, with the encouragement or discouragement of parents, carers and teachers. However, it is at the level of tertiary or vocational education that the distinction really starts to bite. Arts students, science students and business students may attend the same universities but they live in separate worlds. One of the criticisms of specialized arts and media degree programmes is their alleged failure to prepare arts graduates for the commercial realities of managing their creativity as a business asset. Only rarely do artists grasp the commercial nettle. Andy Warhol's background as a commercial designer allowed him to break out of the conventional gallery system and turn experimental art into a commercial commodity, and vice versa, in the 1960s. Damien Hirst benefited from the tutelage of Michael Craig-Martin at Goldsmiths (one of the few UK art schools to introduce artists to marketing and markets) and the patronage of Charles Saatchi to do something similar for conceptual art in the 1990s. But such exceptions are comparatively rare. The separation and specialization of arts and humanities subjects in Western universities has a longer history.

The specialization of Western universities began in the late nineteenth century with the emergence of specialist technical and vocational education. Prior to this period, universities provided a generalist, liberal arts education, directed towards the discipline and adornment of the mind, and catering mainly for the aristocracy and the clergy.

By the 1870s, the 'ancient universities' in the UK and the US were being challenged by an expansion of higher education institutions and new forms of 'utilitarian' professional, vocational and technical education. The new institutions broke with the genteel tradition of a fixed body of knowledge, preserved and perpetuated through a prescribed classical curriculum. Education was now placed at the service of economic and social development, designed to educate the several classes and professions according to their station in industrial society. At the same time, the German research university inspired a new professionalism and a shift in power from the collegiate hierarchy to the faculty 'professoriat'; research was in turn geared towards the improvement of industrial processes in the physical sciences. Finally there was a democratization of education at all levels through successive reforms in secondary, adult and higher education across Europe and the US, partly borne out of idealism and partly out of utilitarianism, leading to an influx of middle class and working class students into universities.

These trends led to a massive expansion of higher education in the last quarter of the nineteenth century. The new institutions were in many cases supported by industrial benefactors and included new faculties and specialisms geared to the needs of industry and agriculture (e.g. metallurgy, chemistry, electronics). Specialist faculties and departments replaced the 'generalist' curriculum, with Harvard introducing its 'elective' system in 1869. Art and design education developed out of a similarly specialized set of interests at about this time. The scholarly curatorial tradition linked art and art history to research institutes and to the museums which began to emerge in the latter half of the nineteenth century, while institutions like the Royal College of Art (founded in 1896) grew out of a more vocational, technical tradition.

In the reforms of the universities in the late nineteenth century, one can see the origins of a specialist education system which allocated students to specialist disciplines and institutions, and how these in turn were linked to emerging class divisions. Today's arts graduates are heirs to an aristocratic educational tradition which values generalist abilities and 'useless knowledge' over specific skills. Today's business studies students have inherited a more pragmatic, practical tradition geared to the emerging needs of industry and to their own professional advancement.

The specializations and separations in education and training have a knock-on effect for the 'great divide' between creativity and commerce. From the education system and into the workplace, labels like 'creatives' and 'suits' allow individuals to avoid responsibilities and stay inside a comfort zone of expertise and competence while at the same time appearing to break rules and conventions. The 'creative' is granted minor exemptions, from breaches in dress-code and etiquette to ignorance of budgets and deadlines. The 'suit' is freed from the need to think creatively outside his or her designated roles and responsibilities and disconnected from the realities of creative processes. Each side feels that it is protecting the other. Yet such disconnections are not only artificial but inefficient. These divisions are unlikely to be resolved through a restructuring of the organization or workplace, given their origins in the formative experiences of education.

Today 'creativity' is as likely to feature on the curriculum of an engineering or business course as in the arts; a creative thinker might be a banker or lawyer as well as a composer or photographer. Teachers, educators and governments are beginning to respond to the growing importance attached to the creative economy by championing creativity in the school curriculum. Yet the tendency to treat creativity as a specialist 'faculty' remains stubbornly entrenched. The dominant mythology surrounding creativity in Western cultures is rooted in a minority of talented individuals, a non-rational / inspirational mode of thinking, and in a narrow field of human activity (the creative industries, scientific discovery, technological innovation, R&D).

The Mythology of Genius

I have argued in the previous section that the specialization of creative education is reflected in an increasingly narrow definition of creativity, based on individualism and innovation. Of course it would be wrong to blame this version of creativity, and its self-conscious separation from commercial realities, solely on our educational institutions and traditions.

The association of creativity with eccentric individualism can be traced back through a predominantly Western philosophical tradition of art, stretching from Plato's 'divine madness' through Romanticism and Freudian psychoanalysis through to the Modernist notion of the avant-garde and into present-day theories of creativity as 'thinking out of the box'. According to this mythology, artists are exceptional individuals capable of extraordinary leaps of invention which transcend rational analysis. Such moments of extraordinary invention have in turn taken centre stage as the basis (or at least the starting point) of our contemporary creative industries, founded on 'individual creativity, skill and talent' (Department of Culture, Media and Sport 1998).

Against this individualistic model of creativity can be counterposed a rationalist tradition which sees art and artists holding up a mirror to nature, society and tradition. In Western cultural theory, this model can be traced back to Aristotle's idea of *mimesis*, through sociological and Marxist theories of art into an analysis of the creative industries based on supply chains, cultural geography and networks. The idea that art and artists follow and reflect collective norms and traditions rather than breaking them through flashes of individual brilliance resonates with non-Western and pre-modern cultures; in African tribal art or in the medieval cathedral, the individual artist is submerged in a collective cultural tradition.

The Western conflation of creativity with individual talent has been mapped and effectively debunked in Robert Weisberg's analysis of the 'genius myth' – see table 1.2. Weisberg (1993) takes several of the leading figures in the mythology of genius (Mozart, Picasso, Coleridge) and shows how their 'genius' can be understood in terms of logical progressions, memory, training, opportunity and sheer hard work. He also indicates how the 'aha!' moment of discovery is framed by other thought processes and how creativity is the result of a combination of thinking styles, not spontaneous invention or divine inspiration.

What is more puzzling is the resilience of the mythology of genius in the face of all the evidence Weisberg and others bring to bear against it, and in spite of our own everyday experience. Here we must understand how 'singular creativity', the

Table 1.2   The myth of genius

Genius	Ordinary thinking
Special kind of thinking	Memory, expertise, craft
Spontaneity, 'breaking set'	Continuity (history, tradition, experience)
Determinism by personality traits	Environmental factors
Consistent level of achievement	Inconsistency, peaks and troughs
Absolute value judgements	Relative value judgements
Genius in the person	Genius in the work
'Aha' moments	Revision and modification
Individualism, self-reliance	Interaction, mutual dependency

*Weisberg (1986, 1993) argues that first-hand accounts of creativity tend to emphasize the 'genius'
elements in the left hand column and underplay the more mundane aspects on the right. This emphasis
is reinforced in the marketing and branding of talent in the creative industries. For the star performer,
inspiration is a more marketable commodity than perspiration.*

conflation of creativity with innovation, individualism and a particular way of thinking, is reinforced by economic, political and personal interests, for governments, for
the commercial creative sector and for artists themselves.

For governments, the notion of an economy based on individual creativity is
undeniably attractive. Because they deal in intangibles, the creative industries are not
subject to diminishing natural resources, and their growth rates (measured in gross
domestic product (GDP), export earnings and employment rates) are outstripping
other parts of the economy. Not only are the creative industries seen to provide employment where traditional manufacturing industries are in decline, they offer a route
into employment which bypasses traditional forms of training and recruitment
through an emphasis on self-employment and self-education. Creative workers draw
on their personal resources and contacts, as cultural consumers and private fantas-
ists, instead of working their way up a career ladder or through the conventional
grind of education and training. This 'just do it' approach to work has made the
creative industries a popular career destination, especially for the young. The
emphasis on God-given talent over hard-won expertise fits with today's cult of celebrity,
ignoring the more laborious, hard-won processes of creativity and the specific skills
and traditions which allow individual talent to express itself.

For governments, an economy based on individual talent also fits neatly with a
neo-liberal perspective on cultural policy. In this version of the future, cumbersome
official cultural organizations are replaced by a vibrant, flexible freelance economy
in which it is possible to 'live on thin air'. Because creativity is seen to be inherently
unmanageable (a stereotype to which we will return in chapter 4), a creative economy
is accordingly best achieved through neo-liberal laissez-faire policies of deregulation
and commercialization. According to the mythology of creative genius, the principal task of cultural policy and cultural management is simply to remove obstacles
and allow talent the space and opportunity to express itself with the minimum of
intervention.

For the commercial creative industries, individual creative genius is a convenient method of branding cultural products and even entire businesses. Individual stars are guaranteed to add box office dollars to a film's value, and to command huge advances and fees from record labels. In terms of sales, these advances seem hard to justify. With a few exceptions, artists of recent years have failed to sustain the multi-album careers which were relatively common in the 1970s and 1980s. Yet the majors continue to stake their business on a handful of blockbuster successes, and super-star signings have a disproportionate effect on company prestige and share price. When Mariah Carey was dropped by EMI / Virgin in 2002, there was speculation that the age of the superstar and the multimillion, multi-album record deal might be coming to an end. In this context EMI's highly publicized £80 million deal with Robbie Williams later that same year can be seen as a defiant statement of intent, reconfirming EMI's major label clout while making Williams 'rich beyond his wildest dreams'. It is debat-able as to whether Williams, operating principally in a volatile teen-pop market, can repay this investment in record sales. However, EMI is no doubt looking to other revenue streams including merchandising and video sales. And perhaps the deciding factor was a desire to reposition EMI as a major player in the industry. The super-star brand remains integral to the majors' business strategy and to their credibility – paying an artist a huge advance is one way of sustaining the myth.

As the commercial creative industries converge technologically and economically, the genius brand works across different media platforms – popular musicians can be used to market television programmes and vice versa. Actors, models and comedians can be used to sell novels. The payment of an advance against royalties is not only a statement of faith in the individual genius brand, it also becomes part of the marketing strategy of the publisher, even rebranding the industry as a whole. When Martin Amis was rumoured to have been paid a £500,000 advance for his novel *The Information* in 1994 the advance itself (and the author's dentistry) became the story. The unprecedented sum and the change of publisher and agent generated much negative publicity for Amis himself and seemed to make little sense in terms of sell-ing and marketing the book. But as with Williams's EMI deal, the accompanying publicity confirmed the commercial reputation of Amis's new agent and provided a marketing coup for his new publisher. It also helped to reposition book publishing as a serious commercial industry, and subsequent high profile signings propagated the idea of publishing as 'the new rock and roll'.

From an industry perspective, the commercial investment in and celebration of individual talent serves a secondary purpose, maintaining the illusion that success for the unsuccessful is just around the corner. This myth of latent or undiscovered genius has been played out many times in the Hollywood storyline of the understudy who becomes a star. It is also repeated by the industry's own publicity machine, a tale of artists plucked from obscurity, chance encounters and fat cheques. The myth of individual talent provides a glimmer of hope for the vast army of underpaid and exploited hopefuls who feed the industry machine. According to the mythology, the moment of success is not earned by hard work, experience or training, it comes from within – an inner talent which has only to be discovered. Such a mythology provides an important source of self-esteem and optimism in a highly exploitative business with virtually no career structure, few permanent jobs and a sporadic, grudging relationship between work and wages. Unpaid, informal, temporary and voluntary work fuels the cultures and networks on which cultural production depends, even if, from a statistical perspective, these workers do not exist. The myth of undiscovered genius provides some of them with a defensive form of self-realization. High profile advances paid to bus-driving novelists are the equivalent of winning lottery tickets – they encourage losers to continue playing the game.

From the perspective of the individual artist, apart from the political and economic justifications, the myth of the talented individual serves a more personal purpose, providing a licence to any self-appointed creative individual. In 1944 George Orwell recognized the emergence of a new form of twentieth-century artist-celebrity in his savage critique of Salvador Dali. According to Orwell (1946), Dali retained the flamboyant gestures and mannerisms of genius, even when his art no longer had the power to dazzle or shock. Despite limited artistic abilities, Dali played the role of celebrity artist to perfection and this talent for self-dramatization granted him a series of exemptions from the normal rules of morality, society and personal relationships.

Orwell was no doubt motivated by political and moral disapproval rather than his knowledge of drawing, but he did pinpoint the extent to which genius in art has become a self-conscious role as much as a talent. Even if the typical 'creative' does not share Dali's acute theatricality, there are opportunities for special privilege, often disguised as pleas of incompetence. An artist may claim not to understand (other people's) money, or that she cannot work to deadlines, or he may stipulate the need to work in certain clothes, at certain hours, with a certain disregard for those around him. As with the outrageous advance, the outrageous behaviour becomes part of the public profile. It also becomes a self-conscious role, a received idea of predictable unconventionality, protecting the individual from self-doubt, secure in the self-conscious eccentricity of the confirmed genius.

Finally, the mythology of genius appeals even to those without a direct political, commercial or personal stake in the business of creativity, providing a mechanism for the non-genius too to feel vindicated. We may tolerate the individual creative genius, but we also acknowledge that such individuals are socially maladjusted, child-like, perhaps mentally disturbed. Genius, according to the mythology, is the result of luck and accident rather than skill and judgement. But it may also be a kind of curse. And so, just as the 'creative' role grants both a licence to misbehave and a form of self-affirmation, so too for the 'non-creative' observer, the absence of genius provides a convenient excuse for inaction and an airy dismissal of those who are successful. The genius figure is to be pitied as much as admired (see the case study, 'The Genius and the Water-carrier').

I have used the mythology of genius to refer to a narrow way of thinking about creativity, in which creativity is conflated with innovation, and creativity is the exclusive property of a particular type of 'talented' individual. I have argued that this view of creativity is perpetuated in a series of myths, embedded in Western philosophies of art and reinforced through our compartmentalized education system. Even though rationally we know that these myths are open to question, they are firmly rooted in political, commercial and personal interests. As with any mythology, the

Case Study: The Genius and the Water-carrier

In 1996 the celebrated Manchester United and France footballer Eric Cantona famously dismissed his team-mate Didier Deschamps as 'merely a water-carrier'. Deschamps was known as the workhorse of the France team, putting in the hard graft which allowed his 'creative' team-mates the time and space to indulge their more flamboyant gifts.

While Deschamps was presented as the epitome of hard work and self-sacrifice, Cantona's flashes of brilliance were punctuated by episodes of self-indulgence and indiscipline. His poor disciplinary record (including a two-footed assault on a fan which resulted in a ban) was justified and excused by his club manager as the inevitable price of genius. Indeed, Cantona's ability to break the rules was precisely what appeared to make him valuable as a player and an off-pitch commodity. Like the other great footballing genius of the day, Diego Maradona, Cantona's undoubted gifts as a player were matched by a seeming ability to break the rules and get away with it. His reputation for inconsistency and eccentricity fitted the stereotype of unmanageable creative genius, the antithesis of Deschamps' reputation for hard work and unspectacular endeavour.

A more generous interpretation can be placed on Cantona's 'water-carrier' comment. In ancient Greece, the water-carrier was honoured as a symbol of creativity – not because of anything he did himself, but because of his ability to inspire and facilitate creativity in others. The original water-carrier, Aquarius, was the cup-bearer to the gods. In cycling, a sport with which Cantona as a Frenchman was probably familiar, the water-carrier is the junior member of the team who supports the leading riders. Perhaps rather than disparaging Deschamps, as had been widely assumed, Cantona was praising him and acknowledging their mutual dependence.

Off the pitch, Cantona was undoubtedly a more valuable commodity than Deschamps. The marketing of individual talent is integral to the business of football. The mythology of genius feeds into an iconography of talent which is exploited through merchandising, image rights, advertising and sponsorship. Cantona, like his successor in the number 7 shirt, David Beckham, understood the role expected of him both on and off the pitch. He led a new generation of gifted young players who helped to establish Manchester United as one of the richest sports clubs in the world. The English top division also became one of the richest football leagues in the world, as a result of the bidding war between terrestrial and satellite broadcasters for television rights during the 1990s. Dour goalless draws featuring hardworking teams do not attract high ratings. Water-carriers do not sell many replica shirts in the club shop. Cantona appeared to understand all of this. He was one of the first players to feature regularly in television advertising deals and one of the first to double up football stardom with an occasional career as a film actor.

Yet on the pitch, the story was different. Flamboyantly 'creative' individuals like Cantona are only as good as the teams around them. Television cameras zoom in on the spectacular strike and the killer pass, but these are only made possible by the feints and runs which happen off the ball and off camera. The unexpected occurs only in the context of the attritional battles which do not make the highlight reel. The players, and the fans in the stadium, see what the cameras are missing. Inside the stadium, the water-carriers are often the real stars of the team.

The story of the genius and the water-carrier is reproduced in many other branches of the media and entertainment industries. Creativity in the commercial creative industries is represented through the branding and packaging of individual talent and the personality cult fostered around stars and celebrities. Yet behind the scenes, a more realistic unit of analysis for creative processes and products is the team or the partnership. At the core of this creative team is the double-act of the genius and the water-carrier. Creative thinking, like football, depends upon a union of contrasting abilities and styles of thinking or playing. While it is not impossible to imagine some of these embodied in one person, more often it is the dialectical tension between different individuals and contrasting perceptions which sparks the unexpected insight or moment of inventiveness, and which allows that spark to catch fire. The challenge for management is to develop the right mix of abilities in the team and to find the right position for each player. As for Cantona, while he played the role of arrogant genius to perfection, perhaps his remarks about Deschamps sprang from a rare moment of modesty and self-knowledge. Every genius needs his water-carrier.

idea of genius protects us from our own doubts and fears, providing a simplified, sanitized explanation of how creativity works. The mythology of genius converges in the notion of a special domain of creative work, known as 'the creative industries'.

False Profits: The Creative Industries

Insisting on a singular definition of creativity based on individualism and innovation becomes increasingly unconvincing in relation to the creative industries. The relative importance of individual creativity and idea generation in the creative industries is open to question. Individual creativity, innovative ideas and products form only one small part in a complex production process. If we examine the revenue streams, value chains and the investment of human and financial resources in cultural production, individual creativity, skill and talent are very much the poor relations. In today's creative economy, ideas are cheap – it is what you do with them that counts. To use the terminology of the UK government (Department of Culture, Media and Sport 1998), the *generation* of intellectual property is consistently less lucrative than the *exploitation* of intellectual property rights. Individual artists, writers, and performers are the sweatshop workers of the creative economy; the real 'value added' comes in the manipulation and development of that content into marketable commodities.

Contemporary accounts of the creative industries are quite rightly more concerned with the cultures and contexts within which creative activity occurs than with the creative act itself. There is a rich literature exploring the geography of the creative industries, and the systems through which cultural production operates, not in linear supply chains, but through complex networks, dependencies and ecologies. These systems of cultural production and distribution offer a challenge and redefinition of traditional business models and processes. One of the aims of this book is to examine management in the creative industries and consider whether there are lessons and models here for other types of business. Rather than attempting to treat creative industries like conventional businesses, I will accordingly focus on their special characteristics. A reliance on individual talent and intellectual property is not in itself a unique characteristic. But I will argue that the ways in which creative processes, talents and products are managed and developed in the creative industries *are* distinctive and that these working methods and models are worth studying.

If we want a workable definition of the creative industries, we need to start with a more sophisticated definition of creativity. Individual talent and original 'content' may be less significant than the ways in which that raw talent is managed and processed. As business models have adapted and markets and technologies have become increasingly sophisticated, 'content' is in many cases becoming less important than the way in which that content is delivered to the consumer. Creativity is being directed towards technological and marketing solutions as much as to the generation and development of raw talent. Our definition of creativity accordingly needs to encompass these aspects of cultural production as a complex process, not just the ideas and talent which provide the raw material.

Abraham Maslow (1968) made a psychological distinction here between 'primary' and 'secondary' creativity; the former works primarily through the spontaneous, intuitive processes also known as 'lateral' or 'divergent' thinking. 'Secondary' creativity requires a more disciplined, conscious effort of the rational mind to shape and modify the initial creative impulse. The same distinction might usefully be applied to different 'levels' of creativity in the creative industries. According to Maslow, creativity is most effective when it succeeds in integrating these different kinds of intelligence into a harmonious whole. One of the difficulties here is the apparent dichotomy, even outright antagonism, between two very different ways of thinking. Reconciling and connecting these contradictory tendencies thus becomes a key challenge for creative industries management.

We might consider that the truly impressive, overlooked and *creative* aspect of the media and entertainment industries is not the products they make, nor even the revenues they generate, but the ways in which creative enterprises are managed and structured. The challenge of managing and structuring creative processes and people centres on the management and tolerance of contradictions. The definition of creativity put forward in this chapter is based on dualism. Creativity has been defined in terms of innovation (novelty) and value (fitness for purpose, usefulness). It has been linked to processes of divergent and convergent thinking, to different types of business process (idea generation and idea exploitation), and to opposing habits of thought and types of people. Creativity contains both a spontaneous, individual act and a deliberate, self-conscious, rational process. For these elements to be reconciled, the creative process must be managed, either by the individual or by an organization or system. This is the unique achievement of the creative industries – not their individual talents or their export earnings – and this is the area I hope to explore in the succeeding chapters of this book.

FURTHER READING

The definition of creativity in this chapter as 'innovation + value' draws upon Margaret Boden's psychological theory of creativity and on Robert Weisberg's critique of the 'genius myth'. While both authors perhaps share a scientific tendency to 'rationalize' creativity, they are representative of a widely held view among creativity theorists that creativity consists of two components, innovation or 'novelty' and value or 'fitness for purpose' (see Boden 1994: 75–117; and Weisberg 1993). Boden's own theory of creativity is elaborated at greater length in *The Creative Mind: Myths and Mechanisms* (1992; see especially pp. 240–60). Abraham Maslow makes the similar distinction between 'primary' and 'secondary' creativity in his *Towards a Psychology of Being* (1968).

In the management literature on innovation, some authors reverse my distinction between 'creativity' and 'innovation', with creativity equating to 'mere novelty' and innovation encompassing the dualism of novelty and fitness for purpose. According to this argument, 'innovation' is about the application of creativity to problem-solving and creativity is a sub-component of innovation. In writing this book, I have preferred to follow the psychological literature on creativity rather than the management literature on innovation. Semantic differences aside, it should be noted that the argument – that two elements (novelty and fitness) are necessary to qualify as innovation / creativity – is fundamentally the same.

Theodore Levitt's 1963 critique of the destructive potential of creativity in management has been reprinted as 'Creativity is not enough' in *Harvard Business Review* (2002). For an account of the difficulties in categorizing and deploying creativity in contemporary organizations, see Banks *et al.* (2002).

The dualism noted by Boden and Weisberg is present in most theories of creativity, from the trait-based definitions of creativity in the 1950s and 1960s through the creativity tests developed by E.P. Torrance and others in the 1970s. For an excellent summary of these and other contemporary theories of creativity, I recommend one of the following edited collections: Sternberg (1988b, 1999); Runco and Albert (1990). For a longer historical perspective, Rothenberg and Hausman (1976) have assembled a compendium of quotations and definitions extending from Plato and Aristotle through to Arthur Koestler.

The genius model of creativity is linked to more negative perceptions of the creative individual as 'special' or 'different', beginning with Plato's decision to exile poets from his Republic and his criticism of poets in his dialogue *The Ion*. Several commentators have since traced analogies between mental illness and creativity – see, for example, Sandblom (1992). Laingian psychiatry questions the relationship between culture, conformity, creativity and mental health – see Jamison (1996). While this approach raises important questions about the way our society identifies and treats mental illness, it is less satisfactory as an explanation of creativity, simply because the range of behaviours and internal and external variables is too complex to allow any easy inference of cause and effect. Freud (1985) suggests a correlation between childhood, repression and adjustment to adult social norms and artistic creativity in 'Creative Writers and Daydreaming'. But responding to Freud's arguments, Anthony Storr (1972) explores the relation between psychology, motivation and creativity among artists and finds no obvious internalized explanation of why artists create.

Henri Poincaré was a late nineteenth century mathematician who developed the sequence of preparation, incubation, illumination and verification to describe the creative process – see Poincaré (1982). This is reproduced in Boden (1992: 240–60). The sequence was later picked up and elaborated by a British psychologist, Graham Wallas, in his book *The Art of Thought* in 1926 and has continued to influence later thinkers. John Howkins (2001: 16) offers an updated version of Poincaré in his RIDER sequence (Review, Incubation, Dreams, Excitement, Reality checks). More recent commentators have identified a similar dualism in the creative process, encompassing different thinking styles (see Weisberg 1986; and De Bono 1982). Neurologists have related this same duality to hemispheric activity in the brain ('right brain' versus 'left brain') and have conducted experiments showing how different areas of the cerebral cortex are used by artists to develop their work (see Hoppe 1994). Frank Barron related creativity to the artist's ability to tolerate complexity and contradiction, which led him to correlate creativity with high levels of 'ego strength' (see Barron 1968).

Boden's discussion of P-Creativity and H-Creativity is in *Dimensions of Creativity* (1994: 75–76). For a contrary view, see Novitz (1999). Novitz suggests that Boden's distinction between 'P-Creativity' and 'H-Creativity' is largely a matter of luck and timing, and therefore of little real value.

The history of university education in this chapter draws principally on two sources: Jarausch (1983) and Kelly (1970). For a more detailed examination of liberal arts education in the US, see Garrison (1979).

The cultural geography of the creative industries has been charted by several commentators including Allen J. Scott, Gernot Grabher and Andy Pratt. For a summary of Scott's arguments, see Scott (1999).

For a detailed analysis of the creative or cultural industries in the UK, see Dave Hesmondhalgh's definitive book, *The Cultural Industries* (2002). The creative industries concept originated in Australia in the 1990s. The UK introduced the term to its cultural policy in 1997 and the UK government's official definition of creative industries, as presented in the Department of Culture, Media and Sport's 'Mapping Document' in 1998, has influenced countries in East Asia, Europe and Canada among others. It has not always been easy for other countries to adapt to a concept of the creative industries, which is based on a Western concept of creativity, as Michael Keane indicates in his 2004 article. In the UK, the journalist James Heartfield has criticized the government's enthusiastic championing of the creative industries. While Heartfield (1998, 2000) is specifically addressing the UK situation, his arguments about the responsibility of governments and the ethics of abandoning traditional manufacturing industry in favour of 'living on thin air' have a wider resonance. There are several academic critiques of the creative industries concept including Jeffcutt and Pratt (2002) and Garnham (2005).

The story of the television drama producer is a personal example of the divided organization, but is echoed in numerous sociological studies by the 'new institutionalists' such as Paul DiMaggio and Walter W. Powell (see, for example, Powell and Friedkin 1986). Keith Negus has conducted similar sociological studies of the divisions and tensions in the music industry (see, for example, Negus 2000).

2 FROM INDIVIDUALS TO PROCESSES: CREATIVE TEAMS AND INNOVATION

In the previous chapter, creativity was defined as a multidimensional process, requiring a combination of thinking styles and a tolerance for contradiction and paradox. This leads us away from an individual, person-based definition of creativity towards a collective model, in which individuals combine into multi-talented teams. In this chapter, I will consider a 'team-based' approach to creativity and innovation and the implications of such models for management.

From Individuals to Teams

Creativity theory has demonstrated a growing scepticism towards individual, trait-based models of creativity of the type propounded in the 1960s. Behaviourist models are criticized for ignoring external conditions. The attempt to develop theories of creativity through the examination of biographies of 'great artists' has become increasingly unfashionable. Attempts to track creative ability from childhood into adulthood by 'testing' for creative competences have proved similarly inconclusive, with inconsistent results revealing no obvious correlation between the identified competences and future performance or career choice. The list of creative traits, behaviours or competences often appear mutually exclusive, or extend into lengthy and contradictory wish lists. It seems highly unlikely that the desired combination of abilities can be located in any one individual. Finally, there is the problem of cause and effect: do certain character traits or competences result in creativity, or do the lifestyle and pressures of creative work result in certain psychological consequences? Psychological studies of the relationship between art and various forms of mental illness raise the question as to whether certain mental conditions or characteristics 'cause' artistic creativity, or whether the artist's lifestyle and working methods have certain consequences for mental health and individual behaviour.

Today's theories of creativity are more likely to be based on processes or systems than the search for the singularly gifted individual. This is linked to a broader scepticism towards 'heroic' or individualized models of human behaviour, both in psychology and in management theory. Contemporary ideas of the creative individual range from 'cognitive' approaches, describing the mental processes which combine new concepts, to social psychology and systems theory. These theories of creativity converge with management theories about team work and innovation, organizational creativity and organizational learning. Connecting all these theories is the framework of post-Fordism, in which networks of organizations, groups and individuals have replaced unitary, integrated organizations as the dominant form of production. In a post-Fordist economy, attention shifts from individual competences to the social and organizational frameworks through which individuals are connected – from know-how to know-who.

| Innovation and Teams

Innovation is at a premium in organizations as the source of new products, new markets and (increasingly) new business processes. The organizational capacity for innovation and creativity has taken on a renewed significance, with the shift from an economy based on material products and transactions towards a 'creative economy' in which ideas and knowledge are the new capital. In the search for the sources of innovation, there is an emerging consensus that team-based approaches are an important area of investigation. Flexible, matrix-based organizational structures which allow managers to assemble and deconstruct project-based teams are favoured over traditional hierarchical, functional models of organization because they fit better with fast-moving, fragmented markets, innovative products and a flexible, highly skilled labour force. They also allow for a rapid redeployment of talent and resources to mobilize new ideas and innovations and make more productive use of the intrinsic talents of the workforce. In manufacturing, product development teams will pull together expertise from across the organization, cutting across the company's divisional structure. In the public sector, task forces and working parties operate in the same way.

One of the most influential arguments regarding teamwork and innovation is the theory of complementary opposites developed by Michael Kirton (1984). The idea that creativity requires a connection between different, apparently opposite, thinking styles was introduced in the previous chapter. Kirton explored this in relation to teams of engineers and found that most teams consisted of 'innovators' and 'adapters'. Innovators would come up with new concepts, but the adapters would develop these concepts into practical models. The most successful teams contained a mix of adapters and innovators. Teams consisting of predominantly adapters or predominantly innovators became blocked – the innovators were unable to progress their ideas while the adapters lacked the initial impetus to get them started. Subsequent researchers have confirmed that homogenous teams, while ensuring quick solutions and instant consensus, do little to stimulate creative thinking.

One can see in Kirton's observation of teams a reflection of Poincaré's creative thinking sequence or Arthur Koestler's 'bisociation'. Again, it is the collision of different thinking styles which sparks the creative process. In terms of team theory,

the key member of the team is not any one individual, since the balance and composition of every team will be different and their needs will be relative. A team
predominantly composed of adapters will be in desperate need of an innovator,
while a team of innovators needs the introduction of an adapter. One might further
surmise that the ideal mix will vary according to the nature of the problem each
team is confronting.

In the creative industries 'adapters' are often in short supply. A colleague attending an arts marketing conference reports a room full of arts marketers taking part
in an exercise to identify team roles at work, following Belbin's framework.[1] Of
the various roles described by Belbin (Shaper, Implementer, Completer-Finisher, Co-
ordinator, Teamworker, Resource Investigator, Plant, Monitor-Evaluator, Specialist),
the participants unanimously identified themselves as 'Plants' – described by Belbin
as creative, imaginative, unorthodox problem solvers. Collectively such a homogenous group would almost certainly lack the diversity to challenge and channel each
other's ideas, or the additional competences to develop and realize the ideas being
generated. We might also surmise that participants choose a role that matches their
aspirations rather than one which reflects their real character, identity and skills. Of
course arts marketers like to think of themselves as creative problem solvers (who
doesn't?) but by labelling themselves as creative individually, they may also expose
gaps in their ability to be creative collectively.

Kirton's theory of complementary opposites has been highly influential on theories
of innovation and in turn on the ways in which managers attempt to organize their
workers into innovative teams. The literature on innovation is dominated by discussions
of team composition, allocation of roles and management of relationships within teams.
There are numerous models of 'complementary but different' individuals working
together in teams. Many of these models share a highly individualized, even deterministic, view of individual human character. Once a role is allocated, it becomes
very difficult to break out of it – once an 'idea generator' or 'resource gatherer', always
an idea generator / resource gatherer. For managers, the key task in managing
innovation becomes one of recruitment. New and potential recruits are screened
through sophisticated psychometric tests, designed to assess not abilities or intelligence but to designate the new employee as a particular psychological type and thereby
slot them into a specific predefined role. Ironically, the team-based organization can
sometimes appear no less deterministic and constraining than the old-fashioned, hierarchical systems of organization based around the functional division of labour, derived
from Taylor's 'scientific' approach to management at the turn of the century and
Weber's 'iron cage' of bureaucracy.

There are a number of practical problems with the team-based approach to
innovation. In a matrix structure where horizontal lines of communication within
project-based teams intersect with vertical lines of communication within function-
ally based hierarchies, there is a cat's cradle of cross-cutting lines of accountability,
leaving plenty of scope for confusion, buck-passing and prevarication. The project-
based team also allows limited scope for organizational or individual learning, with
a lack of continuity and overview preventing the organization from incorporating
the lessons learned from one project into the next. For the individual, the team role

can become a kind of straitjacket, denying the possibility of personal growth and creativity. Finally, by breaking the organization down into teams and the team down into individual roles, the focus of the organization and the individuals within it becomes much narrower, based on specific contributions and outcomes rather than seeing the bigger picture of the organization and the market within which each project or innovation will be applied.

In the end, the 'team-based' approach to innovation has become another recipe for success and like all such prescriptive recipes, it fails to capture the flavour of the original ingredients. The insights derived from Kirton's analysis of team roles are still valuable, but have been forgotten in the pursuit of a 'best practice' approach which sees the management of successful, innovative teams primarily in terms of recruitment. Kirton's emphasis on relativism within the team has been succeeded by a competence-based approach which assigns roles instead of managing relationships. Psychological and aptitude tests screen out diversity and difference, avoiding the 'collision of contradictions' which seems to accompany creative thinking. The team role places a block on creativity, inhibiting experiment and change at the individual level while purporting to support innovation collectively. At its worst, the team-based approach to innovation has resulted in a kind of alienation, with individuals retreating into predefined roles and mutually exclusive stereotypes, avoiding collective responsibility and degenerating into defensive and repetitive patterns of behaviour. Above all, the focus on roles has resulted in a loss of perspective and a disengagement from the collective process.

What can managers of innovation learn about creative teams from the creative industries? In the following section, we will consider the relationship between individuals, teams and creativity in the creative industries, and explore the possibility of an alternative model for team-based creativity.

Beyond Specialization: Creative Work in the Creative Industries

Creativity in the creative industries has always been closely related to individual personalities and relationships, and to self-expression. Organizational structures have tended to be similarly individualistic, with individuals adopting increasingly specialized roles as a result of growing sophistication in technologies, cultural traditions and the diminutive scale of many creative organizations; film credits, CD liner notes and theatre programmes contain an expanding catalogue of specialist job descriptions. Within the sociological patterns of cultural production and systems-based theories of creativity, individuals still play a starring role. And as with the preceding review of team-based organizations, these creative individuals are configured into productive relationships with others.

The myth that the creative industries are the product of uniquely gifted individuals has already been criticized in the opening chapter. Creative individuals are embedded in systems and networks, and this cultural embeddedness is all too often neglected in the celebration of 'individual talent'. The individualization and specialization of creative work results in high levels of mutual dependency, both within and across creative teams, and up and down the supply chain. These collaborative networks will be discussed in more detail in the next chapter. For now, it is worth emphasizing that while apparently rooted in individual skill, creative processes in the creative industries are essentially collective. Indeed it could be said that the high level of supply chain dependency in the creative industries is the direct result of the specialization and individualization of creative work – in such a complex and specialized sector, no single individual or firm can realistically expect to be self-sufficient or self-contained.

Two further structural characteristics underpin this mutual dependency in the creative industries. First, much of the work of the creative industries is project based, particularly in cultural production. Project teams are assembled from networks of specialists. In film and television production, the majority of work will be undertaken on a temporary contract basis. A minority of employees form a bureaucratic or strategic core which is then responsible for recruiting temporary members of the project team. Even quite substantial 'organizations' can turn out to have only one or two permanent staff members. Self-employment in the creative industries is much higher than in other sectors and individuals must adapt to a steady turnover in new roles and new projects. For most of those working in the creative industries the characteristic mode of employment is a kind of serial monogamy, with individuals working together with great intensity and under high pressure, only to split up and reassemble in a new configuration. In this context, specialization must be married to flexibility and a capacity to adapt to other people and contexts.

The other structural characteristic of creative organizations is a tendency towards multi-tasking. Most enterprises in the creative and media industries start small, often based around one or two individuals with an idea. At this stage in the business's life cycle, playing multiple roles is a necessity – everybody has to do everything. A friend who runs his own documentary production company in New York explained to me how he and his partner had allocated each other formal job titles in order to meet the expectations of partners and investors. Each of them took on a series of vice-presidencies and departments, while still running most of their business in each other's apartments. Of course the Vice-President of Marketing in this instance was not necessarily a marketing expert – this was just a way of formalizing the various responsibilities two individuals had to carry in running their own business. The reason that many architectural practices and design agencies are constituted as partnerships is that their business is structured around a federation of self-managing individuals, not a division between managers and creators. This kind of multi-tasking is quite common in small creative enterprises. While it is perhaps born out of necessity, it is also something that most creative entrepreneurs seem to enjoy. As noted in the previous chapter, creative individuals share a capacity to cross boundaries and make connections, both internally in their own heads and externally in their relationships with others. Productive artists and cultural entrepreneurs share a willingness and desire to cross over from one mental state to another, and to embrace different types of experience and different types of thinking.

The project-based nature of creative work and the small scale of many creative 'organizations' (bearing in mind that many such organizations might be sole traders or partnerships) require that specialization is tempered by an ability to see creative problems and business realities from more than one point of view. Just as creative artists draw upon a certain mental agility or 'ego strength' to tolerate uncertainties and contradictions in their work, creative entrepreneurs must be able to connect and adapt to multiple projects and networks. Artists and entrepreneurs are chameleons and shapeshifters, skilled at blending into new habitats and new sub-districts of their own brains. This requires both a kind of empathy and a degree of real practical knowledge of other people's skills and experience.

We tend to see creative people as specialists and obsessive individualists, because of the nature of their skills and talents. But many of them are also generalists, with a broad range of sympathies and connections. As will be discussed in the next chapter, creative individuals understand the importance of acquaintanceship and the strength of 'weak ties'. While creativity is in part a solitary act, it is also a social experience, depending on complicity between creators (and a similar complicity between producer and consumer). To understand the nature of these connections, we need to review the allocation of roles and responsibilities in creative organizations.

Playing Many Parts: Creative Roles in the Creative Industries

From the preceding description, it is clear that the playing of multiple roles in the creative industries is very different from the allocation of team roles in traditional organizations. Team roles in business have been criticized for imposing a very limited and essentially uncreative stereotype onto the individual employee, basing each role on a preconceived system rather than on the complexity and multiple capabilities of real individual people. In contrast the multi-tasking and interchange of roles in the creative industries are seen to be *creative* as well as necessary. When a creative project starts or a new enterprise is launched in the creative industries, roles and responsibilities are loosely defined and communication is informal. Switching roles allows for changes in perspective and introduces an element of unfamiliarity and challenge which stimulates new ideas and approaches. It fits with an informal lifestyle and a DIY aesthetic – everybody is learning, everybody is making it up as they go along. Later it may become difficult to recapture this initial energy and involvement, and entrepreneurs may become nostalgic for the start-up phase of the business. The problems of growing the creative team will be addressed later in this chapter. Here I wish to emphasize the *theatricality* of role-play in the creative industries.

One of Edward De Bono's creative thinking exercises requires a group to use different coloured hats to represent different roles in a decision-making process. By exchanging hats, participants disrupt the expected and familiar roles and highlight some of the expectations and stereotypes which go with specific roles in a group (see 'Six Thinking Hats' in De Bono 1993). While the exercise is consistent with

De Bono's attempt to challenge engrained habits of thought and organizational routines in pursuit of 'lateral thinking' in business, what is striking in this particular exercise is its overt playfulness. Roles are adopted and cast aside lightly, encouraging a certain detachment between actor and role. This self-consciousness is essential to the exercise, allowing participants to observe (and gently mock) the fixed ideas and positions normally associated with each role. Small creative enterprises allow for a similar sense of theatricality in the exchanging and sharing of professional roles. These transition points between different roles and functions allow for a diversity of experiences and thinking styles which are conducive to creative thinking. They also encourage a degree of self-awareness, interaction and empathy within the team.

Role-play is often used in management training, either to illustrate a 'real' scenario, or to allow a temporary release from familiar routines. Over the last 10–15 years, role-play has become an increasingly sophisticated training technique, not just a way of acting out a scenario. Switching in and out of roles allows for changes in perspectives and allows individuals to step out of their roles and see the bigger scenario from another angle. Actors, according to Stanislavski, are trained to maintain two levels of consciousness, engaging with the 'inner life' of the character while simultaneously observing the effects of their performance and the interactions unfolding in real time on stage around them. Role-play thus becomes a way of inhabiting different realities or perspectives simultaneously, and of mining the sub-conscious with conscious intent. Creative thinking, it has been argued in the opening chapter, requires precisely this capacity to accommodate and switch between different thinking styles. Like other aspects of the creative process, acting depends upon a 'divided self'. Without this self-consciousness and self-observation, acting becomes a sterile impersonation, a matter primarily of casting.

The craft of acting is a useful metaphor for creative thinking and team-based innovation. The managerial allocation of roles in team theory is based on casting – finding the right person for the right task. The theatrical approach is based on play. Actors play *with* roles, rather than simply becoming them, moving in and out of character and maintaining a critical distance from their own performance even as they inhabit the role. Similarly, in small creative enterprises, roles are temporary and are taken up and cast aside as necessary, exchanged and merged, played with, not just played. In this way individuals are not trapped within prescribed functions and expectations – they avoid becoming type-cast. They also gain a much broader insight into the problems and abilities of their fellow-players and retain some understanding of the 'big picture' of collective needs and outcomes beyond their own performance.

In today's creative industries, teams are increasingly moving towards a model based on multiple roles rather than the specialized team-based or functional roles (see case study). Some of the structural implications of this shift are considered in the case study. For teams to operate in this more fluid, multifunctional system, members need to split their focus between their own specialist discipline or task and its relationship with the project as a whole. Finding this balance is not easy. Sustaining and managing it, as will be discussed next, is perhaps even harder.

Case Study: Repositioning Creativity in Advertising

Advertising is a business based on creativity, where the key assets are individual employees and the core product is creative thinking on behalf of the client. At the same time advertising is also a multi-billion dollar industry with clearly defined lines of corporate responsibility and control connecting employees, managers, directors and shareholders in global networks. The freedom to be creative and to take risks is contained within hierarchical limits.

The *modus operandi* of the advertising agency manifests a similar paradox. Creative processes are structured within clearly defined roles and relationships. The stereotypical division between 'creatives' and 'suits' referred to at the start of this book is preserved in the advertising agency's separation of creative and managerial roles, with the 'account executive' acting as a managerial buffer between the creative team and the client. Traditionally, the creative function in advertising has been kept at arm's length from the managerial function. The majority of agencies today still follow a divisional structure, based around client services, a creative department and a planning department; in the larger agencies this might be supplemented by a media division, though much of the media buying is likely to be outsourced.

Yet there are signs that this traditional division of labour is beginning to change. Mike Sims is a managing partner at EHS Brann in London, responsible for client services and author of two books on the industry. Sims argues that the separation of creative teams from the strategic and commercial realities is no longer sustainable. 'In the 1980s and 90s, some creative departments would take six weeks to generate some very mediocre creative concepts. They kept themselves apart from the rest of the agency and made up their own rules. It was like a boys' club, very exclusive, lots of in-jokes, no contact with the client. If client services put pressure on them to meet deadlines or to respond to feedback from the client, they were told to back off.' Today, creative departments are much more involved in the client side of the business. Increasingly, the 'creatives' are expected to have client-facing skills, to be articulate about their own work, and to work alongside the planning department to develop customer propositions rather than simply working to a predetermined brief. According to Sims, this involvement of the creative team in the planning and delivery of the service to the client has allowed them to become more effective. 'The idea of the creative department as a hotshop for ideas, which are not specific to the needs of the client, just doesn't work. It's like living in a box. To be creative, you need to be curious and you need to feed your curiosity. You need to be aware of what's going on around you.' Interestingly, while creative departments are still male-dominated, Sims notes the emergence of one or two all-female creative teams as a sign that the exclusive 'boys' club' culture is beginning to break down.

According to Sims, creative teams in advertising today are more fluid and multifunctional. Two factors seem to have driven this trend. First there has been a restructuring of the single integrated agency towards a more disintegrated business model. This restructuring is to some extent cyclical, with large agencies consolidating and then eventually fragmenting as individuals break out to set up business on their own. It is also client-driven, with larger agencies attempting to provide a 'one-stop shop' for the client, bundling together several services including research, advertising, branding, media buying and planning which are then outsourced through a pool of partners and specialist service providers. In this model the agency acts as a shop window behind which the client service team assembles creative partnerships to deliver what the client requires. This has favoured the emergence of a new generation of smaller, more flexible agencies capitalizing on the gaps in provision, demand for specialist services and the inevitable loss of personality and attention to detail among the larger more established agencies. The new generation has evolved a much more collaborative and multifunctional approach to the creative processes of advertising. Creativity is apparent not just in copywriting and art direction but in innovative uses of media and alternative approaches to planning, research and business expansion. Small, innovative agencies in London like Mother and Naked orchestrate creative solutions within and outside the agency by working with partners and building alliances; Naked has even established satellite units inside the buildings of other agencies, a strategy Sims likens to the 'Intel Inside' branding of computer chips inside other manufacturers' computers.

The other driving force towards a more multifunctional, less divisional approach to creativity in advertising has been a less hierarchical organizational structure, a reaction against the corporate mergers and global expansions of the 1980s and 1990s. In 1995 Mike Crossman was responsible for setting up Bates Interactive, a semi-autonomous interactive advertising company within the Bates Advertising agency. The online agency was extremely successful, notably in its work for Carling, and was also recognized as a creative success, winning a succession of awards in the late 1990s. Behind the scenes, however, Crossman found himself having to manage very different expectations and differing perceptions of the value and nature of the business. It became clear that despite escalating expectations of success, the board was reluctant to take commensurate risks in order to reap rewards. Like many others in the late 1990s, the company was excited by the possibilities of new technologies and new forms of creativity, but was still wary of new and unfamiliar territory and still accountable to the bottom line of shareholder value. The battle then became about changing perceptions – trying to present an accurate picture of the new business which cut through the hype and paranoia around 'the new economy', while all the time managing expectations at different levels in the organizational hierarchy.

Crossman's experience points to the difficulties in marrying creative risk-taking with corporate accountability and control. Other agencies experienced similar tensions through the 1990s. One of the most talked about of the new generation of agencies, St Luke's, began life in response to a business merger. In 1995, Chiat Day, a small agency with a maverick reputation, was acquired by

Omnicom and merged with TBWA. Andy Law led disaffected staff in Chiat Day's London office to set up a new agency. More specifically, Law aimed to set up a new type of agency. St Luke's was a cooperative in which every member of the workforce owned shares in the business. Nobody had a desk and everybody was equally involved in business and creative decisions. Instead of being structured around a division of labour, the agency was structured around its clients, with each client allocated a separate 'brand room' in the building and staff 'hot-desking' and moving between 'hubs' in the building.

St Luke's has been one of the big advertising stories of the past decade, and it would take another book to unravel the hype from the reality. My own impression is that St Luke's was a bold experiment which may not in the end be sustainable (few experiments are) but which remains highly influential. The agency was initially extremely successful both creatively and commercially, but the democratic structure also slowed decision making and mired any longer-term strategy. The agency still revolved around the charisma and vision of Law himself, despite its democratic structure and Law's own self-effacing attempt to delegate decisions and control. During my encounters with St Luke's staff, the business culture at St Luke's resembled a religious cult constructed around its founder – St Andy's. Not surprisingly, when Law left (according to some, frustrated by the agency's cumbersome decision-making processes), the business seemed to be in decline. Today St Luke's is back in business, but it is no longer unique. The experiment has been repeated elsewhere and even larger agencies are attempting to set up smaller units and challenging the divisional and hierarchical barriers which keep creativity in the box marked 'creative'.

According to Sims, change is inevitable. Agencies like St Luke's, Mother and Naked have brought creative ideas back into the centre of the business and re-engaged the client in the creative process. Creative teams are no longer insulated from clients or filtered through intermediaries – creativity is no longer the preserve of a single division or department and cuts across everything the agency touches. Clients and staff seem to be happy with the results. It would be an exaggeration to claim that a handful of agencies in London are typical of the industry as a whole – according to Sims around 80–90% of agencies still follow the traditional divisional structure, and the rhetoric of 'flat hierarchies' and 'everything we do is creative' needs to be treated with scepticism. Besides, much of the typical agency's work does not consist of ground-breaking creative concepts but mundane practical tasks – referred to in the industry as JFDI (Just Fucking Do It). Large agencies which have the capacity to offer the full range of services will have an edge over the smaller innovators. Sims suggests that the future may not consist of a new wave of smaller creative agencies and start-ups, but in the traditional agencies becoming smarter and more flexible, learning from the newcomers and replicating their processes.

What does appear to have changed is the way in which creative teams interact with each other and with the totality of the business. Client service teams are having to be more creative in the way they orchestrate creative teams through outsourcing and partnerships. Creative teams must sell their ideas and their business to the client services team or the lead agency and to the client. The market is also becoming increasingly competitive and clients too demand change; Sims estimates that the average marketing director stays in post for about 18 months, and this turnover in staff inevitably results in switches of advertising accounts or diversifying advertising spend across a roster of agencies. In a competitive market, agencies can no longer afford for the left hand not to know what the right hand is doing. The result has been a more integrated, multi-tasking culture with creative thinking no longer locked away as a specialist function of separate divisions and talented individuals. Traditional 'artistic' creativity is still the life blood of advertising and peer approval is still a powerful motivating and legitimizing force; according to Sims 'people would die for a yellow pencil [the annual D&AD (Design and Art Direction) awards for creativity in advertising and design]'. But creativity is also apparent in the way the flow of work is managed, in the placing of advertisements in new locations including new media, in brand-building, in the meshing of data with ideas. Above all perhaps, creativity in advertising lies in the orchestration of relationships within the business as a whole, not in its component parts.

Growing the Creative Team: Familiarization or Specialization?

As teams develop over time, the fluidity between roles and switches in perspective which were possible during start-up become more difficult. As they mature, creative teams face two related problems of over-familiarization and over-specialization. Typically, a team will take time to get to know each other and to work together effectively. Teams need to build a measure of connection and consensus in order to bounce ideas off each other. A basic framework of mutual understanding, agreement and trust makes it easier to disagree and question. But when teams become too familiar with each other, they tip over into routinized habits of thought and assumptions which are rarely questioned. The team starts to drift towards like-mindedness and 'groupthink', smoothing out the internal diversity and 'creative tension' on which innovative processes depend. The team's capacity to innovate will thus follow the familiar upward and downward curve associated with organizational life-cycles.

The second danger is that as teams expand and as their productivity and turnover increase, there will be a pressure to specialize and assume a more tightly delineated set of roles and responsibilities. Distinctive individual perspectives are the grit in the oyster for the creative team, with individuals each contributing something different to the group. Over-specialization describes an excess of individualism, starting with a retreat into the self and a falling back into core competences. Energies and competences turn in onto themselves and individuals become locked into repetitive, defensive, and ultimately destructive routines. Familiar roles provide a comfort zone where we can affirm our own importance and excellence, even while the organization around us crumbles. By focusing on our own corner, we are spared the need to confront the larger problems unravelling around us.

These two problems – over-familiarization and over-specialization – are both exacerbated by organizational growth. As organizations and responsibilities expand and new members are recruited, the informal, overlapping roles become more sharply delineated and individuals become locked into their own areas of expertise. At the same time successful experiments and projects are repeated and absorbed into routine procedures and tacit knowledge. Over-familiarization leads to an easy consensus around certain assumptions and routines, making it harder to break out of familiar habits of thought. The organization's framework of possibilities is narrowed and the capacity to innovate is eroded. Over-specialization is the flipside to this process, with the same accretion of habits and perceptions occurring at the level of the individual. As the organization expands, individual roles shrink and individuals retreat into themselves and their own narrowly defined expertise and tasks. The creative team starts to fragment into a disconnected aggregate of self-absorbed individuals, refusing to share information or step outside their own personal narratives. Internal communication starts to break down into cliquishness, introversion and a cult of expertise. If over-familiarization blocks the capacity to innovate, over-specialization blocks the capacity to absorb innovation. In an over-specialized team, individuals find it increasingly difficult to understand, accept and build on other people's ideas.

The paradox here is that organizational change is not the same thing as organizational growth. As organizations expand and become more successful, they become less likely to change – naturally it is harder to justify change and experimentation if something appears to be working successfully. At the point when they should be enjoying the first fruits of success, creative teams begin, almost imperceptibly, a process of implosion – death by entropy. The literature on organizational change, examined in chapter 6, refers to the problems of the growing organization as a succession of crises and adaptations. Much of the management literature on organizational change is concerned with how managers can intervene to pre-empt these crises before they occur and prolong the successful phases of the organizational life-cycle. In creative teams, flexibility and multi-tasking are relatively easy to manage at the start of a process, project or organization. During the start-up phase, individuals are still learning about each other as individuals and about their collective relationships, boundaries and objectives. What can managers do to sustain this dynamism and fluidity into the future?

Managing the Creative Team

According to the preceding discussion, managers of creative teams face two principal challenges. First they must sustain diversity and flexibility within the team, overcoming a tendency towards conformity and complacency. The second challenge is to avoid over-specialization and fragmentation, ensuring that the parts do not distract from the whole and that team members retain a balance between specialist expertise and generalist understanding.

Innovative teams generate and develop ideas by switching frames of reference and challenging each other's preconceptions. This is a very different rationale from the uncritical process of 'brainstorming', which aims to remove constraints in order to release novel and surprising ideas. Innovation requires a more rigorous approach with an emphasis on the quality and value of the ideas generated rather than quantity. Where brainstorming is based on a refusal to challenge or censor ideas, innovative thinking requires a dialectical process, challenging assumptions from one frame of reference by layering in criticisms from another. The element of surprise comes not from random inventiveness but from discovering a connection between habitually disconnected concepts and frames of reference.

Managers might achieve this dialectic by attempting to micro-manage the creative process itself. More productively, rather than intervene in the process (which can be messy and confrontational), managers can intervene in the composition of creative teams, both by selecting the individual members and by identifying and modifying the roles and relationships within the group. Switching roles and perspectives disrupts the internal pattern of the creative team and prevents the steady accretion of habits and assumptions around individuals and around the group as a whole. Creative teams depend upon a tension between individual focus and collective process. Too much of one or the other begins the slide into over-specialization or over-familiarization respectively. If managed effectively, it should be possible to maintain that balance by allowing people to step outside their roles and exchange places with somebody else, and by encouraging the 'dual focus' which is the mark of a good actor. Much of the literature on organizational change aims to realign the organization with its external environment. For innovative teams, the key problem is the internal alignment between the team and its members. Achieving this alignment means managing internal tensions, between centrifugal and centripetal tendencies (over-specialization and over-familiarization).

Managerial interventions towards achieving this balance will be considered in more detail below. First I will consider how managers can address the problem of 'over-familiarization' through recruitment and human resources and through mediating or 'brokering' relationships within the team. Then I will consider the opposite problem of 'over-specialization' and suggest that this can be tackled through communication, training and recruitment and organizational structure.

Disrupting consensus, encouraging diversity

Alan Rivett, the director of Warwick Arts Centre, likens his approach to recruitment to casting actors in a play. Rather than looking at the actor and the part, his first focus is on the organizational *mise-en-scène*. There may be a checklist of competences and tasks, but the more important task is to discover the individual's 'character' and the likely impact on the rest of the cast. The question he asks himself at this point is not 'who is the best person for the job?', but 'what kind of character does this organization need today? Who do I want to cast and why?' Each new recruit will change the way the organization functions and provides an opportunity for recasting others. Playing with roles, recasting the key players, exchanging and stepping outside prescribed roles can help to maintain a greater self-awareness and reinject diversity and unpredictability back into a repetitive system.

Realignment of the creative team can of course be achieved through recruitment, varying the composition of the team by switching members between teams, or introducing new members. When teams become too familiar with each other's methods and mindsets, introducing a new member can disrupt consensus and increase creative capacity. Managers can play a more sophisticated role in collective creative processes by orchestrating or 'brokering' relationships within the team, reassembling the existing members into new configurations. Here the manager's role of bringing together different people is analogous to Koestler's definition of the creative process as 'bisociation' between two unfamiliar frames of reference.

This intermediary role is often undervalued within creative teams; the most visible contributors to the creative process are those who generate or perfect the idea, rather than the person who connects these two functions together in the first place. Consequently, senior managers sometimes fail to recognize the contribution of those who manage relationships within the team, seeing only the 'productive' members of the team rather than the productive relationships which connect them. This has led to a tendency to strip out some of the intermediate managerial roles in an organization. The practice of 'downsizing' or 'delayering' of organizations during the 1980s and 1990s targeted those people who seem to belong neither to management nor to practice, who sit between functional and hierarchical divisions in the organization. The implication was that these intermediaries were not productive and therefore disposable. This was short-sighted, especially in relation to managing creativity. In creative teams it is often the unseen, apparently unproductive member who is the invisible catalyst for the rest of the group and who is effectively 'brokering' the relationships which connect the group together. Again this perspective depends on a notion of creative teams as multifunctional processes rather than as aggregates of talented individuals.

Creative teams require active managerial involvement, not through directly controlling and leading a process of innovation, but more indirectly through monitoring and modifying the relationships which underpin that process. This role of 'brokering' creativity is well rehearsed in the creative industries, manifest in the intermediaries and Svengalis of the music industry who assemble 'manufactured' pop bands, or in the producers and impresarios who assemble crews and casts in television and film. By connecting disparate talents not only with each other but also with co-creators, resource providers, critics and audiences, creative intermediaries ensure one-hit wonders enjoy extended careers and perpetuate the relationships and networks which allow individual talents to thrive. The brokering function extends beyond the initial phase of assembling the team or group, into an ongoing readjustment and interaction, reinjecting diversity and manipulating creative tensions in the group.

Making connections, seeing the big picture

By intervening in the composition of the team, by 'brokering' creative relationships, a manager can disrupt the drift towards like-mindedness and over-familiarization. The flipside to this problem lies in the opposite extreme of over-specialization. As organizations move towards increasingly decentralized, individualized structures, the scope for confusion increases. Team-based organizations are especially vulnerable to an excess of diversity and complexity. Project-based teams encourage individual employees to focus on the immediate project and their immediate problems rather than on the larger aims of the organization. Like a bad actor who is focused only on their own performance, the individual employee determined by their own role may know their own lines but fail to notice or respond to what others are doing around them.

The tendency towards over-specialization is especially pronounced in the creative industries because of their reliance on specialist technologies and skills, the project-based nature of much creative work and the fragmentation and disintegration of their supply chains. This can encourage workers to see themselves and their tasks in a narrowly functional perspective, disconnected from the contexts which give their work meaning and value; as Marx noted of the first industrial revolution, specialization begets alienation. One of the first tasks of the manager is therefore to make connections between individual and collective achievements. In the creative industries, this often comes down to connecting individual specialized tasks with the completed product. Let the person who designed the door handle see the completed building. The completed product provides a vindication for the piece-workers who provided the components, but it can also provide a critical context. Once the individual understands the context within which their work will be used, they are better able to adapt and frame their own contribution.

The credit sequence at the end of a feature film testifies to the specialization and fragmentation of contemporary film production and the industry goes out of its way to acknowledge the parts which make up the whole, through awards ceremonies, credits, acknowledgements and social gatherings. As film production becomes increasingly dependent on computer-generated imagery, it is easy for the technology to become an end in itself. Yet one of the world's most successful animation and CGI studios, Pixar, goes out of its way to place technology and specialist expertise at the service of the medium. This is only possible because the company's star animators and designers can step back from their own specialist expertise and acknowledge the bigger narrative in which their work will eventually take place.

Much of this depends of course on the individual. Placing one's gifts at the service of the project rather than using the project as a showcase for one's talents requires a degree of modesty and self-awareness. What managers can do to encourage this attitude and capacity is to build a collective culture where individuals are motivated to care about the bigger picture, beyond their own immediate task and function.

Accordingly the first priority of the manager seeking to overcome over-specialization in the creative team is to develop a strong internal culture and to build connection and communication between members. Internal cultures in the creative industries are often modelled around aesthetic or social values, or around shared enthusiasm for the company's products. This can result in a fluid, informal style of communication which cuts across hierarchies, but can equally break down into distinctive sub-cultures, cliques and pockets of expertise, perpetuated by the kind of internal barriers noted in the previous chapter. Managers can address these divisions by fostering a stronger sense of collective ownership and involvement in the larger project, and by replacing hierarchical communication with an open conversation about the company's priorities and values.

The second area where managers need to address the problem of over-specialization is in training and recruitment. As noted in the previous section, the dynamics of creative teams and creative organizations mean that new members must not only match the skills and characteristics specified in the job description but must also fit into the complementary skills and characteristics of others. This is not a demand that new recruits should be 'one of us', quite the reverse – their contributions and competences will always be relative to the context in which they must operate, and they may need to deviate from existing norms and assumptions in order to galvanize those around them. What it does mean is that individual excellence is only half the battle – creative workers (and those who recruit them) need to understand how their role fits with everybody else's. The same argument applies to training. As skills become more granular and technical, managers need to train people to apply these skills in a non-specialist context. Somebody who has superlative IT skills but has no understanding (or interest) in how their programs and systems will be applied by others is of limited usefulness.

The problem of over-specialization is especially pronounced in the technical aspects of the creative industries, particularly in new media, but applies also to those who specialize in more 'creative' functions. If granular skills are not mediated by an understanding of the bigger picture, they are likely to be wasted. Technical skills and the acquisition of 'granular' knowledge play well in our divided culture. Technique feels safe, where creativity feels risky. Specialist expertise provides a comfort zone, from which we can safely dismiss or ignore the skills of others. Specialist skills also provide a marketable commodity and an entry point to employment. Consequently, 'training' in the creative industries tends to focus on the acquisition of skills with limited attempts to develop a broader understanding of the productive context in which those skills will be applied. A friend working for the BBC comments on the difficulty of finding employees who can engage with the business of broadcasting; graduates who are technically well qualified, even over-qualified, lack a rudimentary understanding of how their skills will be deployed, and to what end.

This specialization is of course consistent with trends in formal education, as described in the previous chapter, and with the casting of creativity as a specialized, individual skill, rather than a collective process. Managers may not be able to redress these traditions and assumptions entirely, but they can support a greater sharing of tacit knowledge within the organization and encourage exchanges of ideas and information in a language understood by all. Small creative enterprises typically lack the time and resources for training and do not follow formal career structures. Yet they are less vulnerable to over-specialization simply because they are small enough to be able to communicate with each other and to share ideas outside their own areas of expertise, and to understand how their separate contributions mesh together as a shared enterprise.

The final area in which managers can facilitate creative teams is in managing the structure of teams and organizations as they grow. As creative teams expand, the elements on which their success is based become diluted. Lines of communication based on informal contacts and shared experiences are replaced by formal systems and redefined roles. Growing a hierarchical system follows a simple geometry, adding layers to the pyramid or subdividing a unit, with individuals progressing through the hierarchy. Growing a team-based system requires a more sophisticated approach, with each new recruit demanding a subtle realignment of the existing talents. If individuals have grown too attached to their roles, or been type-cast by management, it becomes very difficult for the organization, and the individuals within it, to progress. Managers cannot solve all of these problems, but they can consider very carefully the alignment between individual and collective change. If the group starts to expand while leaving the individual members trapped in familiar roles, or if the individuals develop their own expertise beyond the capacity of the group to absorb and respond to them, that alignment is broken. When this happens, the resulting over-familiarization and over-specialization will undermine individual motivation and the integrity of the team. The dynamics of the creative team require that managers re-orient their human resources effort to address the relationships between people rather than the people themselves.

Creative Tension and the Need for Trust

In this chapter I have argued against the idea of creativity as an individual, specialist 'skill' and suggested that creativity is better understood as a process rather than as an individual trait – something we do, rather than something we have. Team-based innovation is an attempt to build a collective model of creativity and remains the key unit of activity in creative industries such as advertising or games development as well as in the research and development and new product development departments of mainstream businesses.

Nevertheless, the person-centred theory of creativity remains influential in 'team theory' and in the creative industries. One reason for this continuing emphasis on individual achievement is professional self-interest. The division of labour into separate specialisms supports the pre-eminence of individual professionals, and allows them to position themselves according to hierarchical systems of prestige and seniority within their peer group. But in the end such a division of labour, like the separation of creatives and suits referred to in the case study, is not very creative. If creative people remain locked into their specialist fields, however successfully, they risk entering a downward spiral towards homogeneity, predictability and entropy. Creativity requires diversity and contradiction as the raw material for unexpected lateral connections and 'bisociative' leaps of recognition between disconnected frames of reference. Opposition and difference within the creative team are the start-ing point for new and unexpected combinations of ideas. At a more pragmatic level, the processes of cultural production in the creative industries require an ability to switch between different ways of working and to connect the detail with the big picture. Such an internalized diversity is only possible if organizations and teams can tolerate opposition and difference.

Arthur Koestler describes creativity as the perception of a new idea in two self-contained and habitually disconnected frames of reference. Koestler calls this 'bisociation'. Instead of the linear connections possible within associative thinking, bisociation requires a shift of perspective between apparently incompatible 'matrices' or 'codes' of possibilities. So instead of recognizing an associative connection between objects within a pattern, the creative mind introduces a new set of reference points and reconfigures the original pattern. According to Koestler, the point of connec-tion between unfamiliar elements is where the act of creation occurs.

Koestler makes a further distinction between scientific and artistic creativity. Where scientific discovery depends upon 'synthesis', artistic creativity depends on 'juxtaposition'. The idea that art produces dissonance rather than resolution recalls the definition of creativity not as problem solving but as problem finding – the seeking out of difficulties and questions rather than the pursuit of order and integration. According to this definition, creativity requires a certain perversity. The act of creation depends not on the moment of discovery which sees a connection where others see only dissonance – it is the desire to seek out that dissonance and discon-nection in the first place.

In this chapter I have argued that in order to make new 'bisociative' connections, the innovative thinker must have access to alternative frames of reference or perspectives. The first danger to innovative thinking, especially in a team, is the steady accretion of consensus around shared values and habits of thought, sometimes described as 'groupthink'. In this chapter, I have suggested that managers and recruiters need to find ways of disrupting consensus and re-injecting diversity into systems which naturally tend towards repetition and convergence. They also need to prevent team members from becoming so self-involved and so narrowly focused on their area of specialization that they are unable to step back and see the connections between their individual talents and alternative perspectives and frameworks.

In order to achieve this creative friction between different individuals and different frames of reference, the missing ingredient is perhaps mutual trust and respect. From a managerial perspective, the dissonance, disruption and counter-intuitive juxtaposi-tion contained in the creative process are challenging. Innovation is not a comfortable project. Those involved are likely to be 'difficult', argumentative, passionate, disruptive. They will not fit the comfortable notion contained in that old standby of job descriptions, 'good team player'. They will disrupt rather than seek consensus. No doubt these tendencies to disruption and dissidence will need to be 'managed' and countered by attempts to socialize the team, to establish shared languages and com-mon understandings. But they are necessary.

Building complexity and diversity into the organization thus becomes a core task of organizational design. When Greg Dyke, the Director-General of the BBC, described the corporation in 2001 as 'hideously white', his concern was perhaps not only the problem of 'institutional racism' in British public life, but the danger of homogeneity and like-mindedness in a creative organization. In creative teams, members must 'agree to differ'. In the creative industries, opposing points of view and different criteria and frames of reference can result in passionate disagreements. It would be easy for creative processes to fracture into mutual animosity – and of course this does occasionally happen, in the well-publicized 'creative differences' which leak out from film sets, recording studios and the offices of lawyers and publicists. My own experience of theatre is that the people I work best with are the ones I argue with and disagree with most vehemently. The emotional stress of creative work might explain why creative partnerships do not always last. The content of creative work, based on ideas and emotions, and the context, based on intensive, short-term projects, encourages high levels of emotional and intellectual commitment. Rows are inevitable. Yet underpinning these arguments (hopefully) there is an underlying trust and intimacy which allows each side to risk upsetting the other in the first place.

This might explain why social networks, friendships and emotional bonds form an important bedrock for creative work. Theatre performers are often derided for their emotional promiscuity – why are they always and so quickly on first name terms, why are they so overbearingly friendly with casual acquaintances? The answer may be that this is an insurance policy for their professional work. In order to take risks in performance and in rehearsals, actors have to build trust and intimacy, often from a baseline of distrust and mutual animosity. The smooth sociability outside the theatre is a necessary counterweight to disagreements and the clash of egos when they get down to work.

Framing this relationship between disagreement or 'creative tension' and mutual trust in terms of creativity, it is clear that individual diversity and dissonance can generate innovative ideas and new frames of references. But unless these ideas can be developed and tested through integration and dialogue, they are unlikely to be made valuable. Divergence must be balanced by convergence. Friction and conflict in creative collaborations are only sustainable through mutual trust and respect. As in the opening chapter, creative processes seem to require a tolerance for contradictions.

How can these contradictory tendencies be nurtured within the creative team? At the managerial level, I have argued that managers can and should intervene in the composition and communication system within the team. On the one hand, a productive team depends upon a level of mutual trust and understanding – only if there is a base line of shared norms and expectations can individuals feel free to differ. On the other hand, by responding to group dynamics and through changes in personnel, managers can re-inject diversity and surprise into systems which tend towards repetition and consensus. Creative teams depend upon constructive disagreements, not smooth harmony or mutual indifference. Managers must develop connection without consensus.

At the individual level, team members need to maintain a dual consciousness, mining their own internal resources for new ideas, but also deploying them tactically in response to the other players in the group. Here I believe the metaphor of theatrical role-play can be productive, in particular an approach based on playing *with* roles rather than playing *in* roles; 'character' becomes a means of sparking interactions with other players, rather than an end in itself. Too much inward focus on the role blocks out the other actors. Too many individuals speaking out in the creative team means that nobody is heard and promising ideas remain blocked or undeveloped. Trust and intimacy provide a context within which individuals can express themselves but also hear voices other than their own.

Creative Teams Need Uncreative People

I began this chapter by arguing that the creative team is the key source of innovation for industry, whether in the so-called creative industries themselves or in research and development and new product development in manufacturing and engineering. The creative team provides a bridge between individual inventiveness and collective creativity. In the creative team, ideas are not only generated but tested, developed and applied. Spontaneous, intuitive processes come up against rigour and rational argument. Creative teams connect new ideas with the heritage of past experience and performance, and rule-breaking with rule-making – teams will be more effective if they work to a brief and if they retain some organizational memory of previous projects. Without knowing the rules and precedents, it is impossible to deviate from them.

Perhaps the most important creative contribution of the creative team is not the spectacular moment of 'breakthrough thinking' (which can, after all, be an individual experience too), but the recognition and development of half-formed ideas. Teams need listeners and idea adapters as well as idea generators, they need convergent thinkers as well as divergent thinkers, they need a 'problem-solving' capacity as well as a 'problem-finding' capacity. Above all they need to retain a sense of 'fitness for purpose' and an understanding of how their proposals will mesh with the broader realities of the organization, in terms of resources, objectives and markets. Understanding the big picture is more likely to provide an incentive for idea generation than a block on creativity. Creative teams need to be integrated into the overall organizational system, not seen as free-floating satellites. Intermediaries and brokers who stand at the transition points within the organization thus become a key resource for knowledge transfer and idea development.

Beyond the composition and management of the creative team, ideas about team-based innovation reconnect with some of the earlier concerns raised in this book. Too often, team-based innovation follows the 'genius' model of talented individuals and breakthrough thinking. If we place too much emphasis on the purely novel aspects of idea generation we risk ignoring the less glamorous process of idea recognition and value creation. If we focus exclusively on the composition of the team, we ignore the organizational and managerial context through which that team is manipulated and supported. Some of the most important functions and the most important members of the creative team do not appear to be especially 'creative' in themselves. Yet the combination of these different elements is what allows creative processes to occur.

In this chapter I have argued that creative people are not characterized by any specific characteristic or combination of characteristics. Creative thinking is characterized by a combination of different thinking styles, in particular a dialectic between rational, incremental thinking and spontaneous, intuitive thinking. Beyond this combination of thinking styles, creative thinking is also characterized by an ability to connect different elements into new forms and to make rapid transitions between perceptions and experiences. Following on from this, creativity theory lends itself to complex, 'multi-tasking' individuals, to collective models of creative work and to organizational structures based on teams. However, where creativity theory departs from a management theory of team roles and matrix organizations is in the notion of role-*play* and 'divided selves'. Creative teams require a chameleon ability to switch roles, to inhabit the other person's mental space at the same time as occupying our own.

Creative teams move the focus from individuals to groups. They also point away from a person-based theory of creativity towards an approach based on collective systems. Instead of attempting to cultivate or recruit a particular type of 'creative' person, managers in the creative industries seek to design collective systems and structures where individual creativity can be enabled and made effective. In the next chapter, the focus will broaden further to take in the networks and communities which connect individuals, teams and organizations and the managerial and policy interventions which support them.

FURTHER READING

The best known proponent of 'team theory' is perhaps Belbin (1993). For an excellent critique of Belbin's position, see McCrimmon (1995). The discussion of creative teams and innovation in this chapter draws on a variety of articles including Bilton and Leary (2002), Kirton (1984), Thompson (2003) and Amabile (1998).

The best-known proponents of 'trait-based' approaches to creativity were Howard Gardner and Frank Barron. Barron identified the contradictions in this approach and came up with a model of creativity based on an ability to inhabit different perceptions and positions rather than on any single personality type (see Gardner 1984; and Barron 1958). For an example of the 'creative testing' approach, see Torrance (1988). The best-known psychometric testing technique is the Myers-Briggs Type Indicator, which correlates cognitive styles to Jungian psychological types – this system is frequently used by HR professionals to identify and measure individual creativity.

Systems theories of creativity attempt to place the internal psychological or behaviourist approach to creativity in a broader context. Systems theories will be discussed in more detail in the next chapter.

Arthur Koestler's defines bisociation in *The Act of Creation* (1976: 35–50). Koestler initially describes bisociation in terms of humour – a pun is based on 'the clash of the two mutually incompatible codes, or associative contexts, which explodes the tension'. This differs from the more normal process of association, where we make connections between concepts within the same associative context or matrix, because it connects together two separate frames of reference which appear to be governed by incompatible rules or 'codes'. The concept of bisociation becomes the basis of an extended meditation on various forms of creativity and creative thinking in art and science. Margaret Boden's theory of creativity as 'transforming

ıal space', in *Dimensions of Creativity* (discussed in chapter 4) echoes Koestler's
d methodology.

1   Muɪɾay Belbin's 'team roles at work' model has been very influential on management
    approaches to team building. See the notes in the Further reading section, or visit the
    Belbin website (www.belbin.com).

3 CREATIVE SYSTEMS: IMPLICATIONS FOR MANAGEMENT AND POLICY IN THE CREATIVE INDUSTRIES

> *All ideas originate with individuals, but their ideas must fit into a matrix of innovation before progress is made. The innovation matrix extends across groups of researchers and, in many cases, across nations and the world.*
>
> (Sir Alec Broers, cited in Leadbeater 2000: 14)

> *Creativity is not the product of individuals, but of social systems making judgements about individuals' products.*
>
> (Csikszentmihalyi 1999: 314)

In the opening chapter, I proposed a psychological model of creativity as a complex combination of different thinking styles. Such a model deflects attention away from the creative individual towards the 'system' or 'art world' within which creative work takes place. This in turn leads to a sociological model of creativity involving a combination of different types of people, and a growing interest in the environment, organization or ecology which enables creativity to happen. These sociological, systems-based theories thus build upon the cognitive, psychological theories of creativity in broadening the definition of creativity to encompass multiple dimensions and levels *outside* the individual as well as within.

Just as systems theories of creativity have shifted focus away from trait-based models of creative individuals towards the communities and relationships which define them, studies of the creative industries have become increasingly concerned with the geographical networks which connect creative organizations and individuals. Cultural production is seen to be embedded in and made possible by specific geographical and historical contexts. This has implications for management and policy in the creative industries.

The creative and media industries are increasingly characterized in terms of networks and clusters of activity, some spontaneously formed by groups of individuals and businesses, some artificially engineered by policy makers. Scholarly attention has focused on the localized geography of the creative industries and the extent to which creative work is rooted in communities and cultures. From a policy perspective, 'clustering' of the creative industries has become increasingly fashionable, with commentators claiming that local hotspots of creative activity, especially in cities, will produce a ripple of benign social and economic impacts on local economies and communities. From a managerial perspective, a systems view of creativity leads to an interest in organizational design and networks, and away from a preoccupation with individual talent.

In this chapter I will begin with a brief exploration of how and why creative networks occur in the creative industries. I will then consider the relationship between creative networks and creativity from a more conceptual perspective, based upon the workings of complex adaptive systems. I will conclude with a summary of the implications of these theories for management and policy.

The Cultural Geography of the Creative Industries

Psychological and sociological definitions of creativity alert us to the network of relationships within which individual moments of discovery happen. According to a systems theory of creativity, the bright sparks of illumination only catch fire when the right combination of elements is assembled. Creative individuals are embedded in informal networks of collaboration, expertise and influence.

These networks extend in two dimensions, horizontally, through peer-to-peer relationships with organizations and individuals, and vertically, through supply chain relationships which contribute to the different phases of cultural production and distribution. These horizontal and vertical relationships in turn describe the geography of the creative industries, in which cultural production is embedded in predominantly local networks and face-to-face communities, but also extends upward and downward into global patterns of ownership, distribution and consumption. They also correspond respectively to systems of production and idea generation, and systems of consumption, reputation and idea exploitation.

Horizontally, individuals and organizations develop their ideas through informal collaborative relationships with their peers. These relationships are based on an accumulation of 'social capital', a mutual exchange of information and ideas which creates goodwill and eventually repays the giver. They also invest in a shared pool of talent and knowledge accessible to all. Crucially, because transactions and transfers of knowledge are not tangible, they are not usually recorded or accounted for. There is thus a tendency to take horizontal networks for granted, or simply to ignore them. Contact lists are used as an individual resource in the creative industries, but rarely audited or managed in any systematic way by organizations, still less by policy makers.

Vertically, creativity does not begin and end with the idea. The creative process requires us to take a concept through a series of phases, drawing on different mental resources at each stage. In a sociological analysis of the creative industries, each stage in the development of an idea also draws upon networks of resources, people and organizations. Compared to the 'invisible' horizontal networks of idea generation, these vertical networks of idea exploitation and development in the creative industries are transparent. The processing of ideas into commodities is achieved through a series of intermediaries ranged along the supply chain and measured through a series of transactions for the buying and selling of intellectual property rights.

The disparity between horizontal and vertical networks in the creative industries is also one of power and scale. At one end of the value chain, idea generation draws upon informal, local networks of collaboration between individuals, groups and organizations; at the other end of the scale, vertical relationships are funnelled through a handful of global media and entertainment companies. This disparity is also geographical. Vertical networks providing access to capital and markets are global; horizontal networks, providing access to clusters of creative activity and a pool of resources and skills, tend to be more localized.

There are obvious challenges here for policy and management in the creative industries, to which we will return, particularly the management of capital flows and access to markets. First I wish to consider in more detail the 'horizontal' patterns of collaboration which underwrite creative activity.

The Strength of Weak Ties

Granovetter's analysis of relationships within networks led to the counter-intuitive discovery that networks depend primarily on the 'weak' ties of acquaintance, rather than the 'strong ties' of kinship and membership (Granovetter 1973). At one level this is simply a reassertion of Metcalfe's Law and its underlying premise, that in a network, quantity of relationships is more important than quality.[1] When we become locked into strong mutual relationships, our broader circle of acquaintances shrinks – so strong ties tend to undermine weak ties and in the end contract the network. But Granovetter's analysis is also relevant to a sociological or 'systems' view of creativity; strong ties tend towards duplication and like-mindedness, with both parties likely to share similar concepts and values. Weak ties on the other hand allow for more diverse, less familiar connections – the frisson of the unexpected encounter.

A related hypothesis concerns the different types of relationships which occur at the centre and periphery of a network. Networks can obviously take many forms, but it is obvious from a geometrical perspective that the nodes at the centre of the network will be more connected than those at the periphery. On the other hand those nodes which find themselves at the periphery will have greater opportunity for rubbing up against *other* networks. The hypothesis following from this analysis in terms of creativity is that the peripheral actors in a network will have greater access to unexpected, non-habitual connections than those at the core. They are also more likely to span boundaries between networks, and are therefore likely to be more 'creative'.

Putting these insights together, a third hypothesis emerges: as networks expand and as the initial membership becomes more integrated and central to the network.

their ability to access new paradigms and perspectives, and hence their creative capacity, will decrease. Through a process of familiarization, proximity and information sharing, they will drift towards the centre, and weak ties will become strong ties. Gradually they will tend towards greater conformity to the norms and values established by the network and they will lose their peripheral ability to make unexpected connections. Hence their creative capacity will decline, even as they accumulate prestige among their peer group.

One could object that this drift to the centre is premised on a rather static and two-dimensional view of networks, assuming that there is a single centre to the network and a stable configuration which is not affected by the gravitational pull of other networks around them. If we accept that individuals and organizations belong to multiple networks, some of which intersect and others of which do not, the 'core-periphery' structure of networks and its accompanying hypotheses start to look less convincing. Nevertheless, the core-periphery model of networks contains challenging perspectives for collective creativity. The drift towards core assumptions at the centre of the network echoes the tendency towards like-mindedness in creative teams discussed in the previous chapter. Furthermore, if creative people are good at crossing between different networks and value systems, we should look for creativity in the transitions between systems at the periphery of the network rather than in the stable, familiar relationships at the centre.

Networking and clustering, as noted at the beginning of this chapter, are fashionable concepts in the creative industries and in management. The sociological theory of creativity has been converted into a series of apparently incontrovertible assertions. First, creative work, by virtue of its reliance on specialized skills and individual talents, is dependent on multiple connections. Secondly, it follows that for creative activity to thrive, many connections are preferable to few. Thirdly, networks and clusters must therefore provide a fertile breeding ground for creative ideas. There is some truth in these assertions. But if policy makers and managers attempt to intervene in the delicate ecology of networks, especially in the creative industries, there is a danger that they end up centralizing and locking down networks which were previously fluid, transient and complex. This ignores the strength of weak ties and results in stable, centralized networks where 'like-mindedness' outweighs the peripheral, unexpected connections on which creativity depends.

In the previous chapter I argued that members of creative teams need a kind of 'dual consciousness' allowing them to switch between their specialist tasks and expertise and the broader context of the organization. There is an analogous relationship between the organization and the network in the creative industries, with members switching affiliations between the specific organization and the wider network. The network provides a needed source of continuity in a sporadic project-based system. The organization and its members are continually realigning themselves, switching between the relationships within the creative team and their broader contacts and affiliations with the network outside. Indeed, to speak of organizations at all may be missing the point. In a creative system an organization is just a temporary system of communication which allows a specific project to occur – it may not have any longer-term purpose beyond this project, at the end of which it will simply rejoin the cultures and communities which gave rise to it in the first place. Trying to fix this process into a known quantity of organizations is therefore problematic; 'mapping' the creative industries by auditing the formally constituted organizations is like trying to measure the bubbles on the surface of a boiling pot.

The visible peaks of the creative industries are underwritten by a mess of informal creative activity which precedes and facilitates them, and by a value chain which extends upwards and outwards beyond them. If we accept the systems view of creativity, our unit of analysis should no longer be the individual or even the individual business, but the system or ecology which supports them. Individuals and businesses come and go – this has led many observers (especially investors) to lament the notorious instability of the creative and media industries. How can they invest in a record label or film production when the stars might walk out tomorrow, or start suing each other? How can governments 'map' the creative industries when much of the activity takes place offstage, in non-commercial transactions and sociability? Yet despite this apparent volatility, the overall system retains a measure of momentum and continuity, beyond the sum of its parts. A group of freelancers and micro-enterprises converge on a particular project, then split up once the project is completed, disappear for a while, then re-emerge in a new configuration around a new project. From the outside it might appear that businesses are dying and being born at an alarming rate – but on closer analysis, familiar names and faces recur. A cluster of enterprises, a network, or a city thus accumulates a cultural dynamism which is difficult to attribute to specific individuals or organizations.

Locating creativity in a system or network rather than in a gifted individual also connects back to the redefinition of 'creativity' proposed in chapter 1. According to this perspective, creativity lies as much in organizing a system of relationships as in 'the act of creation' – and the act of creation is itself dependent upon a system of relationships. Individual skill or talent in the creative industries is less important than the ability to select talented partners for a given project. The 'internalized otherness' of the creative individual described in previous chapters is here externalized into relationships with a wider circle of acquaintances and contacts (see case study). Just as artists orchestrate and manipulate their thought processes and thinking styles within a complex and apparently contradictory 'divided self', creative managers must learn to tolerate diversity and complexity, brokering relationships across boundaries and identifying unlikely connections with other actors across the network. The line between 'management' and 'creativity' thus becomes blurred and, especially in the creative industries, increasingly unnecessary. The distinction between creative individuals and creative managers seems to come down to a question of scale and the 'unit of analysis'. Individual creativity stems from a self-conscious, deliberate process of observing and responding to multiple internalized 'subselves'[2] and linking together different thinking styles. Organizational creativity is concerned with making connections between individuals and organizations within a creative network or 'system'. In either case the key to creativity is the ability to manage complexity and contradiction.

key to creativity

Case Study: Theatre as a Creative System

Susan Fenichell is a theatre director based in Brooklyn, New York. Her work has taken her all over the country, from Oregon and Seattle to New York, Philadelphia and New Jersey. Formerly an associate artistic director of the Intaman Theatre in Seattle, she is now the artistic director of her own ensemble, Hopeful Monsters, but most of her work today is as a freelance. Over the years she has built up good working relationships with a pool of fellow professionals – designers, writers, actors, lighting designers, composers and producers. She also has a reputation for a certain way of directing, reworking classic texts and finding in them a contemporary political or cultural resonance.

Theatre is a collaborative medium both in its production process and in its economy. Much of Fenichell's work comes about not through a formal commission but through a collaborative interaction with her colleagues, many of whom she has worked with before. Ideas are generated informally before they turn into productions with budgets. In these circumstances it is difficult to identify the division between 'paid' and 'unpaid' work, between employment and unemployment. What ends up being pitched to the producing theatre as a fully conceived production begins life as an informal conversation between individuals. The initial exchange of ideas is also a pooling of contacts. The first conversation might involve an outsider approaching Fenichell or one of her associates, but soon extends outwards to involve other potential collaborators from her network.

Theatre and film director Sam Mendes, while he was still directing student plays at university, observed that 90 per cent of the success of a production depends on good casting. Admittedly this remark applies especially in the context of a limited pool of student actors, but can be extended more generally into the production process of theatre and to the development of a professional career. All collective creative work involves an element of casting. When theatre professionals choose who to work with, they are simultaneously constructing a CV and a source of future employment. As a freelance, Fenichell's livelihood is dependent on her network. When producers approach her they are not only hiring her, they are also buying access to her creative team of associates. Her reputation and track record are thus built on the quality of her own work but also on the reputation of previous associates, and on her choices of collaborators and projects. These relationships are reciprocal – there is no hierarchy between members of the network and the invitations to come on board a specific project can come from directors, designers, producers, even actors.

From the outside the 'networking' of the theatre industry can appear incestuous or exclusive. Given the risk of mounting any creative endeavour, there is a natural tendency to prefer the trusted former colleague over the untried talent. In the absence of any formal career structure, individuals must also rely upon a steady accumulation of contacts to construct reputations and status and to gain employment. Yet for networks to evolve and grow they also need to be sufficiently porous to allow new talent into the system – Fenichell and her colleagues do not want to become locked into a set rotation of contacts. Different projects demand different talents, and they also demand new sources of ideas and information. As a director, Fenichell has recognized opportunities for rejuvenating texts by incorporating non-theatrical sources (testimonies, documentary material), into some of her productions. As a theatre professional, she also has to find ways of replenishing her network and plugging into new contacts and new relationships. One way of doing this is to reposition herself on the periphery of the network rather than allowing herself to drift towards the centre. In Fenichell's case, this was perhaps achieved by physically relocating from the west to the east coast, or by her recent forays from theatre into opera. For Mendes, a similar relocation came with the decision to leave the Donmar Warehouse in London for a new career in the US as a film maker.

What we see in the theatre is a good example of a complex adaptive system. In the transition from informal, sometimes random encounters into formal theatre productions with a list of credits, order emerges at the edge of chaos. Yet the 'edge' is necessary to retain the vitality and dynamism of the product. There is a dilemma here; theatre professionals rely on a pool of trusted collaborators to construct their careers and reputations, but creatively they also depend on the 'weak ties' of diverse acquaintances and chance encounters as sources of new inspiration. This perhaps underlies Fenichell's decision to reposition herself as a freelance director rather than working exclusively with her own troupe or seeking a permanent position with a repertory theatre. It is also reflected in the movement by theatre directors into other media (opera, film, multimedia) where they are forced out of their comfort zone.

From a management perspective, the challenge is to find a way into this complexity without unravelling it. Theatre production depends on a delicate ecology of collaborations between individual talents. If a producer or a producing theatre attempts to assemble a creative team without understanding this ecology, or to launch a project without allowing it to emerge from a gradual accretion of ideas and contacts, the creative process is shoehorned into a linear, predictable pattern. Top-down interventions can provide a catalyst for new projects, but they cannot pre-empt the connections and inputs which will eventually result in a completed product. Delegating decisions on personnel and content downwards to those directly involved in the process rather than attempting to control or pre-empt them requires a hands-off management style and a long-term approach to developing new work.

Theatre managers are aware of the need to provide space within the system within which unexpected encounters and unplanned outcomes can germinate. Many theatres create an informal support network for writers and directors developing new scripts, providing new writing programmes, workshops, studios and rehearsal spaces for devised work. Some employ 'dramaturgs' to broker connections between these informal networks and the main theatre; interestingly the equivalent position exists in some European orchestras too, but is comparatively rare in the commercial creative sector.

Of course such development work and networking efforts are expensive for the theatres and do not deliver any immediate or obvious returns for investors, sponsors and funders. In a climate of increased accountability and scarce resources, the decision to invest in peripheral resources, spaces and people outside the core business is hard to justify. Such programmes only make sense in relation to the evolution of a creative system, and cannot be measured through the specific outcomes of singular projects. Whether operating in the commercial sector or in the subsidized system, theatre managers have to persuade their backers to take a long-term perspective on developing new ideas and talent.

The collective system of theatre also depends on trust and reciprocity. Theatre is a gift economy where institutions and individuals invest time and resources in supporting an invisible, informal creative community or network. In the short term, new writing projects and studio spaces may not yield any 'product'. Even if they are successful, institutions cannot guarantee to reap the rewards of the ideas and talents they helped to develop. Similarly the time Fenichell spends talking to colleagues may not result in any immediate paid work, or her idea might be hijacked or taken forward without her. Mutual trust is obviously important here. Yet even if the individuals and institutions concerned do not enjoy any immediate benefit, there is a tacit recognition that such investments are necessary for the overall health of the system, because this system in turn provides the life blood of the network, a pool of contacts and projects which flows between and underneath the visible outcomes of plays, contracts and pay cheques.

In the theatre industry, individuals and institutions depend on their networks. Investing in and diversifying these networks is a collective necessity. Practically speaking, these investments are risky, for the individual and for the institution, because there is no obvious, immediate or guaranteed return. Yet by constructing and developing a network, freelance directors and producing theatres are building a creative system and sowing the seeds for their own future livelihoods.

Implications for Management

The first implication for management in a systems theory of creativity is to focus again on the value chain. Where Porter's original discussion of the value chain envisaged an internalized value chain within an integrated firm, that value chain has now been externalized and is conducted through partnerships and strategic alliances between firms rather than within firms. This disintermediation of the value chain is especially pronounced in the creative and media industries, where the 'chain' is better described as a network, with an overall shift in the centre of influence towards the customer or end user. The linear movement 'upstream' and 'downstream' between producers, *"sticking and knitting"* Complex!

intermediaries and markets is now more complex and unpredictable, with organizations closest to the customers pulling in sources of value from multiple suppliers and repackaging these to meet the needs of an increasingly demanding and fragmented market.

This reorientation of the value chain might be considered to be broadly applicable to any industry which is moving towards a 'post-Fordist' system of production and consumption. Indeed the restructuring of the Hollywood film industry from the integrated studio system of the 1950s to the networks of specialized firms outsourcing and collaborating in today's industry has been presented as a classic case of post-Fordist industrial structure (Storper 1994). This restructuring and disintermediation goes further in the creative industries because notions of 'value' are dependent upon the subjective, individual interpretation of 'symbolic goods' in the mind's eye of the consumer. Consequently, the creative industries have to work much harder to engage with and manipulate customer perceptions of value, through critical reappraisal, customized marketing and innovative modes of packaging and delivery. Intermediaries and opinion formers (DJs, critics, fan clubs) play a critical role in positioning the product in its market. New technologies for digital distribution of film, music, games and information have changed the relationship between producers and consumers, allowing and demanding greater customization, faster response times and new forms of value added at the point of consumption (mobility, convenience, transferability of content between devices).

One consequence of this reconfiguration of value chains and networks in the creative industries is to shift attention away from 'content' to the ways in which that content is filtered, packaged, delivered and consumed. This is reflected in the 'vertical' structures of distribution in the creative industries and the high cost of marketing relative to production. I will return to the question of marketing and 'creative consumption' in chapter 7. At this point I want to focus on another aspect of the creative industries' value chain, the high degree of dependency between firms.

In a systems theory, creativity is dependent upon the relationships *between* individuals and organizations, not the competences *within* individuals and organizations. The creative industries themselves are characterized by high levels of mutual dependence and a high proportion of their creative work takes place outside the boundaries of traditionally structured organizations, undertaken by a variety of intermediaries, from freelance individuals to specialist organizations who act as aggregators of other people's products and information. To be successful in the creative industries it is not enough to have a good idea or product. The successful realization and delivery of that idea rests on a network of contacts and intermediaries who lie outside our immediate control. According to a systems theory of creativity, the network of critics, retailers, marketers, agents, editors, broadcasters or talent scouts outside the firm are as crucial to the successful reception of the product as the product's originators.

A good deal of management theory and practice, including Porter's own theory of competitive advantage and value chains, is based on consolidating the firm's unique competences and strengths, in competition with other rival firms. In the creative industries, this concentration on core competences, also known as 'sticking to the knitting', is just not possible. So much of the value of the firm's products is

the connecting with the customer is much more difficult.

All about networking which is not in our control.

dependent on variables, individuals and organizations which lie outside the firm's immediate orbit. Porter's strategic response to this problem is to take control of the firm's value chain and seek to align the firm's competences with suppliers and buyers upstream and downstream, locking them into impregnable, interlocking partnerships and ensuring that the core aims and values of all the participants are harmonized. The solution in the creative industries is more pragmatic, using techniques such as viral marketing, peer to peer networking and 'open source' software to hand over control of the product to a network of intermediaries and collaborators. This goes beyond mere 'outsourcing' or 'disintermediation' to a real devolution of power and responsibility. As will be discussed further in chapter 7, consumers and their representatives use a variety of media such as fanzines, user communities, clubs and websites, reviews and blogs to take control of products and redefine their meaning and value.

As a result of this reorientation of the value chain, the creative industries are characterized by a core-periphery structure, polarized between very large conglomerates primarily concerned with distribution and exploitation and smaller firms and individuals who orbit around them, concerned primarily with generating content. As already noted, this core-periphery structure is an efficient way of dealing with creativity, because the organizations at the edge of the network, the 'independents' or 'fringe' elements are free to develop new alliances and new forms of content which are fed back to the centre. In the music industry, for example, the independent labels provide an informal artist development service for the majors, building new acts to the point where they are ready to cross over into the mainstream. Independent film producers enjoy a similar relationship with larger independents like Miramax, who in turn are linked into the major studios for purposes of distribution and finance. Independent retail and distribution channels can also complement the mainstream market by repositioning and reinterpreting mainstream products for niche audiences. One of the possible defences for Napster's illegal music download services, not submitted in evidence by Napster's lawyers, is that Napster and other similar services provided a niche marketing channel for the major record labels. Having fought to close Napster down, a year later one of the major labels (BMG) decided to invest in a new service, Napster 2.0. In a separate development Napster's founder Shawn Fanning set up a new company, Snocap, helping the majors to develop legal peer-to-peer music download services. Such collaborative ventures are more representative of the creative industries than mutual antagonism and lawsuits – and more productive.

This cooperative network structure starts to unravel, however, if those at the centre attempt to centralize control over the periphery. Continuing with the example of the music industry, if the majors attempt to intervene in the decision making of the independent sector, the peripheral innovative capacity of the network as a whole is undermined. As the transition between innovative fringe and mainstream success is accelerated, the creative industries risk losing the innovative capacity of the network. In today's highly competitive creative industries, new talents are rushed onto the big stage before they have time to develop, receive their fifteen minutes of fame, then vanish into obscurity. Televised talent shows like *Pop Idol* and its many variants and franchises around the world do not so much discover or nurture new talent as absorb it. Individual eccentrics are moulded into manufactured pop stardom. Entire careers are telescoped into a matter of months, from discovery, first exposure and chart success through to repetition, boredom and a rapid return to obscurity. From a systems perspective, what is happening here is that the periphery is being sucked into the centre, and the autonomy and unpredictability of the network is being streamlined around the core objectives and competences of a handful of dominant organizations. In this context the music industry's initial attempts to shut down illegal file-sharing networks like Napster, Gnutella and Grokster, while legally and morally justified, were commercially short-sighted.

In fairness, the major players in the creative industries have for the most part tended to resist this temptation to over-centralize. Large organizations have always looked to buy a stake in smaller organizations and used these alliances to tap into new sources of talent and new markets; the structures of film, music, television and publishing are a cat's cradle of cross-media ownership, part-ownership, alliances and joint ventures dominated by a handful of corporations. But the underlying approach to ownership has usually been light touch – less control, more collaboration. For example, when Sony acquired a 49 per cent stake in Alan McGee's independent record label Creation Records, they nevertheless waived their option to acquire complete control of the business, hoping that McGee would continue to do what he did best, discover and develop new talent. Only when McGee himself wound up Creation did Sony inherit what remained of the business and the bands still on the Creation roster; it was an outcome for which Sony cannot in the end be held responsible.

However, as the new creative and media landscape is overshadowed by a dwindling oligarchy of cross-media giants, this light touch is under threat. Global corporations like News International or Time Warner–AOL are now stretched across so many separate media and territories, some rationalization and strategic centralization is inevitable. The temptation to seek synergies, to impose a strategic blueprint, to realign the value chain, to milk the junior partners until their creative juices dry up, grows more plausible with each successive round of mergers and acquisitions. As these new behemoths extend their reach, their understanding and respect for their new acquisitions diminishes, replaced by the need to extract maximum shareholder value from each deal as quickly as possible. Major labels began to encroach on independent territory during the 1990s, aggressively buying up independent labels and setting up their own 'pseudo-independent' subsidiaries. Major label involvement does not of course necessarily mean a loss of aesthetic independence and it would be naive to assume that 'indie' music is the preserve of independent labels. But even if they have given birth to temporary artistic successes, forced marriages between majors and independents have seldom been lasting or happy.

The model of systems theory suggests that this centralization of control is a mistake. Attempting to control too much and to ensure a strategic alignment of the supply chain will kill the creativity of the system. Better to leave some space for the system to evolve its own rules and relationships. Creativity depends upon a hidden network of collaboration – again this is especially true in the creative and media industries as a result of the fragmentation and specialization of creative work. The temptation, according to classic management theory, is to seek a better 'fit' between the strategic core and the peripheral partners. Underlying this principle is a desire to control resources and focus on outcomes rather than inputs. But in the creative industries, the correlation between inputs and outcomes is highly unpredictable; the only thing we can be sure of is that a multiplicity of inputs – in other words, complexity – is more likely to result in quality of outcomes. Rather than seeking to centralize the network, managers need to foster complexity and diversity at the point of idea generation. This relaxation of strategic control requires a degree of humility. Total involvement across the supply chain is simply not practicable in a system as complex as the creative industries. The relationship between core and periphery in the creative industries can be mutually beneficial, provided those at the centre do not attempt to control and pre-empt the periphery, and that those on the periphery avoid being sucked into the centre. Major corporations and independent enterprises can cooperate successfully in the creative industries provided they keep their distance.

Managing Creative Systems by 'Brokering' Knowledge

Knowledge management has become an important topic for managers, particularly as we edge towards a 'knowledge economy' where tacit knowledge and culture ('know-how') are seen to be as important as the explicit knowledge contained in technology and products ('know-what'). In the creative industries, 'know-how' is replaced by 'know-who'. It is not necessary to possess all the attributes of creativity within oneself, or even 'in house', within one's business. Far more important than the possession of talent is the ability to recognize and support it in others, and to know where to find it in the wider network.

In terms of knowledge management, managers have attempted to 'leverage' a firm's internal knowledge base – in other words, to make the tacit knowledge explicit and available, and to ensure that the firm builds on its accumulated memories and experiences. This management process is supported by theories about analysing and managing information, and by practical interventions in communications technology. Most managers are aware of these theories and practices, and have done their best to turn their businesses into 'learning organizations' and make sure that knowledge and ideas inside the business are shared by the many rather than hoarded by a select few.

The creative industries require a greater emphasis on external knowledge management. With the decentralization of cultural production and the fragmentation of integrated supply chains, knowledge has become similarly dispersed. Products and technologies are no longer distinct and self-contained. Industries and markets bleed into each other as a result of new synergies, technologies and emerging hybrid cultural forms. Amidst this complexity, it is no longer possible to know everything about the business – some pessimists go so far as to suggest that in the creative industries nobody knows anything. Knowledge is no longer an internally managed commodity – it is out there, among consumers, collaborators and competitors. Above all it is handled by the new 'infomediaries' – the connectors, standing between organizations and individuals, between ideas and resources. These intermediaries are the switching centres within the network, where the ideas and synapses of the total system are filtered and processed.

Some of these knowledge brokers are former insiders, team members made redundant because their knowledge was deemed surplus to requirements, now touting their knowledge and contacts for hire. In UK television, for example, former executives of the BBC play a prominent role in the independent sector, not least because they are better placed than most to connect independent productions with the commissioning editors of the major broadcasters. As noted in the previous chapter, the contribution of middle managers, intermediaries and idea champions (as opposed to idea generators) is often underestimated in creative teams and organizations. Having stripped out this 'unproductive' layer of middle management (or seen it depart of its own accord, lured by greater autonomy and better wages), creative organizations may find themselves forced to hire it back in again. Conversely outsiders also become sought after by those on the inside for the opposite reason, because they have a perspective or expertise which the corporate centre lacks. Shawn Fanning, the archetypal poacher turned gamekeeper referred to earlier in this chapter, is a good example of this sharing of knowledge and expertise across the network between former industry opponents.

It would be futile to try to reproduce this continually shifting and expanding knowledge base internally. Leveraging internal knowledge therefore takes second place to managing external contacts. Much of the business of the creative industries takes place among informal contacts and chance encounters across the network, not in boardrooms and offices. Rather than seeking knowledge within the firm's own knowledge base, the challenge for those on the inside is to tap into what's happening outside in the network – a reversal of 'inside knowledge'.

Exchanging ideas and making connections is much easier in small, informal groups where face-to-face communication is the norm. As organizations expand and adopt more formal structures, these informal networks of communication and trust extend outwards. When this happens, managers have to play an increasingly active function in identifying channels of communication and connection. The importance of internal connections and intimacy within the creative team was identified in the previous chapter. Managers must extend this network externally. In the absence of intimacy, managers must try to recreate these informal contacts and relationships themselves. At first sight much of this 'knowledge brokering' looks like wasted time. A significant challenge for management lies in recognizing the productive potential in communication and interaction which is not bounded by the immediate tasks and needs of the organization. The social culture surrounding creative and media businesses can seem self-indulgent and non-productive from the outside, an endless round of schmoozing, partying and 'hanging out'. Yet partly because the formal working relationships are dispersed through the specialization of creative work, social interaction provides a needed communication network where ideas can be exchanged and deals made. Much of the business of Britain's film industry takes place in bars in Soho, not in offices. The same could be said of other creative hotspots, from the artistic communities of Brooklyn and lower Manhattan to the parties and restaurants of Los

Angeles. As with the 'redundant' intermediary in the creative team, what appears to be unnecessary or irrelevant may turn out to have critical importance.

For many businesses today, 'knowledge management' has turned in on itself. The demand for internal data in today's organizations has escalated to the point where key messages are buried under repetitive, pointless details. In the subsidized arts (and in universities!), increased accountability has resulted in an increasing demand for information, but this constant flow of information does not result in increased understanding of the business or an exchange of ideas. Data collection is concerned with control rather than knowledge. The same 'data smog' of internal communication prevents external connections, or even unexpected connections across and within the organization. Lines of communication follow hierarchical patterns of accountability and control, rather than opening up fresh connections. Part of the problem here may be the shift towards electronic communications, especially e-mails and intranets. The need to respond to internal messages is all-consuming, blocking out a more open-minded, proactive approach to communication. Face-to-face communication can perhaps still offer a greater scope for the unexpected connection than electronic forms of interaction. In recent years some organizations have banned internal e-mails in an effort to get staff talking to each other again.[3] The paradox here is that the supposed connectivity of e-mail and intranets results in a kind of introversion and prevents us from accessing other networks and systems. Intranets are the enemies of 'extranets'.

Whatever the mode of communication, offline or online, internal or external, the key task for managers is to clear some space for outward-looking, non-task oriented communication. With the intensification of internal communication networks, 'strong ties' of loyalty, hierarchy and accountability are replacing 'weak ties' of sociability, curiosity and unpredictability. Communication has to extend beyond an internal system of monitoring and controlling data into a willingness to engage with ideas and realities outside the organization. What is needed here is a thin layer of casual contacts across a wide network rather than a narrow inwardly focused communications system – fewer meetings, more conversations.

A systems theory of creativity challenges preconceptions about the role of management. Competitors are also potential collaborators. Some of the relationships with other players in the network appear unproductive or wasteful. Relationships and partnerships with other organizations and individuals are not always tied to strategic objectives and outcomes. Much of the manager's role is focused not on the objectives of the single firm, but on sustaining complexity within a live network. New ideas grow out of complexity, and complexity within the organization and the network is essential to innovation. If managers attempt to align the network to their own strategic objectives, they risk subverting or destroying the connections and complexity which underpin creative work.

So what can managers do to support creative systems? First, in moving from a person-centred view of creativity to a systems view, the role of the manager within the organization changes. The person-centred view of creativity assumes that innovation emerges suddenly and spontaneously and leads managers to regard creativity as an issue for recruitment and training (creative people) rather than organizational design (creative systems and incremental processes). Engineering such a system becomes a key role for management, enabling connections across boundaries and encouraging people to exchange ideas and talents and to collaborate in their mutual development. Such connections require an active involvement from managers, not in the creative process itself, but in setting up the connections which precede and facilitate that process. Rather than attempting to control or manage the process, managers must use their contacts and their knowledge-brokering skills to tap into the knowledge and creativity which is spread across the network. This requires a much looser, less centralized approach to supply chain management and knowledge management.

In a systems view of creativity, the functions of management and creativity converge. Both are essentially concerned with establishing connections between ideas (novelty) and outcomes (value), by building alliances between individual talents, experiences, technologies and people. Both are manipulating and exploiting ideas; the process through which value is added is no longer by way of the linear 'value chain' but by creating a space within which individual talents, experiences and perceptions can collide in interesting ways. Within the creative industries, the functions of management and cultural production blur together; the key task is engineering the relationships within and between different individuals, between ideas and resources, and between different types of thinking within the creative process.

Implications for Policy

The tendency for policy makers to see the creative industries and creativity in terms of individual talent was noted in the first chapter of this book. This tendency isolates one element or phase in the creative process – the talented individual who comes up with innovative ideas. What this model leaves out is the more complex, more painstaking process of value creation which we find in the psychological process and in systems-based theories of creativity. It also ignores the pragmatic realities of the creative and media industries.

The genius model of creativity is reinforced in European cultural policy by a tradition of investing in cultural production. Cultural policy has evolved in relation to traditional arts sectors such as the performing arts, where high production costs and market failure mean that many art forms and arts organizations are simply not economically viable. Consequently, an important goal for cultural policy has been to subsidize the costs of cultural production.

Applying this model of production subsidy to the creative industries is problematic. Cultural production is only a small part of the overall creative system – indeed it has been argued that European cultural policy traditions have led to a crisis of *over*-production in the creative industries, especially in the film industry. As with the EU agricultural policy, production subsidies in the audiovisual sector have resulted in over-supply and a surplus of product with no market or distribution system to support them – films which nobody wants to see. Cultural production in the commercial creative industries is not always the most expensive part of the process, nor the most effective point of intervention for public subsidy. In many cases, ideas are relatively cheap, and the initial phases of idea generation and product origination in the creative and media industries are not in themselves expensive. We are all familiar with tales of films shot for $500, hit records recorded for £50, sketches on napkins. The expensive part is realizing, marketing and distributing these products – at which point public funding can rarely keep pace with commercial investment and becomes marginal or irrelevant.

If policy makers do want to support the creative and media industries, the key will be to intervene not in cultural production *per se* but in the horizontal and vertical networks which allow cultural production to happen. Yet it is not always easy to artificially engender these creative systems. The policy-based 'creative clusters', business districts and cultural quarters in today's cities attempt to mimic the characteristics of self-organizing creative systems, in particular the clustering of creative activity in metropolitan districts and artisanal communities. The problem with such a top-down approach is that officially sanctioned creative networks rarely succeed in encompassing the unexpected connections and contradictions on which creativity thrives. There is a danger here of a sanitized, officially sanctioned creativity which achieves security and like-mindedness at the expense of risk and diversity.

Horizontal networks do not necessarily occur directly between creative organizations. More often, connections are made through social networks and 'third spaces' – bars, clubs, cafés. Policy makers need to think laterally. By taking a broader approach to cultural policy they might succeed in nurturing the social networks and communities in which creative organizations thrive. This might extend into areas such as licensing of entertainment venues, rent control and housing policies, transport, childcare provision, links to higher and further education, welfare and unemployment benefit, youth and community development. This in turn challenges the compartmentalized structure of policy-making institutions, which manifest many of the cultural divisions noted in the opening chapter. Building alliances across different policy streams including economic development, social development and cultural development requires that policy makers themselves become 'networked' organizations in order to make effective interventions in creative systems. That old political mantra, 'joined up thinking', needs to extend horizontally across departments, not just downwards from strategy to implementation.

Alongside these horizontal connections across networks, policy makers need to identify and understand the vertical channels which connect cultural producers and markets. While cultural producers are 'horizontally' embedded in informal local networks and sub-cultures, they remain 'vertically' dependent for the most part on global patterns of distribution for access to the market. As already noted, access to the market is channelled and controlled through a handful of gatekeeper organizations. This in turn restricts access to capital, since major investment depends upon access to major markets. Local cultural producers are sucked into global systems of exploitation and distribution. For policy makers this makes it difficult to retain and benefit from creative activity at local, regional or national level.

Policy makers can identify and support alternative patterns of distribution and consumption which might give cultural producers a genuine alternative route to market. At local level, there may well be a strong sense of connection or community between producers and consumers; one task for cultural policy is to tap into these local, niche markets and allow producers and consumers to make effective use of them. Smaller organizations do not always have the resources, expertise or inclination for this, and cultural policy might open up connections by setting up or supporting joint marketing initiatives, training networks, local venues and infrastructure. Showcases of local film makers by regional cinemas, municipally run music venues and recording studios or subsidized artist studios and exhibition spaces all provide a channel through which creativity can reveal itself rather than attempting to discover or manufacture creativity by intervening directly in cultural production.

Policy makers can also open up new channels for investment by providing sources of capital. The creative industries are dependent on a fragile, unpredictable market. Investors are reluctant to lend money or buy equity in organizations which appear to have few tangible assets and the financial sector remains suspicious of lending against intangible assets such as intellectual property rights. For independent cultural producers, the temptation is to make a deal with a larger organization, mortgaging future intellectual property rights in return for immediate access to capital. By opening up alternative sources of capital investment, regional and local agencies can help cultural producers to develop their business without surrendering their right to profit from their own ideas. At regional level in the UK, economic development agencies have set up specialist venture capital funds and attempted to educate investors on the value of intangible assets and the revenues which can flow from investing in somebody else's ideas.

Before attempting to intervene in creative systems, policy makers need to start by identifying and understanding the activity which already exists. Despite energetic attempts to 'map' the new cultural geography through local, regional and national surveys of the creative industries, research into the creative industries has been hampered by a lack of clear definitions. In the UK's Creative Industries Mapping Document, it has proved difficult to get past the visible outcomes towards an understanding of the invisible infrastructure, especially at regional level. As this map and its underlying methodology are being reproduced at local level in the UK and in other countries around the world (Singapore, Taiwan), these blinds spots are getting bigger and more widespread. Rather than simply listing the businesses which comprise the local creative industries, it might be more useful for policy makers to explore and document the systems within which such firms operate, in terms of facilities, resources and connections with the informal cultural sector. Of course this would require a more long-term and broadly based research methodology than a simple mapping exercise. But the unit of analysis for cultural policy must be the system or network, not the individual business.

A final policy issue raised by a systems theory of creativity is the need to sustain a shared pool of ideas and products from which future creators can draw inspiration. One of the stated aims of intellectual property law is to ensure a public right of access to the products of the arts and sciences; indeed, the private rights of individual creators are protected not as an end in themselves but in pursuit of a public good – providing an incentive for future creators to be creative. Several commentators have noted that successive reforms have extended copyright protection for existing

"pool of ideas"

individual and corporate owners of copyrights, at the expense of a shrinking public domain or 'creative commons' which might provide a resource for future copyright creators. Intellectual property law requires a delicate balancing act between competing economic, social and aesthetic rationales and competing interest groups. The most recent attempts to create a new 'global' standard of copyright protection in the new media age, specifically the Digital Millennium Copyright Act in the US and the EU Copyright Directive, have tilted the balance in favour of rights owners rather than rights creators, and the public domain has consequently been cut back. The primary beneficiaries of changes in copyright law appear to be corporations like Disney; the extension of copyright to lifetime of author plus 70 years appears to turn copyright from a strictly limited and *temporary* privilege into a semi-permanent property right which favours established artists and their descendants rather than emerging talents. From a systems perspective, restricting access to a cultural commons or public domain closes off the connections and channels which facilitate creativity and narrows opportunities for exchange and collaboration. There is an urgent need to review intellectual property law, especially copyright, in the light of these criticisms.

Based on a systems theory of creativity, certain policy imperatives occur and it is perhaps worth pausing to summarize them:

- Direct interventions in sub-cultural, informal systems of creativity are unlikely to hit the mark. A more effective strategy for cultural policy will be to recognize and engage with the often invisible local networks which allow creativity to happen.
- Horizontally, policy makers can encourage greater connectivity within the cultural sector, by identifying and supporting clusters of activity, disseminating information, taking a 'joined-up' approach to social, economic and community development and providing a supportive environment for informal, horizontal networks to form between businesses and between creative activity and a broader social infrastructure.
- Vertically, policy makers can help to identify and build alternative routes to market for cultural producers, first by supporting local distribution and delivery platforms which provide an opportunity to sell cultural products closer to home, and secondly by using virtual networks to extend the reach of local cultural producers into global markets.
- Instead of directly targeting individual creative organizations and the process of cultural production, a systems-based theory of creativity directs cultural policy towards recognizing and supporting a viable infrastructure – an 'art world' – within which creativity can thrive.

Systems and Sustainability

In this chapter I have argued that a systems approach to creativity moves us away from creative individuals towards questions of organizational design and structure. For policy makers and for managers, the key to a sustainable creative system is in building connections and channels between individuals, groups and organizations – even if the purpose and value of these connections is not immediately measurable in terms of outcomes. Over a longer period, organizations with a complex, rich diversity of internal communication, both formal and informal, are more likely to generate new ideas and to respond to and capitalize upon these ideas effectively.

There is considerable interest among managers and policy makers in how to make creativity happen. A lot of effort has focused on supporting creative individuals (education and training) and individual creative businesses (investment and business support services, mentoring, mapping). It is extremely difficult to measure the effectiveness of such interventions, because the individuals and businesses do not stick around long enough for us to measure the results. Cultural production and creative businesses proceed on a project-by-project basis and are only as good as their last piece of work. There are many risks in building a business around talented individuals – as David Ogilvy once remarked of the advertising industry, the assets of the business go up and down in the lifts. Similarly, trying to identify and support individual creative businesses is extremely difficult for policy makers – the stock of the creative business can rise and fall just as fast as the lifts in an advertising agency. Investing in and supporting systems may turn out to be a better strategy than targeting the individual components of the system. This means building infrastructures and cultures through which individual creativity can thrive.

Systems theories of creativity are especially challenging for managers and policy makers, because they suggest that complexity and dispersal are preferable to focus and efficiency. We need to let the weeds grow in the garden. Too much order, a hierarchical and focused management style, will have the paradoxical effect of closing down the scope for individual agency and interaction. Complexity, on the other hand, will in the end result in a new form of order – the 'order for free' which emerges from complex adaptive systems. Managers and policy makers must find more subtle, oblique forms of intervention and take into account the network or system as their unit of analysis rather than the single organization. Direct interventions may undermine the self-organizing, generative potential of complex systems. One important priority for managers, especially in their communication strategies, is to ensure that communication does not become too overtly strategic; scope is needed for the unexpected connections and multiple networks layering outwards from the immediate organizational priorities.

The success stories of creative individuals and creative organizations burn brightly, blinding us to the creative networks which lie behind them. Based on creativity theory and the cultural geography of the creative industries, I have argued that these bright sparks grow out of years of unspectacular, invisible endeavour and from a network of informal contacts and associations. If we focus on the visible successes of the creative industries, the places where money is being made and jobs being created, we are unlikely to be able to devise successful strategies for supporting them. The bright lights will fade away or catch fire somewhere else. We also ignore the history and the context which lie behind them. High-profile individuals and organizations are the public face of collective creative systems. Individual creativity and talent are worthless without a system of developing, delivering and disseminating their products. Creative organizations are embedded in horizontal networks of collaboration and informal, unpaid work and in vertical networks of supply and demand. It is these relationships and networks which should be the focus of policy and management in the creative industries, not the individual talent or single business.

FURTHER READING

For an introduction to 'systems' theories of creativity, see Csikszentmihalyi (1988). For a sociological perspective on systems theory, see Becker (1982). Becker exposes the relationships, dependencies and value systems which underpin individual artistic creativity. Drawing on Marxist cultural theory, Janet Wolff argues in *The Social Production of Art* (1993) that individual creativity is embedded in social structures of cultural production and consumption.

Pierre Bourdieu is arguably the most influential sociologist in the field of cultural studies. In *The Rules of Art* (1996), Bourdieu emphasizes that the charismatic individual creator is only one element in the field of cultural production and that the individual is never entirely autonomous of this broader context and its associated rules. Turning to the field of cultural consumption, Bourdieu argues that consumption is likewise determined by a sociological context. In *Distinction: A Social Critique of the Judgement of Taste* (1984), Bourdieu claims that cultural consumption is a means of signalling and acquiring social status through the accumulation of 'cultural capital'. Our tastes are accordingly determined in large degree by the cultural capital we acquire through education, especially at school, and hence by our social class.

Bourdieu's work is a core element in the curriculum of cultural theory and the sociology of culture, but not often read by management students. Richard Florida's work on the creative class (2002) can be read as a popularization of Bourdieu's work for a wider audience more concerned with managerial practicalities than critical social theory. Florida locates the geography of the creative industries in a bohemian urban middle class. I will discuss Florida's work further in chapters 4 and 8.

In *Competitive Advantage: Creating and Sustaining Superior Performance* (1985), Michael Porter emphasizes the systematic links between firms, arguing that 'supplier linkages mean that the relationship with suppliers is *not a zero sum game* in which one gains only at the expense of the other, but a relationship in which both can gain' (Porter 1985: 51). More recently Porter's integrated model of the value chain has been reconfigured in several directions. From the perspective of global commerce, Gary Gereffi (1994) argues that we are moving from supply chains to 'buyer-driven networks'. From the perspective of post-Fordism, especially in the creative industries, the value chain has been rearranged around decentralized networks of flexible, specialized firms – see Piore and Sabel (1984) and Dicken (1998).

Porter's theories have also influenced economic and cultural development agencies, notably his arguments about 'clusters' as a new locus for competitive advantage – see Porter (1998). Clustering has become the new orthodoxy not only in economic development but also in urban cultural policy – see Landry (2000). As indicated in this chapter, some of the assumptions regarding the relationship between clusters and creativity are open to question, especially in the context of urban planning and policy.

For a discussion of networks and systems in the creative industries, see Grabher (2002), Storper (1994), Blair and Rainnie (2000) and Hesmondhalgh (1996).

Suggested reading on complexity is included in the further reading section at the end of chapter 5. For a helpful summary of complexity theory from an organizational perspective, see Stacey (1996a: ch. 1 'Organisations are complex adaptive systems').

Western managerial approaches to knowledge management have been driven by a perception that Japan's successful manufacturing industries reflected an ability to 'leverage' tacit knowledge and thereby empower their workers to be more productive – see Nonaka and Takeuchi (1995). This perception led to a new emphasis on organizational learning or 'the learning organization' – see Senge (1990).

Granovetter's theory of weak ties is explained in 'The strength of weak ties' (1973); some of Granovetter's arguments reappear in Malcom Gladwell's *The Tipping Point* (2000). For an examination of the relationship between creativity, teams and the core-periphery of networks, see Mumford and Gustafson (1988), Perry-Smith and Shalley (2003) and Sutton and Hargadon (1996).

Further reading on cultural policy in the creative industries is included in the final chapter of this book. For a more detailed examination of the tension between creativity, access and ownership in intellectual property law, see Barlow (1992), Lessig (2001), Thierer and Crews (2002), Bollier (2002) and Vaidhyanathan (2001).

NOTES

1   According to Metcalfe's Law, the utility of the network is equal to the square of the number of users – so as new members join the network the 'value' of the network increases exponentially. This recalls the old joke that the real breakthrough in telecommunications came not from the inventor of the world's first telephone, but from whoever invented the second.

2   I am grateful to Mark McGuinness for introducing me to this concept – for further discussion see Rowan (1989).

3   In 2002 Liverpool City Council banned internal e-mails because it wanted to encourage its employees to talk to each other. In 2004, John Caudwell, chief executive of Phones4U, Europe's largest independent phone retailer did the same. The avowed intention was not to prevent 'waste' (though no doubt this was also a key factor) but to make communication more efficient – encouraging employees to talk to each other and solve problems rather than 'batting the problem into cyberspace'.

4 MANAGING CREATIVE WORK THROUGH RELEASE AND CONTROL: THE MYTH OF THE SELF-MOTIVATED CREATIVE WORKER

To throw away all constraints would be to destroy the capacity for creative thinking. Random processes alone, if they happen to produce anything interesting at all, can result only in first-time curiosities, not radical surprises.

(Boden 1994: 79)

Did I not tell you just now that we are different from the persecutors of the past? We are not content with negative obedience, nor even with the most abject submission. When finally you surrender to us, it must be of your own free will.

('Big Brother', in Orwell 1954: 204–5)

The World Turned Upside Down

In pursuit of creativity, today's managers are encouraged to reject control and hierarchy in favour or release and individualism. According to the new orthodoxy, the role of management is to enable the individual autonomy and self-actualization of the employee, not to control the workforce by setting limits and deadlines. Hierarchies are flatter, organizational cultures are self-consciously 'casual' and managers have removed their neck-ties. In this system of creative management or 'soft control', managers seek to remove constraints in order to free individual workers to express themselves, to take risks and to challenge conventional thinking. Consequently their employees will, of course, be more productive and inventive. Freedom and autonomy are tolerated not as ends in themselves but in the belief that, in the long run, they will enhance corporate objectives. The new managerial ideology is based on economic liberalism, not social liberalism.

The change in management style is linked to a neo-liberal faith in markets and a belief that markets, and organizations, are self-organizing systems. By removing constraints and by letting workers express their own individual ideas, managers believe they will improve performance. Management has thus become a form of non-management, or laissez-faire.

The new management style is also based on a partial and stereotypical view of creativity as 'freedom from constraints' and 'individual self-expression'. The discipline and systematic organization required for real creativity (innovation + value; divergent thinking + convergent thinking) are omitted from the equation. Consequently the new management confuses the style of creativity with its substance. Today's managers are self-consciously iconoclastic and painfully hip. Television advertisements reflect this rebranding, showing managers as down-to-earth democrats (sharing a lunch in McDonald's) and streetwise communicators (startling their employees by turning a podium speech into rap for NTL). Managers embrace alternative philosophies (Orange) and fly balloons (Richard Branson). The 'suits' are now wearing casual shirts and chinos, a new 'creative' uniform. Meanwhile 'creatives' are dressing up, hoping to be taken seriously. But underneath the casual dress code, is today's management any more creative than the command and control model it affects to despise?

Today's 'creative' managers are the delinquent teenage offspring of the old 'scientific', rational managers, and now they have taken over the family firm. Like all rebellious teenagers, today's alternative, 'creative' managers have more in common with their parents than they like to admit. By denigrating the old-fashioned attitudes of a previous generation, they seek to legitimize themselves, flamboyantly rejecting the old management style while still clinging on to some of the old management substance (see the case study 'Changing Management Styles at the BBC').

Case Study: Changing Management Styles at the BBC

When Greg Dyke succeeded John Birt as Director General of the BBC in 2000, there seemed to be a symbolic transition from old management to new. Birt's regime at the BBC (lasting from 1992 to 2000) was associated with rigid top-down control, cost reduction and strategic centralization. Cost-centred accounting and the 'internal market' were introduced, so that the corporation no longer provided a free resource for programme makers. Under Birt, all resources and internal transactions had to be accounted for, to such an extent that staffers complained that it was easier to buy a CD from the high street than rent a piece of music from the corporation's own sound archive. Partly in order to meet government requirements on competition and efficiency, Birt also opened up the BBC to the external market, with in-house production teams competing for contracts against external independent production companies, and the BBC in turn competing with other broadcasters in the global market through co-productions and programme sales. Mindful of the need to win government approval in the run up to the renewal of the BBC's charter, Birt set out to reduce internal costs and to outsource activities and services if cheaper options were available outside the corporation. At the same time Birt was keen to reposition the BBC strategically with the shift towards digital channels and the possibility of becoming a global player in the market for subscription and various forms of pay-to-view broadcasting. The attempt to restructure and reposition the BBC as a digital broadcaster, which in retrospect seems to have been more than partially successful, proved hugely unpopular within the corporation since it took the emphasis away from programme-making. As part of this strategic vision, it had proved necessary to centralize strategic thinking and bring in external management consultants, a further provocation to the BBC's 'creative' workforce.

Events at the BBC need to be seen in a broader international context. At the same time as the BBC was implementing 'Producer Choice' in 1993, China's main national broadcaster, China Central Television (CCTV) introduced a similar system of 'Producer Responsibility' *(Zhipianren Fuze zhi)*. CCTV's new management system replaced an employment system based on hierarchy and quotas with a new accountability. Henceforward, CCTV producers and journalists were forced to pay close attention to ratings and to their own production targets, not just to senior colleagues and their political masters. In Europe through the late 1980s and early 1990s the last few remaining national publicly owned broadcasters were privatized and rules governing ownership, competition and commercialization on terrestrial, satellite and cable broadcasting have continued to be relaxed. These changes were driven by a variety of cultural, social, technological and economic objectives and by a range of constituencies seeking greater diversity, democratization, accountability and choice. Seen purely from a managerial perspective, the new broadcasters are designed to be leaner, more competitive and more efficient in an increasingly competitive international market. Deregulation of public service broadcasting is in turn part of a more widespread marketization of public institutions, underwritten by global agreements on free trade in goods and services.

When Dyke arrived at the BBC, he was greeted by demoralized staff as a breath of fresh air. Dyke's background was established by the media as a programme maker. He emphasized shortly after his arrival that his priority was to make the BBC a more creative, fun place to work. He introduced a new culture change programme called 'Make It Happen', in which staff were encouraged to contribute their ideas for improving the BBC. Part of the programme was the now infamous 'cut the crap' yellow cards which staff were encouraged to produce at meetings if they felt creative ideas were being blocked. The divisional structure of the BBC was reconceived as a 'petal' pattern, with the various divisions fanning out from a central node occupied by Dyke himself; the implication was that any member of the corporation, however lowly, could contact the senior management personally and would, eventually, receive a response. He was known by all as 'Greg', a significant change in style from the more formal manner of his predecessor. While stopping short of any explicit criticism of the old regime, he acknowledged the corporation's low morale and made a point of criticizing the 'old guard'. He made a short film about the 'Bafta Bastards' who pursued their own careers while exploiting the contributions of others. As noted in the previous chapter, he also publicly criticized the 'hideously white' monoculture of the corporation, not just on equal opportunities grounds, but also in line with his belief that a creative culture needed to be democratic, inclusive and culturally diverse.

When Dyke eventually resigned in 2004 as a result of a controversial news report on the war in Iraq, staff were vocal in their expressions of support, sympathy, even grief. The moment of his departure signalled how, to an extent unimaginable for his predecessor, Dyke had effectively become 'one of us'. The impact of his brief tenure on programme making and creativity, and on his avowed aim of making the BBC the most creative organization on the planet, remained unclear. What was clear was the transformation in management style and culture. Dyke epitomized the new management orthodoxies – informality, creativity, empowering the workforce, approachability, populism. But when we look more closely, what was the management substance behind the management style?

Dyke and Birt knew and respected each other, having worked together at London Weekend Television. To a considerable extent their aims were complementary, not contradictory. Both were iconoclasts, challenging programme makers by making them more accountable, whether creatively or financially. Both were accused of 'dumbing down' the BBC, in other words of putting on programmes which would appeal to large audiences instead of attempting to challenge and educate audiences with more 'difficult' output in the Reithian tradition of public service broadcasting. Both used managerial gimmicks to outflank and alienate the old guard, from the 'internal market' to 'cut the crap' and 'Bafta Bastards'. The approach to management and to public service broadcasting fits with a broader shift in the television industry towards democratization through deregulation, imposing 'democracy' through accountability to the market. Under Birt and Dyke, this marketization was approached from different angles. Birt sought to open up the BBC to market forces, while Dyke sought to open up the BBC to a different kind of competition through bottom-up criticism. In different ways they attempted to enlarge the circle of the BBC to include audiences, independent production companies and ordinary employees and to 'empower' these participants to make their own choices. Both implied that audiences and ordinary employees were better judges of quality and excellence than the traditional guardians of BBC traditions and values.

The divisional 'petal' structure introduced by Dyke placed the Director General firmly at the strategic centre of the BBC; indeed the model can be viewed as a traditional hierarchy, seen from above. Dyke sought to democratize the BBC and empower ordinary workers, but he also relied on an inner cadre of trusted senior colleagues and (like his predecessor) on an army of consultants to push through his reforms. The style was more consultative, and he was no doubt less isolated than Birt as a result. Yet he could also be ruthless in exposing and outflanking his opponents and critics. The goal of employee creativity, like Birt's goal of management efficiency, was pursued through the insidious 'soft control' of accountability, responsibility and self-management. It is ironic that for all their apparent differences in personality and tone, Birt and Dyke were both representative of the new management orthodoxy of operational autonomy and strategic centralization. The new boss, despite the accent, the clothes and the style, was not so different from the old boss.

In this chapter I will consider the origins of the new 'creative' management style in a more employee-centred approach to management which originated in the 1960s, based on Abraham Maslow's theory of 'intrinsic motivation'. Maslow's arguments have also influenced theories of creativity, most notably in the work of Professor Teresa Amabile at Harvard Business School. The new management style is therefore based on certain assumptions about human behaviour and creativity. In this chapter I will examine these assumptions and suggest that creativity is not only achieved through the removal of constraints, but that it also depends on a measure of control. Empowering individuals by releasing them from formal organizational constraints may not in the end be the best recipe for creativity. Similarly 'freedom from constraints' does not in the end amount to a genuine freedom for employees. The rhetoric of empowerment has been accompanied by a corporate centralization and concentration of power, not least in the creative industries. Working in the creative industries does not equate to a life of freedom. The methods of control and containment have simply become more sophisticated.

Finally I will argue that creativity and creative management are not achieved by removing constraints and breaking the rules but by inventing new rules to the old games. By integrating the traditional functions of management (setting boundaries, fixing budgets and deadlines) with the creative function (problem-solving, innovation, adding value), it may be possible to come up with a more convincing approach to managing creative work.

Not chaos !

Whistle While You Work: Changing Theories of Employee Motivation

The contemporary prophets of the new management style are management gurus like Tom Peters, with his upper case exhortations, or Charles Handy with his folksy anecdotes. But the source of the new management thinking is actually rooted further back in psychological theories of motivation. The core assumption of the new management style is that 'extrinsic' motivation – the external pressure to meet targets, expectations and criteria imposed from above – is less powerful and effective than 'intrinsic' motivation – the internal desire to complete a task to our own, not others' satisfaction. This humane approach to management was described in 1960 by Douglas McGregor (1960) as 'Theory Y', in response to the older hierarchical approach described by McGregor as 'Theory X'. According to Theory X, workers will only respond to the carrots and sticks imposed by management – without being goaded by constant external pressure, they will underperform. Theory Y argues that workers who are self-motivated (and hence to some degree self-managing) will in the end be more effective and productive. McGregor pointed out that workers who work only under duress according to Theory X may meet minimum standards, but they will never strive to exceed them – consequently the full human potential of the individual employee will never be realized.

Maslow's hierarchy

McGregor's arguments drew upon Abraham Maslow's definitions of intrinsic and extrinsic motivation. Maslow argued that higher level needs (the need for 'self-actualization') will become more influential than basic needs, once those basic physiological needs (safety, shelter, etc.) have been met. So in a relatively affluent society, especially in industries where work is becoming more skilled and sophisticated, employees will be driven increasingly by the intrinsic desire for 'self-actualization' or fulfilment through their work. This in turn drives workers to ever greater levels of achievement, inspired not by fear or management approval, but by an internal sense of pride and fulfilment. It should be noted that these arguments reflected a specific social and economic context. McGregor was writing in the 1960s, a time when British and American societies appeared on the brink of a new period of prosperity after the lean post-war years, driven by new technologies and increased consumerism. The idea of a less authoritarian, more caring management style also fitted with a more idealistic, youth-centred culture. The arguments of McGregor and Maslow resonated with managers and politicians of the time.

In the context of today's economy, with the shift from heavy manufacturing industries to information, service and technology sectors, and from mass employment to self-employment and flexible labour, it is perhaps not surprising that a similar 'human' approach to management should predominate. The psychological emphasis on individual self-expression and intrinsic motivation as the basis of work, especially of creative work, has infiltrated almost every aspect of the new management style. Transactional leadership, based on systems of reward and promotion, has been replaced by 'transformational' leadership, or 'leadership from the back', in which charismatic leaders no longer tell workers what to do, they attempt to inspire them with a vision and values which will make the workers *want* to complete their tasks (and to exceed the minimum requirement) out of a shared sense of mission and belief. Organizational cultures encourage informality and self-expression, allowing workers to play games in the workplace, to *enjoy* their work and find satisfaction in it. Employment patterns are more flexible, with an increase in telecommuting and home-working and a growth in self-employment and part-time work. These new arrangements are not only more cost-effective for employers, they claim to offer employees a better work-life balance, allowing them to construct their working identity around their own personalities and lifestyles, rather than the other way around.

trans-formational leadership

Behind the rhetoric of empowering individual employees, there are hard-nosed commercial reasons for allowing greater autonomy and flexibility to the employee. The individual is the core asset of the new corporation. Loyalty is valuable and recruitment of highly skilled and trained employees is expensive. Tangible assets have been replaced by intelligence, knowledge and creativity. Managers must now work to empower and enable front-line entrepreneurs, not to monitor and control them. In making the individual the ultimate organizational asset, the new management style has actually effected a more complete incorporation of the individual personality than was ever possible in the old hierarchy. Before employees were simply doing what they were told. Today they must learn to love their work.

Out of Control: The Myth of the Self-motivated Creative Worker

The emphasis on intrinsic motivation in management is echoed in creativity theory. Attempts to understand the motivation behind artistic creativity are confounded by the apparently self-contained, intensely personal nature of artistic work. The external rewards of artistic and cultural production remain so pitifully small and unpredictable for the majority, that intrinsic motivation seems the only possible explanation for creative work. From an anthropological and historical perspective, the professionalization of artistic work is a comparatively recent phenomenon. The folk arts of primitive and indigenous peoples demonstrate a pursuit of beauty and self-expression which cannot be explained by purely utilitarian arguments. In nineteenth-century Britain, William Morris argued that a similar intrinsic pleasure in the beauty of art was part of the pre-industrial way of life, until the Industrial Revolution when commodification of art and the industrialization of labour broke the connection between aesthetic beauty and everyday use and experience.

Even in today's commercial creative industries, it is clear that 'intrinsic' motivation is going to be more than usually important. The workforce in the creative industries is highly skilled and highly specialized. Achievement is not easily measured against minimum benchmarks since creativity inevitably involves an element of the unexpected and unprecedented. Work is often project-based and self-employed, with limited continuity from one project to the next and no obvious career structure. Task-fulfilment, the sense of satisfaction which comes from a job well done, is an important motivation for creative activity and may well precede any offer of external reward in terms of money or reputation. Many creative careers in music, theatre and writing begin in amateur, semi-professional or unpaid work; later, once the individual's reputation and contacts are better established, it might be possible to recycle or reincorporate amateur content into a marketable product. Rejected first novels and youthful compositions may thus eventually become commodities, but this may not have been their original motivation.

The desire to create has been traced back to childhood, predating any commercial exploitation of creative work; even commercially successful artists are likely to have begun their careers working for love not money. This association between childhood and creativity reflects in part a Romantic idealization of childhood and of primitive, impulsive desires. In contrast, creativity in adulthood is associated with psychological illness and maladjustment. In mythology these arguments combine in tales of wise children, *idiots savants* and holy fools. These two elements, childhood play and adult repression and neurosis, converge in Freud's writings on art and artists. According to Freud (1985), artists have not learned to repress the play instinct from childhood. This results in their alienation from mainstream society, but also drives their creative output. External interventions into this internalized system are not likely to affect the internal drive. Indeed, from a psychoanalytic perspective, if artistic creativity is driven by psychological imbalances and maladjustments, then we might end up 'curing' the artist of the desire to create through psychoanalysis.

managers do nothing?

Harvard Business School professor Teresa Amabile does not adopt a Freudian view of creativity, but she does associate creativity with playful childhood impulses and has a similar argument regarding the repression of creativity in adulthood. According to Amabile, the creative impulse is something most children share, until it is slapped down by adult interventions from teachers, carers and parents. Following this logic, if intrinsic motivation is the key to creativity, then external interventions will be at best irrelevant and at worst damaging to the creative process. In Amabile's empirical experiments, 'extrinsic' forms of motivation, whether rewards or punishments, are, in most cases, an irrelevance to the creative process; offering people rewards for creative tasks may at best have a secondary, reinforcing impact where 'intrinsic' motivation is already strong, but at worst the rewards will undermine intrinsic motivation and so defeat their own purpose.

Given the importance of 'intrinsic motivation' in the creative process, it would be easy to conclude that the best thing a manager can do for creativity is to do nothing. To this extent, psychological theories of intrinsic motivation converge with a theory of creativity rooted in internal psychological drives. Taken together these theories appear to vindicate a non-interventionist approach to management, because creativity cannot be deliberately engendered or controlled, only 'released'.

These theories of motivation and creativity are modelled around an individualized, romanticized notion of creative work. But in reality, 'releasing' creativity is not as easy as turning on a tap, nor is the individual necessarily going to be any more creative if left alone to their own devices. Indeed, many artists share a fear of absolute creative freedom – the tyranny of the blank page or empty canvas. The myth of a pure, unfettered individual creativity is part of the mythology of genius. In practice this mythology may be a block on creativity rather than a source of inspiration. In the first place, the pursuit of a perfect state of absolute freedom allows a continual procrastination, deferring action until we find the perfect time and place to start, as in Bukowski's poem 'air and light and time and space'. For most artists, this perfect place does not exist. Moreover, even if it was achievable, it is questionable whether the release from constraints would have the desired effect. The result might be the paralysis of too many possibilities rather than spontaneous inventiveness. The expectation of an effortless, spontaneous release of pure inventiveness is a burden rather than a gift.

> air and light and time and space[1]
> by Charles Bukowski
>
> 'you know, I've either had a family, a job,
> something has always been in the
> way
> but now
> I've sold my house, I've found this place,
> a large studio, you should see this space and
> the light,
> for the first time in my life I'm going to have a place and the time to
> create'.

Splitting of creative and managerial work

no baby, if you're going to create
you're going to create whether you work
16 hours a day in a coal mine
or
you're going to create in a small room
with 3 children while you're on
welfare.
you're going to create with part of your mind and
your body blown away,
you're going to create blind
crippled
demented
you're going to create with a cat crawling up your back while
the whole city trembles in earthquake,
bombardment,
flood and fire.

baby, air and light and time and space
have nothing to do with it
and don't create anything
except maybe a longer life to find
new excuses
for.

The Isolation of Creative Work

The assumption of intrinsic motivation and innate creativity leads to a splitting of creative and managerial processes. In practice, once industry turns creativity into a commodity and creative processes into a commercial activity, it cannot avoid external constraints, rewards and deadlines. The managerial solution to this dilemma is to isolate creative processes and creative teams from commercial realities. The process of designing or creating a new product is consequently broken into two distinct phases, the creative process which is kept at arm's length from the realities of the market, and a management process which deals exclusively with budgets, deadlines, clients and customers. Examples of this isolation and containment of creative processes and creative teams have been noted in previous chapters, from the 'buffering' of creative teams in traditional advertising agencies to the separation of idea generation and idea evaluation by the early proponents of brainstorming. Underpinning both the specialization of creative work and the deferral of judgement in brainstorming is the assumption that creative people and processes are self-sufficient and self-motivated, and that any attempt to manage them will 'kill' their creativity.

This separation and specialization of creative work results in the isolation of creative workers from the rest of the organization. It also imposes a crude supply chain logic on a complex, multidimensional process. Creative ideas and idea generators are separated from the management decisions and the commercial contexts which

Isolation of workers

frame them and give their content meaning and value. Screenwriters frequently complain that they are excluded from the decision-making process which leads up to their work being commissioned or accepted. They are still less likely to be consulted on questions of marketing and distribution and are even routinely excluded from production decisions around casting and directing. In one case a writer friend visited the set of a television drama he had written and attempted to challenge some of the director's decisions. This intervention breached the invisible professional boundaries which separate the different stages in the production process. An embarrassing confrontation ensued and the writer and director, previously close friends and colleagues, have not spoken to each other since. Another screenwriter comments that writers in British television are at the bottom of the industry food chain, isolated and excluded from the production process; he compares this with the status of writers in US television comedy and drama, where writers work collectively and are frequently awarded executive producer status. In the US the hierarchy is simply reversed, with writers calling the shots and the director as the hired gun.

It is ironic that in what is held to be a collaborative medium, these professional demarcations and levels of responsibility should be so tightly and hierarchically defined. The managerial assumption is that these separations are necessary to protect writers, directors, actors and producers from each other and from straying outside their own area of competence. Perversely this protection and isolation is presented as a kind of freedom, 'letting the writer/director/producer get on with their job'. The barriers are further reinforced by professional rivalries, with professional associations of screenwriters and directors arguing over the authorship rights and credits sequences to films, a throwback to the 'auteur' theory of European cinema in the 1960s.

Yet it does not have to be this way. I have already argued that the separation of creative and management processes is counterproductive. This separation assumes that 'creativity' consists exclusively in the generation of new ideas, not in their selection, development and application. Many of the most successful talents working in the film industry take a more holistic, collective approach to their work. The British film director Mike Leigh argues that a screenplay is only a work in progress, not a self-contained product. His own working method is to work collaboratively with his actors to devise or rewrite the screenplay and to collapse the roles of writer and director into one. Sam Mendes generously attributed the success of his debut feature film to the veteran cinematographer Conrad Hall, while in his theatre career at London's Donmar Warehouse he combined the roles of director, manager and entrepreneur. Artistic directors in British theatre are increasingly required to take on commercial responsibilities. Decisions about plays, casts and directors are inextricably linked to decisions about budgets, markets and strategy.

In this book I have argued that multi-tasking and crossing boundaries between managerial and creative responsibilities is an inherent characteristic of the creative process and of creative people. While the new management style is premised on the unmanageable individualism of creativity and the separation of managerial and creative tasks, many small creative enterprises in advertising, theatre, film, music and design are moving in the opposite direction, seeking a closer integration of 'managerial' concerns (budgets, deadlines, strategies, markets) and 'creative' processes (idea generation, the release of individual creativity, spontaneous invention). At the individual level too, creative decisions about form and content are inseparable from commercial and operational decisions about materials and resources; to this extent all artists are required to make managerial decisions about their own creative output.

Creativity is a dualistic process which requires an integration of thinking styles and a pooling of talents. By isolating the moment of creative breakthrough from the conditions which precede it and the applications and developments which follow it, managers are limiting the creative possibilities, not 'releasing' them. By attempting to insulate the creative team or individual from the rest of the organization and from the boundaries, constraints and expectations which give their work value and meaning, managers are restricting their ability to be creative. The freedom on offer through the removal of constraints and evaluation is in reality a kind of disempowerment through isolation and containment. 'Freedom from constraints' is a temporary fiction. The commercial realities are not removed from the creative process they are simply deferred to a separate meeting attended by a separate group of people.

In practice, external rewards and boundaries are an inevitable part of the creative process. Artists operate within commercial and practical constraints, but they also operate within self-generated formal rules and reputation systems. Even if we could strip away all external rewards and expectations, artists would construct their own rules around process and impose their own expectations around outcomes. Frank Ferrie is a Scottish painter based in Geneva. Because of his personal circumstances he has very few boundaries to structure his work: no immediate financial pressures, no clients or galleries demanding he work in a certain way or at a certain speed, no local network or peer group. His work is abstract and unique to him, with few traditions or conventions to guide him. Working on his own, he has his own self-imposed rules and routines. He paints for between 10 and 12 hours each day in 3-hour bursts, working on many pieces at once (as many as 30). His technique involves scrubbing away and retaining layers of acrylic paint on paper, a laborious process of experimentation and correction which he describes as 'flying in many different directions at once'. He rejects about 75 per cent of this output, but his self-criticism fuels the continual experiment rather than discourages it. Left to his own devices, the artist is a hard taskmaster and a harsher critic. Freed from all constraints, he invents new ones of his own. The challenge for management is not to remove all constraints on creativity but to incorporate these constraints into the creative process.

Bounded Creativity: Creativity through Control and Constraint

In the literature on extrinsic and intrinsic motivation, there is a tendency to assume that extrinsic motivation is about the imposition of constraints and conditions, whereas intrinsic motivation is about the removal of constraints. Yet as De Bono (1982) has recognized and Bukowski confirms in his poem, the blocks inside our heads may be far more intimidating than those imposed by our managers and colleagues. At a practical level, artistic creativity appears to depend upon self-generated formal rules and structures, providing a framework of possibilities within which ideas can be explored. At a theoretical level, creativity theorists such as Boden and Weisberg suggest that creative thinking takes place within a bounded conceptual space or a specific artistic domain combining expertise, tradition and experience.

We can perhaps make a distinction here between self-imposed constraints (form, structure, rhythm, genre) and externally imposed constraints (deadlines, budgets and organizational objectives). But even this distinction is blurred, because the artistic choices result in external boundaries; thus certain genres of films fit with certain markets and budgets, placing expectations and conditions around the decisions of the film maker. One of the key differences between artistic creativity and scientific discovery is that boundaries and criteria for artists are more fluid and negotiable. A scientific discovery is either novel and useful, or it is not – the criteria and cut-off points are relatively easy to establish. An artistic breakthrough is measured by more subjective criteria – we can reposition the novelty of a painting or piece of music within different traditions, we can measure its value according to different responses and markets. The boundaries, criteria and rules which govern artistic creativity can be manipulated and reconfigured. Most artists are aware of this and either self-consciously or intuitively play with the rules and conventions which govern their work. Musical forms and film genres are continually being modified and subverted – this regenerates and develops the genre, but it also provides a stimulus for the creator. This playful deviation from norms and expectations helps to define the novelty of the work and its value to an audience. A similar process of boundary-tweaking and manipulation of constraints can be applied to the management configuration of objectives and conditions.

If our definitions of creativity are linked to conceptual boundaries and stretch-ing or breaking rules and expectations, it makes little sense to attempt to insulate creativity from the outside world. Creative thinkers understand and acknowledge the context in which they are working, and recognize the constraints imposed by genre, technique and tradition. Having recognized these constraints, they push up against the limits of the possible, testing the boundaries of their field and eventually trans-forming that field from the inside out. The moment of transformation comes not from thinking outside the box but from rethinking and redefining the shape of the box from within. Working to order does not preclude inventive solutions within the parameters of budget, deadline and objectives. As demonstrated in the case study 'Musician for Hire', it is possible for a creative process to work through, not against, the requirements set out in the brief. At a more conceptual level, if a creative idea is to challenge existing parameters and redefine a problem, it must first engage with the existing boundaries and rules.

In theory and in practice, creativity works through breaking and making rules, sometimes working within conventions and expectations and sometimes outside them. It is through the transitions between different modes of thinking and sets of rules, and between conditions of release and control, that creative processes emerge,

rules are needed for creativity

Case Study: Musician for Hire – Boundaries for Musical Composition

Roger Bolton is a composer of film and television music. Almost all of his work is commissioned in response to a brief from a producer or director. Usually the music is one of the last elements to be added to a production, at a point when time and money are tight. Entering the project at the post-production stage, the composer's work has to follow the rhythms and timings dictated by the director and editor. The space for manoeuvre is thus extremely limited.

Within these very tightly demarcated boundaries, the challenge for Bolton is not only to satisfy his clients but to surprise them. Yet in many cases clients either do not know or are unable to communicate exactly what they need or want. The client wants a solution that is unexpected or novel, but which is still rooted in an understanding of their needs. Consequently, the programme maker is not going to be entirely satisfied by an outcome which merely delivers on expectations or follows the brief to the letter.

Bolton's first task is to tease out the sub-text to the client's initial brief. One of his methods is to list all the adjectives contained in the brief on a separate sheet of paper and use these as a jumping off point. He also makes it a rule to avoid discussing music with the client (his other rule is never to discuss his fee until the work is completed). Instead he attempts to communicate in a visual language or speaks of the emotions a scene is attempting to evoke rather than of musical motifs and structures. He approaches the brief as a screenplay which must be deconstructed and re-imagined rather than as a template to be followed.

Bolton emphasizes that even in the most apparently banal jobs, he will try to find an unexpected creative angle. This is partly a matter of professional pride – if the client wanted an obvious solution to the brief, they could find this from any competent musician for hire. As noted above, Bolton believes that his job is not only to satisfy expectations but to transcend them. He also sets himself this task because of his own personal pride in his work as a composer and his passionate belief in the emotional truth of music. Just because he is working to a brief does not mean he is not engaged in an artistic process.

To illustrate the point, Bolton cites the example of 'the cheetah chase'. Hunting scenes like this are a staple of natural history programming, with the film maker cutting between an unwary antelope and a prowling cheetah, then using faster editing and camera movement to build a crescendo of expectation and excitement, leading up to the moment when the predator kills or the prey escapes. Visually, the sequence is a cliché. The temptation is to respond with a musical pastiche of the camerawork. Instead Bolton claims that the composer has a 'responsibility' to come up with an alternative solution which deviates from the expectations of the viewer and surprises the film maker. In the end too, he aims to satisfy not just the client but his own belief in music and in himself as a composer.

Bolton becomes angry with some of his fellow-professionals who take a less idealistic approach to their work. He argues that composers who cannot discover some intrinsic satisfaction within the extrinsic demands of the brief are doing themselves and their profession a disservice.

How far do you try to give the customers what they want, and how far do you attempt to provide an unprecedented experience (which the customers didn't know they wanted, but recognize when they see it)? Creativity is a multifunctional process. In order to provide something which is both innovative and valuable, creators have to challenge as well as meet expectations. The demand for Bolton's services among producers and directors is an indication that his approach is not merely self-indulgent, but strikes a chord with his customers. The paradox here is that in seeking to satisfy himself, and by going beyond the explicit instructions of the client, he ends up satisfying the client. Intrinsic motivation and extrinsic motivation here work in tandem.

Bolton's dilemma is not uncommon in the creative industries. Designers, architects and advertising agencies are all working to a client's brief, yet there is usually an expectation that they will deliver something beyond the job as specified. This after all is their 'value added' to the customer – if the creative professional merely enacts or fulfils the brief, the client might as well have delegated the job to an intelligent machine. The key is to understand which parts of the brief are negotiable and which are essential. Successful composers, designers and architects are not necessarily the ones with the best portfolios but those who can negotiate these boundaries successfully.

One of the important skills of the hired creative professional is an ability to communicate outside their own specialist discipline. As noted in chapter 2, creative individuals are multi-taskers, able to tap into alternative modes of experience and expression. Bolton shares this ability to communicate outside his professional vocabulary and to get under the skin of what customers want, as opposed to what they say they want. He admits that a major part of his work is not about music at all, it is about psychology and communication. One could add that much of what he does is a form of management, both of his own creative process and of the inputs, intermediaries and relationships which frame his work.

'Work for hire' in the creative industries describes a particular relationship between the client and the artist, where the customer sets the boundaries of the creative work and owns the resulting intellectual property rights. The creativity of the composer or artist in this context appears tightly constrained. Yet Bolton's experience and the response from his clients indicate that constraints do not have to limit the creative process. By stretching the limits of what he is asked to do, he ends up not only meeting minimum requirements but exceeding expectations. Creative professionals identify opportunities and problems as well as solving them. Boundaries and constraints are not merely a challenge or stimulus but an integral part of the creative process.

allowing problems and concepts to be taken apart and reassembled. Given this inter-play between release and control, the idea that creativity correlates simply with the removal of all constraints and barriers seems at best only half true. Certainly a highly constrained organizational culture might not be the best context for creativity, but an anarchic, individualistic culture might be equally counterproductive. De Bono (1993: 34) emphasizes that his lateral thinking approach to creativity might work for bureaucratic cultures but be entirely inappropriate for a group of artists. Businesses may need to think laterally in order to break down formalized, hierarchical man-agement systems and inject diversity and surprise into predictable systems. Artists on the other hand may need to think a little more vertically – in De Bono's terms, they may need to 'dig a deeper hole' rather than 'dig another hole'.

Just as the central assumptions of neo-liberal management are spun out of a core argument about the motivation of employees, much of the rhetoric of genius derives from assumptions about the motivation of artists. Theories of management and creativity overlap in this debate over the extent to which motivation is driven or discouraged by the constraints and expectations imposed upon us. There is an assumption that constraints undermine self-motivation and creativity, leading some proponents of creative thinking and creative management to embrace transgression, rule-breaking and individual freedom as a recipe for individual creativity. This is of course part of the mythology of individual creative genius outlined in the opening chapter. I have argued that creativity actually depends on constraints, boundaries and on rule making as well as rule breaking, and I contend that this echoes the majority view both in creative theory and in creative practice. But the rhetoric of liberation and individual self-actualization remains a powerful mantra in popular management books. If constraints are actually an integrated feature of the creative process, what might be the consequences of the freedom and autonomy offered by the new management style?

False Freedom: The New Management Style in Practice

Popular management books frequently emphasize individual autonomy as a route to creativity. Like the self-help books promising regimes for self-improvement, this literature is targeted in part at the aspirations of individual readers. The possibility of taking control of one's life and career is a seductive myth, and is projected into a management style based on empowering individuals for creativity. The assumption that the individual is the right unit of analysis for organizational creativity has already been challenged in the previous chapter. Two further assumptions characterize the genre. First, it is assumed that individuals and individual creativity will be centre stage in a new knowledge-based creative economy. Secondly, it is assumed that in times of 'turbulence' and uncertainty individual initiative is a better guideline than collective precepts, and we accordingly need to liberate individuals from oppressive bureaucratic control in order to release their creative potential.

Alongside popular management books, business magazines and newspaper sections eulogize a certain brand of maverick entrepreneurialism. If the trade press is to be believed, today's managers are in thrall to charismatic leaders and self-made creative gurus. Men like Steve Jobs, reinstalled at the head of Apple and now also building a new creative empire with Pixar, epitomize this new faith in visionary creative management. Even Bill Gates, demonized by some of Jobs' disciples as the pinnacle of corporate empire-building, goes out of his way to present himself as a maverick entrepreneur in his writings, in his public profile and even in his choice of clothes and music. These celebrity CEOs represent management as it likes to see itself – as entrepreneurial free spirits who don't play by the rules. Much is made too of the creative manager's passionate resolve to empower the workforce by purging bureaucrats, encouraging risk-taking and seeking inspiration from the lowliest employee. This is myth as wish-fulfilment, reflected in the Hollywood iconography of management, from *Wall Street* to *Big* (see case study).

Case Study: Management in the Movies – Wise Children and Men in Suits

The rebranding of management as liberating and creative has been highlighted in some of the television advertising referred to elsewhere in this chapter. Many of these simply present managers as self-consciously 'cool', dressed down and democratic. At the same time the commercial realities occasionally crack through the surface. IBM has worked harder than most to reposition itself as a 'cool' brand through its advertising. One campaign featured graffiti spray-painted onto the sidewalks of major American cities, a classic reappropriation of rebellious sub-culture by a pillar of the establishment. In another television advertisement a creative geek (he wears glasses, he talks too fast) is describing 'cool stuff' (IBM systems technology) to a sceptical manager (he is older, he wears a suit). The manager appears bored and unimpressed. Finally the geek blurts out that the new technology will save the company millions of dollars. After a pause, the manager replies: 'Cool'. The message here is not only that IBM is a cool brand which saves the customer money, it makes the point that the coolest stuff of all is not creativity or technology but money. The manager will tolerate the geek's eccentricities, provided the new technology delivers real economic benefits.

The IBM campaign (there were other advertisements in the series) illustrates the weary tolerance shown by managers to new ideas and creative employees. The creative employee can play with their toys, but freedom to play is conditional on results. One of the best examples of the iconography of 'creative management' is captured in a fictional film, *Big*, starring Tom Hanks as a 13-year-old boy, Josh, trapped in a man's body. With his childish insights, Josh becomes the *faux-naïf* creative genius of a toy manufacturing company, leapfrogging placemen who play by the corporate rules of hierarchical subservience, smilingly tolerated by the boss for his 'creative' eccentricities. The manager of the company, played by Donald Sutherland, is something of a father figure, and his indulgence of his childish employee echoes the attitude of the manager in the IBM ad.

To some extent this is Hollywood painting business in its own image as a world of rule-breaking, freedom and self-expression. The underdog outsider who dares to challenge the system and eventually becomes the system is a standard Hollywood plot device. But *Big* also recalls Freudian theories of creativity as a natural childish playfulness which adults learn to repress. One female executive, the Hanks character's 'good' colleague and love interest, is taught to play again, casting off her hard-bitten professional personality and getting back in touch with her inner child. At the same time, Josh's 'bad' colleague and rival treats him with that mix of praise and condescension reserved for artists and children – Josh is a genius, but he is too naive to understand why and how his ideas work. He is, after all, still only a child. And at the end of the film he reverts to his real childhood self.

Managerial attitudes to creativity are not so different from the portrayal of Hanks' character in *Big*. Unconventional behaviour will be tolerated, provided that it serves a useful corporate purpose. The creative individual will be included in the brainstorm, but is unlikely to 'fit' in the boardroom. Like Josh, the creative individual has been given licence to play – up to a point. Josh genuinely does not understand the toy company's business. He understands only how to play with toys. This fits with a paradox in our notion of genius, as noted in chapter 1. Genius makes creativity seem easy, a natural facility which has not really been earned. The possessor of genius is somebody we similarly praise and patronize. Like a child, the genius can have the ideas, but somebody else has to turn the ideas into a marketable commodity.

The freedom granted to creative play in business takes place within similar limits. The freedom to play without worrying about the commercial consequences comes at a cost. 'Buffering' the creative individual or team from managerial realities is also a way of excluding them from management decision making. Autonomy around the creative process is achieved by separating the creative task from the objectives and outcomes which precede and follow it. Creative freedom thus becomes a form of isolation, reinforcing the 'great divide' between 'creatives' and 'suits'. As noted in chapter 2, the fragmentation and specialization of creative work makes this separation of means and ends all the more plausible in the creative sector. The creative child-genius is in the end alienated from the management process; at the end of *Big*, the boy-man Josh is left confused and isolated, and his wish to revert to the innocence of childhood is miraculously granted. The ending of the movie signals that there is a time and a place for childish things. In the end the creative employee must learn to grow up and play by management's rules, or face a future outside the industry.

One of the paradoxes of the new freedom in management is that decentralizing and devolving operational activities is often accompanied by a centralization of strategic control. Hierarchical management structures evolved around the needs of the multi-division corporation. Today's multimedia, multinational corporations are more likely to be structured around networks of businesses and business interests, held together by a tightly defined managerial core. These networks continue to expand both through merger and acquisition activity and through strategic partnerships with suppliers and distributors. Profits and equity are not used to expand or shore up the core business but to buy up equity in other related businesses. Operational activities and production costs are outsourced and new businesses are spun out of existing ones. All of this is done in the interests of efficiency and appears to delegate power and responsibility downwards. But the strategic core remains intact.

This core-periphery structure is present in Charles Handy's 'shamrock' organization (Handy 1991: 70–92), where work is split three ways between a permanent strategic core group, contracted specialist workers and temporary staff. Such a structure is well adapted to the creative and media industries, due to the specialized, project-based nature of cultural production, as described in previous chapters. It also reflects the need for 'flexible labour' in a post-Fordist network economy, the capacity to mobilize or redeploy workers around specific projects for a specified period in response to market demand. In the creative and media industries, Handy's shamrock has stretched into a more uneven pattern. The strategic core has decreased in size but increased in influence. The flexible workforce has expanded to encompass most of the employees. The distance between core and periphery has stretched, as mergers and acquisitions have concentrated power in a handful of global media and entertainment corporations. As these giant multinationals extend their tentacles to encompass new businesses, the strategic core has become increasingly remote from front-line operational decision making. Here the only common language is the bottom line of financial accountability. Thus while devolving operational responsibility and outsourcing production, corporate control in the creative and media industries consists primarily in the setting and monitoring of financial targets.

Creative work is especially prone to this structural dynamic. Today's creative and media industries are characterized by unusually high levels of self-employment and micro-enterprises. The freedom and flexibility of the freelance economy are paid for by high levels of insecurity. Risks which might have been absorbed into central budgets are now outsourced to freelancers – creative work is funded on a project basis, allowing dips in demand and business failures to be borne by individual projects, not by the core business. Living on their wits, the creative individual or micro-business must fund their own R&D, passing on the benefits to larger companies once the product has proved its value. The risks of the creative process are thus shared unevenly across the value chain.

At the level of the individual firm, the same imbalances can be observed between operational decentralization and strategic centralization. Creative work is granted a degree of autonomy around process, but the outcomes are monitored and measured. The removal of constraints, like the deferral of judgement in a brainstorm, is only temporary. While devolving operational responsibilities, the core function of senior management is to control outcomes through rigorous surveillance of financial outputs, targets, deadlines and budgets. The creative worker's individualism and insubordination will be tolerated, provided he or she delivers, on budget and on time.

Richard Florida has described the management approach of the creative industries as 'soft control':

> The no-collar workplace runs on very subtle models of control that rely on people's intrinsic motivations. As companies try to motivate and persuade us rather than boss us or bribe us, they're basically seducing us to work harder – and we are most willing to be seduced. (Florida 2002: 134)

It is ironic that the new 'creative class' which Florida describes as the dominant social stratum in the new creative economy should itself be subject to a new form of self-policing managerial control. Junior advertising executives do not *have* to work later than their superiors. They are not *compelled* to stay for a drink with the boss. Nobody forces theatre directors to socialize with actors and audiences in the bar, to attend conferences at weekends, to take their work home with them, to talk shop with their friends and family. Some of this they do because they want to, but mostly because it is expected of them – it is part of the job, and if they are unwilling to fulfil these unwritten obligations, there are plenty of other young wannabes waiting to take their place.

How does the 'freedom' of the new management style play out in practice in the creative industries? There are two answers to this question, reflecting the hollowed-out structure of the creative industries, polarized between small creative enterprises on the periphery (the idea generators) and global multimedia corporations at the centre (the idea exploiters).

The freedom offered to the majority of those working in the creative industries is double-edged. Workers and creators are 'empowered' to make their own decisions and take responsibility for their own actions. The comfortable hierarchy of permanent employment, promotion and patronage has been replaced by the scramble of the freelance economy, the democracy of the market. What is presented initially as freedom, flexibility and autonomy actually becomes a form of alienation. Freelance individuals in the creative economy, small creative enterprises orbiting multimedia corporations or creative teams in the organization all enjoy a degree of creative freedom, but are at the same time excluded from the strategic processes which define and demarcate the purpose and value of their work. Creative workers can play with their toys but they are playing by somebody else's rules.

The freedom offered by neo-liberal management has different implications for the CEO who presides over the outcomes of this creative process. The new management style fits with the structure of the new economy. Operational autonomy is contained by strategic and financial control. Flexible labour is a self-policing market, driven not by managerial hierarchy, but by the desire and need to outperform the opposition. The freedom to work flexible hours and to set independent targets and objectives becomes a new tyranny, made all the more insidious by its voluntary character. This 'soft control' is especially powerful in the creative industries, where a vast army of unpaid, ambitious and overqualified people is waiting in the wings, jealously observing the performance of the 'self-motivated' creative worker.

As a system of control, the new, relaxed, arm's length management style is extremely effective. Whether it is creative is another question, to which I will now return. I want to conclude this chapter by reconsidering the place of managerial rules and boundaries in the creative process and the possibility of a less divisive approach to the management of creativity.

Beginnings and Endings

Constraints, whether externally imposed or internally devised, provide a necessary framework for creative activity. These are the boundaries within which the creative effort can be channelled and against which the edges of possibility can be tested. These boundaries provide both a starting point and an end point for the creative work. At the start of a project, rules and deadlines provide a framework of possibilities around which random impulses and suggestions can be processed and organized. At the end of the project, these devices provide cut-off points and closure. Without this framework, the absolute freedom of creativity is both intoxicating and paralysing. Beginning and ending the creative task, already perhaps the most difficult parts of any endeavour, would become almost impossible.

Intrinsic motivation precedes extrinsic motivation, in the sense that this is where the creative impulse begins. Whether or not we accept a Freudian view of creativity as reflecting an inner neurosis, the 'intrinsic' desire to create can appear unhealthy, at least from the perspective of 'normal' human behaviour. Artists often discuss their work in terms of an inner compulsion which they are powerless to resist. In a commercial context, external expectations ensure that minimum standards, budgets and deadlines are met. Internally generated constraints and standards are more rigorous, driving the creator to exceed expectations, to go beyond what is required in the brief, to add the element of surprise which will later be identified as the 'value added' of their creative input. The core of the creative process is thus 'intrinsic' – the pride, obsession and self-esteem of the creator.

Intrinsic motivation and self-imposed standards of excellence may produce the desire to begin work, but they often result in an inability to finish what has been started. Artists revisit their work continuously and pre-empt external criticism with a savage internal self-analysis. Even when a work is 'finished' it does not necessarily produce satisfaction, only a desire to return to the same subject and surpass the previous effort. This obsessive pursuit of perfection can be a major block on creativity, with the fear of future failure reflected back into the present and freezing the creator in indecision and self-doubt. For many artists, a work of art is never complete, and the constant process of revision and reconstruction becomes the work of a lifetime.

If intrinsic motivation provides a starting point for creativity, extrinsic motivation provides an exit strategy, a reason for seeking closure even if it means sacrificing the possibility of perfection. And whereas the constraints around starting a project are often self-imposed and self-generated, the constraints around closure are more likely to come from outside, from cold commercial realities or from a third party's assessment. The outside eye may provide a judgement which the creator, blindly caught up in the process, can no longer make. The relationship between manager and creator at this point is a cooperation based on mutual trust and respect, analogous to that between writer and editor.[2]

At different stages in the creative process, different types of motivation and different types of constraint will be called upon. Managerial interventions and 'extrinsic' forms of motivation in the form of targets, evaluation, rewards and penalties are likely to work alongside internal compulsions and desires. This combined approach reflects the view of creativity advanced in this book as comprising different thinking styles and competences. In particular, managers might provide a catalyst for moments of synthesis and clarity in the creative process, complementing the more digressive and divergent processes of problem-finding and deconstruction.

Contrary to the myth of self-sufficient creative genius and the ideology of neo-liberal management, managerial intervention can play a significant part in the creative process. Intervention here does not simply consist in the imposition of deadlines and targets, but in a more deliberate manipulation of beginnings and endings in the creative process. Roger Bolton, the composer referred to in the case study, describes setting his computer to automatically delete a passage of music if he has not completed it within ten minutes. This is his game with himself, not the result of a deadline or a requirement of technology or musical form. Lucy Neal, the theatre producer and former co-director of London International Festival of Theatre, refers to 'deadline magic' – the point of pressure where a work comes together in an accelerating sequence of 'just-in-time' decisions. Sometimes these cut-off points are real, sometimes they are arbitrary, but they are absolutely necessary for the work to reach fruition.

While intervening in the creative process is likely to inhibit creativity, setting 'strategic targets' may well enhance creativity. This is the opposite of 'buffering' creatives from the managerial realities, and provides a clear set of parameters for the creative process, defining the goal without attempting to prescribe the means. Rather than seeing management and constraints as external, 'boundary-setting' thus becomes part of the creative process. Creators and their managers are engaged in an analogous process of manipulating the limits of a problem in order to come up with a genuinely radical solution. By incorporating managerial controls and management personnel into the creative process, we are more likely to achieve such a transformation.

For the manager of the creative process, the challenge then becomes judging the correct moment to intervene. If the intervention is made too soon, it can crush the seed of an idea and prevent it from flowering. If it comes too late, the idea may already be dead on the vine. There is no obvious rule to follow here, other than to learn from experience. In improvisation, these fine judgements are continually being negotiated. Once an actor or musician initiates, it is up to the others to follow. Chris Johnston is a practitioner, teacher and writer on theatre improvisation based at the University of Warwick. Watching him work with an experienced group of improvisers from theatre, dance and music, one of the remarkable aspects is the sense of timing – first the split second complicity between the performers, but also the sense in which the group uses endings to initiate new beginnings. As soon as something appears to be winding down, it opens up a new set of possible interventions and new beginnings. Because of the nature of improvisation, it is seldom possible to describe the work as 'finished' and Johnston notes that the group seems to have more trouble with endings than with beginnings. Perhaps only somebody or something external to the group – for example an audience – can signal when that moment of closure is reached.

What this means in practice is a much greater empathy between managers and 'creatives'. In the divided organization, managers define problems and creatives solve them. In a genuinely creative organization, managers and creatives need to negotiate the boundaries and parameters around the problem together. They must also acknowledge that creative solutions will occur up against the wire, when 'deadline magic' becomes the mother of intervention. The closer they can operate to these edges, the more likely they are to come up with a genuinely creative solution.

The Rules of the Game

Managing creativity requires a balance between release and control. This chapter began with a critique of the neo-liberal management style which equates creativity with a removal of all constraints. By liberating creative individuals from bureaucracy and hierarchy, it is assumed that the latent creativity in organizations will be released. This stereotype of creative individuals and strict managers fits with an oversimplified, individualistic model of creativity. It may serve to legitimize corporations and neo-liberal ideology as inherently liberating and creative, but it bears little resemblance to the reality of creative practice in the creative industries, nor to creativity theory. The promise to 'release' creativity simply unleashes the private demons of obsession and compulsion or the paralysing blankness of too many possibilities. At the same time, the emancipatory rhetoric of the new management style belies a steady accumulation of strategic control by and within a handful of corporations, notably so in the creative industries.

Difficulties occur when the managerial setting of parameters is abstracted from the creative process and regarded as a self-sufficient and independent system. This removal is one consequence of the specialization of management, a problem discussed in the opening chapter of this book. In the creative industries management decision making has been elevated to a separate plane in the organizational hierarchy and distanced psychically and geographically from the creative decision making on the ground. This asynchronicity between managers and creative teams is not resolved by withdrawing managers from the creative process and adopting a laissez-faire management style, or by 'buffering' the creative team. On the contrary creative managers need to find ways of drawing managers and creators closer together.

One of the consequences of the new managerialism in the cultural sector has been to elevate management as a specialist discipline and to reinforce the importance of measuring the efficiency and effectiveness of the organization. Without any specific knowledge or experience of the messy business of cultural production (and possibly without much interest in it either), the new generation of cultural managers have concentrated on what they know best: the control and monitoring of inputs and outputs in pursuit of centrally agreed strategic targets, measured through financial data and performance indicators. This retreat into a strategic core indicates a bunker mentality in cultural management – make sure the figures are right, and let the art manage itself. As a consequence of the structural divisions between managers and creators in the creative sector and the specialization of managerial and creative exper- tise, targets and strategies have been abstracted from the cultural context in which they must be delivered. The growing split between operational reality and strategic vision is in turn reinforced by the physical and psychic distance of the strategic core of decision-making from the rest of the workforce.

At the same time creative work is excluded from the strategic processes and out- comes which give it value and purpose. Autonomy and freedom are meaningless if that freedom does not extend upwards and outwards into the setting of targets and evaluation of outcomes. Real creative freedom encompasses not just the right to play the game but the possibility of challenging and redefining the rules. Creative practice and creativity theory extend into decision making and problem setting, not just idea generation. By separating out creative process and managerial outcomes, manage- ment restricts the possibilities of creativity and of management, ignoring the extent to which these processes inevitably overlap.

Creative processes cannot function without some boundaries and constraints, whether these are internally generated (formal rules, genre conventions) or externally imposed (the requirements of the brief). From this perspective, creative workers and their managers are engaged in an analogous process of negotiating and stretching the limits of what is possible or allowable, working within the rules of the game in order to reinvent them.

If we attempt to abstract the process of boundary setting from the process of cre- ativity, boundaries become barriers instead of challenges. Managers find it difficult to set parameters for the creative process, because outcomes and processes are not linear or predictable. There is a choice here, between attempting to rein in the creative process according to artificially constructed timetables and targets, or tak- ing the generative systems of creativity as the starting point. From this perspective, deadlines and targets need to be seen for what they are – a means for stimulating creativity, not an end in themselves. Managers and creators need the confidence to manipulate and play with the rules rather than simply playing within them. By mov- ing the goal posts we might invent a new game.

One of the aims of this book is to challenge the separation of managerial control and creative freedom. Where the new managers like to present themselves as creative free spirits and mavericks, they have failed to understand that creativity is messy, complex and painful. The analogy between management and creativity is not that management is inherently 'creative', it is rather that creative work, like management, requires trade-offs between release and control, and takes place within systems and boundaries, not in a fantasy world of absolute freedom.

FURTHER READING

The chapter's critique of neo-liberal management theory and its roots in neo-liberal political philosophy draws on Thomas Frank's *One Market under God: Extreme Capitalism, Market Populism, and the End of Economic Democracy* (2001). For an application of this critique to public sector broadcasting, see Colin Leys, 'Public Service Television' in *Market-Driven Politics* (2001: 108–64). For 'Theory X and Theory Y', see McGregor (1960).

The idea of breaking rules and 'thinking outside the box' is identified with Edward De Bono and his concept of 'lateral thinking' – see De Bono (1982 and 1993). Many standard creativity tests and creative thinking exercises reinforce the importance of breaking taboos and thinking outside the boundaries of the problem for a solution. A number of these exercises, and the rationales behind them, are brought together in James L. Adams's *Conceptual Blockbusting* (2001). Creative thinking games such as the 'nine dot problem' or the 'ball in the pipe problem' are designed to disrupt our rational, normal perceptions[3] and encourage us to break rules.

Other theorists challenge this perspective on creativity as 'breaking out' of old patterns of thought. Robert Weisberg in *Creativity: Beyond the Myth of Genius* (1993) argues that creative thinking depends not on a sudden and dramatic change of perspective but on a logical, analytical process, combining memory and knowledge within the individual's domain of expertise and experience. Margaret Boden describes creative thinking as challenging and ultimately transforming a 'bounded conceptual space' from within. It is only by working within a set of existing parameters and definitions that we can eventually transform them. The paradox here is that in order to change the rules governing a conceptual space or way of thinking, it is first necessary to accept them. Creative thinking requires that we identify these rules and limits so as to press up against them. So Picasso might push the rules of perspective and composition to a point where the approach is entirely redefined, at which point a new conceptual space ('cubism') is born, together with a new set of rules. But if Picasso did not initially identify and work within the existing conceptual space of contemporary painting, this new method would not emerge – instead of creativity, the result according to Boden would be random innovation, innovation without value or meaning (Boden 1992: 75–9).

Creativity theorists agree that boundaries and constraints have some important correlation to the creative process. Where they differ is in the extent to which creative thinking deviates from or conforms to a set of boundaries, expectations and conventions. For Weisberg, creativity takes place within a specific domain of experience and expertise. Boden argues that the boundaries around that domain are stretched and challenged by the creative thinker, leading ultimately to a redefinition of the conceptual space or genre. For De Bono, creative thinking requires a deliberate transgression of the borders.

Freud's theory of creativity, childhood and repression is summarized in 'Creative Writers and Daydreaming' (Freud 1985). For a more extended discussion, see also the essay on Leonardo da Vinci in the same volume. By locating creativity in childhood play, Freud challenges the perception that creativity is in some way dysfunctional or 'abnormal'. Instead of Plato's 'divine madness', Freud describes an 'ordinary madness', locating creativity in mental states and experiences we all share. Whereas most adults learn to repress or sublimate their childhood impulses, artists continue to play – like the Tom Hanks character in *Big*. For a critical discussion of Freudian theories of creativity and motivation, see Storr (1972: esp. chs. 3, 2 and 4).

Teresa Amabile's experiments to measure levels of intrinsic and extrinsic motivation are described in 'Within you, without me: The social psychology of creativity' (1990). See also Hennessy and Amabile (1988: 11–38).

Charles Handy's shamrock organization is described in *The Age of Unreason* (1991: 70–92).

Big (dir. Penny Marshall) starring Tom Hanks was released in 1988. For a very British take on the childlike quality of genius see also the 1960 comedy *The Rebel* (US title: *Call Me Genius*), starring the comedian Tony Hancock as a bored suburban office worker transforming himself into a Parisian artist and founder of a new artistic movement, 'Infantilisme'. Notable Hollywood portraits of the artist as maverick outsider include Kirk Douglas as Vincent Van Gogh in the 1956 movie *Lust for Life* and Charlton Heston as Michelangelo in *The Agony and the Ecstasy* (1965). Perhaps the most intellectually coherent film portrait of alienated, non-conformist genius was Gary Cooper's portrayal of the architect Howard Roark as Nietzcheian *ubermensch* (purportedly based loosely on American architect Frank Lloyd Wright), in King Vidor's *The Fountainhead* (1949), faithfully adapted from Ayn Rand's book.

NOTES

1   'air and light and time and space' from *The Last Night of the Earth Poems* by Charles Bukowski. Copyright © 1992 by Charles Bukowski. Reprinted by permission of HarperCollins Publishers. Thanks to the novelist Gonzalo Enriquez-Soltero for introducing me to this poem during a discussion of 'intrinsic motivation' and creativity.

2   Thomas Wolfe describes such an intervention from his editor, informing him 'with quiet finality that the book was finished whether I knew it or not'. The author, on the brink of despair, reacts with relief and recognition: 'He told me so, and suddenly I saw that he was right' (Ghiselin 1985: 201–2).

3   The nine dot problem requires that we connect nine dots arranged in a 3 × 3 pattern, using four straight lines, without lifting our pens from the paper – the solution requires literally 'thinking outside the box'. The 'ball in the pipe' problem requires that we remove a ping pong ball from a metal pipe embedded in a bare concrete floor, using various pieces of mostly irrelevant equipment. The most elegant and popular solution here involves the passing of bodily fluids – participants are thus encouraged to overcome their feelings of impropriety and cultural taboos, and accept a 'rule-breaking' approach to the problem.

5 SEEING THE PATTERN: STRATEGY, LEADERSHIP AND ADHOCRACY

The message is that there are known knowns – there are things that we know that we know. There are known unknowns – that is to say, there are things that we now know we don't know. But there are also unknown unknowns – there are things we do not know we don't know. And each year we discover a few more of those unknown unknowns.

(Donald Rumsfeld, 2002)[1]

Nobody knows anything . . .

(Goldman 1983: 39)[2]

The Strategy Wars: Orientation versus Animation

The idea that strategy can be seen as a creative process has become increasingly fashionable. What this means in practice depends on how we define our terms. Before considering 'creative' strategy, we must consider what is meant by strategy. Attempts to clarify the meaning and purpose of strategy all too often succeed only in muddying the waters. It is questionable whether fine gradations between competing strategy schools or internal arguments between professors of strategy are of much practical use to managers. The distinction proposed by Cummings and Wilson (2003) between 'strategy as orientation' and 'strategy as animation' offers some welcome clarity. Strategy as orientation attempts to establish a strategic position and direction for the business as the basis for sustainable competitive advantage. Typical of this approach would be Michael Porter's (1985) concept of generic strategies used to differentiate a firm from its competitors. Strategy as animation is more concerned with the energizing effect of the strategic process on the organization, resulting in a common sense of purpose and vision. Representative of this approach would be Mintzberg's concept of 'emergent strategy' (Mintzberg and Waters 1985) or Quinn's 'logical incrementalism' (1978).

Orientation and animation encapsulate an opposition between strategy as position and strategy as process. These strategic tendencies are linked in turn to different models of structure and leadership, and to different ways of thinking about organizations and markets. Over the last twenty years, there appears to have been a shift in the overall balance of power from strategy as orientation towards strategy as animation. Some of the structural changes have already been noted in this book, for example the shift towards a more individualistic, 'empowering' and flexible concept of the workforce and towards more flexible, less hierarchical structures. As described in the previous chapter, leaders are no longer expected to lead from the front, but to 'animate' their workforce to become more creative and self-motivated. In the more recent literature on strategy, there has also been an implied change in the way that managers see markets, towards a recognition of escalating complexity and unpredictability. In this new environment, where forecasts, data and knowledge have become increasingly unreliable and messy, a strategic approach based on 'orientation' is difficult, if not impossible.

During the 1980s and 1990s, these criticisms of the 'orientation' approach turned into an outright attack on the discipline of 'strategic planning'. Strategic planning, typically the domain of a handful of senior managers and analysts, had evolved to meet the needs of large, multidivisional corporations competing in relatively stable markets. Such an approach seemed to detach strategy from implementation. Like armchair generals dispatching soldiers into battle, armchair strategists were accused of making plans at one remove from the frontline. How would the planners cope with more entrepreneurial, individualized businesses competing in turbulent markets? Above all, this approach to strategy seemed to offer no space for risk, creativity, or individual initiative. Managers began to suspect that competitive advantage might lie not in the long-term, strategic approach but in the fleeting moments of individualism, risk and opportunism which strategy as orientation explicitly excluded.

In his 1994 book, *The Rise and Fall of Strategic Planning*, Mintzberg attempted to lay traditional top-down strategic planning to rest, arguing that strategic planning was not the key to sustainable competitive advantage, merely an idea which had evolved to meet the needs of the times. That time was now past. Mintzberg's alternative approach to strategy centred on the concept of 'adhocracy', a term introduced by Alvin Toffler to describe the new organizational forms of the future, and developed by Mintzberg in a series of articles in the 1980s. Adhocracy in strategy meant not simply an acceptance of chaos and uncertainty, as Mintzberg was at pains to point out to his critics, but a bottom-up process which allows strategy to emerge from operational decision making rather than forcing operational decisions to conform to strategy.

Despite the title of his 1994 book, Mintzberg's real achievement was perhaps to describe the fall and rise of strategy rather than its rise and fall. Businesses still needed to plan for the future. But now they would use a very different set of tools from Porter's three generic strategies. Mintzberg had not given up on strategic planning, merely changed the rules. Having set out to bury strategic planning, Mintzberg returned to praise it.

Strategy and Creativity

The two versions of strategy described in table 5.1 are allied to the conflicting definitions of 'creativity' considered in this book. Strategy as orientation requires a kind of

Table 5.1 Two models of strategy

Strategy as orientation	Strategy as animation
Differentiation, fixed position	Emergence, evolving pattern
Strategy as a specialist skill	Strategy as shared process
Leader as visionary	Leader as orchestrator
Divergent thinking	Divergent *and* convergent thinking
Revolutionary change	Evolutionary change
Fixed position, perfect fit	Many positions, changing shape

creativity based on originality or 'thinking different' in relation to the competition. In order to orient the business around a uniquely differentiated competitive position the strategist must discover, against all the odds, a unique and visionary perspective on the market or product. This differentiation is the key to Michael Porter's 'generic' strategies.

Like the genius model of creativity, a highly differentiated strategic position is based on a capacity to reject conventional thinking and 'think outside the box'; pushing the analogy further, the strategic thinker may be seen as a visionary, creative individual, or at least as the product of an individualistic culture. The need for differentiation escalates as markets become more crowded, competitive and unpredictable, and the 'creative' strategist's stock also rises. Visionary business leaders who can steal a march on the competition through singular insight, a moment of daring or an individualistic, unexpected solution to a problem are highly sought after – even if the reasons for their success or failure are more complicated.

Porter's approach to strategy nevertheless requires certain 'trade-offs'. In order to achieve differentiation from competitors, there is less scope for internal differentiation. Once a position of strength has been identified, strategy must be implemented across every area of the business. In order to consolidate their differentiated position, managers will have to turn down or trade off other options, making short-term sacrifices in pursuit of long-term gains. Differentiation requires a precise alignment across the whole business. Various divisions and levels of the organization will need to be monitored against strategic objectives to ensure consistency and continuity. The hierarchy of objectives will usually, though not necessarily, be reproduced through an organizational hierarchy, with strategy being determined by senior management, then filtered down through the organization. Those at the base of the pyramid will not need to see the whole picture, but provided they meet their discrete targets, the overall strategy will be maintained. In other words, while the product of this strategy may be 'creative' in the sense of 'different' or 'original', the underlying process appears almost wholly uncreative. All of the 'creativity' is concentrated into the person who sets the strategy and the moment where that strategy is first conceived. Everything else is implementation and control. This isolates the leader of the business, leaving the CEO to take credit and blame for success and failure (for which in truth they may not be responsible), while devaluing and demotivating any broader participation in the strategy process.

At its worst, the 'creativity' of differentiated strategy can lead to an emphasis on novelty rather than value. Of course, differentiation is justified initially in terms of competitive advantages, resources and an assessment of the market – being different is not an end in itself. Porter himself is quite clear on this point. Nevertheless, an emphasis on 'thinking different' in strategy can contribute to a fascination with bold, 'visionary' strategic actions which produce little real benefit. This is especially true for organizations seen to be failing or 'in crisis', with the desperate need for 'new ideas' blocking out doubts as to 'useful ideas'. The result is a 'reinvention roller-coaster' with organizations lurching from one strategic vision to the next. The tendency to seek bold strategic statements, disconnected from the organization's history and capabilities, is reinforced by the tendency to buy in strategic thinking from outside the organization, either from a consultant of from a newly appointed chief executive. Outsiders are inevitably keen to make their mark on the business and have limited respect for or understanding of existing strengths and competences.

The leadership merry-go-round at Apple Computers illustrates the problems which follow from attempting to change direction by changing leaders. Apple commands passionate loyalty among its core users and successive leaders (Steve Jobs, John Scully, Gil Amelio and the rest) have been idolized or demonized by users. The Apple board has repeatedly appointed or removed leaders as a way of addressing perceived weaknesses in the company's strategic vision. This has resulted in dramatic changes in strategy and leadership style – in keeping with the company's slogan, 'think different'. Yet it was precisely this inconsistency in leadership rather than the quality of individual leaders which contributed to Apple's strategic failings. In particular, lack of continuity was undoubtedly a factor in Apple's failure to agree a consistent line on the licensing of Apple's operating system and software to other third party producers. In the first place, Apple's attempt to build an exclusive, integrated hardware and software package opened the door for Microsoft to build alliances with other 'third party' hardware manufacturers and software developers. Then when Apple did belatedly license its proprietary software and operating systems to other manufacturers, some of its 'partners' became competitors, and third party 'cloned' products threatened to outsell the Apple originals. Inconsistency in strategy was exacerbated by the tendency for successive regimes at Apple to deliberately 'think different' from their predecessors, rather than building on the legacy of past decisions and strategies. Lack of consistency in strategy and lack of continuity in leadership were fuelled by the personality cults around individual managers.

Mintzberg's notion of adhocracy locates the creativity of strategy in a different tradition. Here, new ideas emerge incrementally through collective activity, not from a singular vision in the boardroom but in the everyday operational decisions of the workforce. Freed from a single overarching vision, individuals in the organization can pursue separate directions. From these one-off decisions, new strategic options are discovered and out of this apparently disorganized system a strategic pattern gradually emerges.

When we compare this version of strategy formation with the creative process, several similarities emerge. First of all, what appears at first to be a random, spontaneous process actually works from a common set of values and assumptions. As

noted in the previous chapter, creative ideas are generated within certain conceptual boundaries or constraints. In a business context, these boundaries derive from
shared values, personalities or a shared organizational history – instead of being determined by an explicit organizational strategy, decisions are framed within an implicit
organizational culture.

Secondly, the process of strategy formation depends upon an ability to synthesize
or make connections between apparently unconnected and intuitive individual
decisions. This synthesis is immediate and ongoing, with participants recognizing
and capitalizing on promising new directions to form a new evolving strategy. The
pattern is ad hoc, not post hoc. It is not enough to observe the strategic pattern with
the benefit of hindsight – those inside the organization must recognize and converge
on new possibilities as and when they occur. Strategy in an adhocracy is a 'synthetic'
process. The participants in the system share an ability to pursue their own agendas
apparently at random, while at the same time recognizing and responding to emergent patterns of relationships.

Finally, it is possible to identify two levels of intelligence at work within the
system. At one level, the process of strategy formation is individualistic, intuitive and
proceeds through a series of apparently random innovations. At the second level,
the participants identify and build patterns from these random innovations and are
influenced, perhaps even subconsciously, by the emerging trends in the organization.
Creativity in an adhocracy is thus multidimensional or 'bisociative' rather than
singular. The combination of experiment and synthesis is comparable to the combination of divergent and convergent thinking styles identified by creativity theorists,
or the 'preparation – incubation – illumination – verification' sequence devised by
Poincaré (see chapter 1). Strategists and creative thinkers are required to walk the
line between random inventiveness and an ability to configure and recognize new
patterns – to think both in and out of the box.

The best known example of adhocracy in action was the decision by Honda to
change its strategy for selling motorbikes in the United States (Pascale 1984). Having
set out to break into the US market for performance motorbikes, Honda dispatched
executives from Japan to investigate operational logistics and markets. Once in the
US, the Honda executives used their own bikes to attend meetings and get around
town. The bikes began to attract attention. Honda had assumed that Americans
would not be interested in the compact, economical machines they sold in Japan,
but reaction on the streets suggested otherwise. In a much discussed strategic u-turn,
Honda decided to follow the hunch of their executives on the ground and begin
producing and marketing small bikes for the American market, instead of following
their pre-planned strategy. The decision resulted in a commercial success and a clearly
differentiated strategic position for Honda in the US market. It also highlighted
certain paradoxes in adhocracy. The new strategy deviated from expectations yet it
also allowed the company to stick more closely to its existing strength and expertise;
one could argue the 'new' strategy was actually more conservative and less risky
than the original concept of striking out into enemy territory. The decision was
initiated from below, but was endorsed and supported from the top. Senior managers at Honda had to recognize and support the strategic pattern emerging from

their own people. Interestingly the Honda case has been claimed by both sides in the strategy wars, with one side claiming the case as evidence that top-down planning does not work, and the other countering that the case shows that top-down planning *does* work, and is more flexible and inventive than its opponents admit. Proof perhaps that in academic arguments about strategy, the evidence is never allowed to get in the way of a good theory, but also an indication that adhocracy is a paradoxical concept.

Creativity in an adhocracy takes on very different connotation from creativity in a differentiated strategy (see table 5.1). The latter follows the 'genius' model of creative thinking, dependent on a particular type of (divergent) thinking and focusing on the creation of a single unifying idea as the strategic blueprint for the entire organization or system. The model is individualistic, associated with charismatic, visionary leadership, and lends itself to a revolutionary approach to organizational change. Strategic thinking is a specialist skill which may be 'bought in' from outside the organization, or imposed from the top of a hierarchy. The strategic vision is totalizing and absolute, requiring complete unity of purpose and commitment, and relies on a disciplined, predictable path from idea to implementation.

In contrast, creativity in an adhocracy is a collective process which requires a dualistic intelligence, deviating a little from the old pattern but also converging on new patterns as they begin to take shape. Strategic thinking requires both divergent and convergent thinking, overlapping and alternating with each other, and reflects a multidimensional process-oriented model of creative thinking. The responsibility for strategy formation is more likely to be delegated through the organization – the role of the leader is to orchestrate the process and help to make connections rather than to dictate or control. The approach to organizational change is evolutionary instead of revolutionary, with the strategic direction continually being modified in a sequence of small steps and modifications. Strategy is not fixed, continually adapting to changing realities and inputs.

Strategy in an Open System

Complexity theory takes its cue from the physical sciences (chemistry, biology, genetics, nuclear physics) and from observations of biosystems in the animal kingdom (beehives, termite mounds) and applies these models to other systems including human organizations. The surprising conclusion of complexity theory is that order emerges from apparently random, disorganized interactions – hence Stuart Kauffman's phrase 'order for free' (1995). Indeed, if we attempt to make purposeful interventions in complex systems, we are unlikely to get the outcome we expect or desire. On the other hand, if we observe the system, we might learn to understand better how it works and adapt our behaviour accordingly. Through these adaptations, complex systems evolve and patterns emerge. The relationship between complexity, emergence and deliberate planning is explored further in the case study of decision making in the film industry.

Case Study: Emergent Patterns in Film Marketing

Complexity theory is concerned with the relationship between apparently random chaotic phenomena and the emergence of simplified patterns. This approach has been applied to management theory, especially to processes of decision making and strategy. As with Mintzberg's 'emergent' strategy, emergent patterns in complexity evolve not as a result of a preconceived plan but through an accumulation of apparently random, individual events. Complexity theory describes this cumulative reinforcement in terms of 'sensitivity to initial conditions' and 'feedback loops'. Applying complexity theory to strategy and decision making, individual decisions can have large and sometimes unexpected consequences if they are reinforced by other events in the system. It thus becomes much harder to track the relationship between cause and effect or intention and outcome, or to assume that strategies can be implemented in a straightforward linear way.

Complexity theory was initially developed in the natural sciences, and is identified with organic systems such as weather systems, the formation of human cells or the flocking behaviour of birds. When we apply complexity theory to the social sciences, questions of relative power complicate these processes. In human systems, decisions to follow the leader or to reinforce one event with another are typically influenced by hierarchy and status. Decision making in closed hierarchical systems tends to gravitate around centres of power, pulling subordinate decision makers into their sphere of influence, and cascading down through an organization. However, in the more open network forms of organization which predominate in the creative industries, decisions can follow a more unpredictable, complex path. If we factor in the high levels of risk and mutual dependency in the creative industries, small decisions can throw up unexpected consequences across the whole system. Decision making in the creative industries thus shares some of the characteristics of complex adaptive systems, but it also retains hierarchical patterns based around power relationships.

A good example of this combination of 'complex' and 'hierarchical' decision making in the creative industries occurred with the release of the 1997 film *Titanic*. Known before its release as 'the most expensive movie ever made' with a budget estimated to be over $200 million, there was predictable speculation as to whether the 'big boat movie' would sink at the box office. James Cameron, the director, had gone over budget and over schedule. The movie was over three hours long. The planned release date had been delayed by six months, missing the lucrative July 4th holiday weekend and held over to the traditionally less busy Christmas holiday period. The studios, Twentieth Century Fox and Paramount, were said to be nervous. When Fox chose to premier the movie in Tokyo, instead of using the more obvious shop window of the London Film Festival, this was seen by many as a defensive strategy, betraying a loss of confidence. The story of a sinking ship provided an easy target for the film's negative critics. Industry gossip likened the movie to Kevin Costner's *Waterworld*, released two years previously and now a byword for directorial hubris, financial excess and box-office failure.

What happened next is a classic example of how small events can have large consequences in a complex system. According to Steve Perrin, head of research at the UK Film Council, during the lead up to the film's release a not unfavourable review appeared on a website. The notion that the film was 'not bad' permeated the advance word of mouth on the movie, gradually transforming a negative expectation into positive excitement. This in turn influenced not only critics but also the studios, pushing them towards a more confident approach in their marketing and release strategy. From a positive but by no means record-breaking opening weekend at the US box office, *Titanic* eventually went on to become not only the most expensive but also the highest grossing movie of all time. Cameron's intransigent refusal to compromise on budget and timetable was rewarded with a Best Film Oscar.

According to Perrin's analysis, this one review on a specialist website did not 'cause' the success of the film. But it was an example of a relatively small and apparently insignificant event having major consequences – the equivalent of the butterfly flapping its wings. What followed was then played out through a series of 'positive feedback loops', reinforcing and amplifying the positive 'buzz' about the movie, gradually building into an unstoppable momentum. The decisions of audiences to watch the film, and the decisions of studio executives on releasing, marketing and supporting it, need to be seen as both cause and effect of this emergent pattern, success at the box office and the perception of success feeding off each other.

Where the *Titanic* story departs from the model of complexity theory is in the underlying sense of hierarchy and centres of power within the emergent pattern. Specifically, once a film is perceived by the studio to be a marketable commodity, the full force of the marketing machine reinforces that initial perception, and the studio's expectations in the end become self-fulfilling. Studio expectations of the audience response influence decisions on marketing and promotion, which in turn influence audience behaviour. Once a film has been positioned in relation to a particular audience and a predicted box office return has been targeted, the remainder of the decision-making process becomes more linear and predictable. But the events leading up to the studio's decision to target a particular market and level of box office return are more unpredictable.

In the story of *Titanic* there are thus two tipping points. The first occurs with the review on a website which builds a positive expectation around the film. This process of mutually reinforcing feedback loops and cumulative yet apparently random events fits with a complex / chaotic theory of decision making. This leads to the second tipping point when the studio decides to launch a full-blooded marketing campaign which eventually becomes self-fulfilling. Here the model is more hierarchical – once the studio has decided how to position the film, the remaining decisions on marketing and prints (i.e. how many copies of the film to print and how many screens to show them on) follow a more predictable trajectory. One can thus make a distinction between an apparently unpredictable, complex series of actions and reactions which precede the decision to position a film in a given market, and a more hierarchical, predictable set of decisions on marketing, prints, exhibition and release dates which follow the studio's decision on target market and expected return.

From a very different starting point, the independent film *The Blair Witch Project* followed a similar pattern. The film was made for a relatively low budget, estimated to be somewhere between $30,000 and $60,000. The initial marketing campaign was coordinated by the film makers themselves, based around an ingenious website which exploited the film's back story as a piece of 'reality film making' and built a viral 'word of mouth' reputation among an obsessive Internet fan base. This was not dissimilar to the growing buzz around *Titanic* – a marginal and apparently insignificant website created an expectation around the film which was eventually picked up by distributors. Again, the next stage in the story follows a more conventional route. The film's distributor, Artisan Entertainment, is estimated to have invested between $10 million and $25 million on marketing the film, including a 60-minute special on the Sci-Fi channel and the usual mix of trailers, TV spots, press advertising and poster sites. A further sum was spent on post-production, tidying up the deliberately rough edges of the production – this took the overall production costs to a figure estimated at between $1.5 million and $2 million. As with *Titanic*, the distributor's decision at this point became more or less self-fulfilling and the remaining decisions on marketing expenditure, release strategy and exhibition followed on logically and predictably from here.

It is worth noting that while production costs for films can vary enormously, the marketing costs are more predictable. Once a film has been positioned in its market, marketing and print costs must be set at a minimum level in order to achieve the right exposure. A low budget independent film like *Blair Witch* eventually requires a substantial marketing budget to reach its target market. A high budget movie like *Titanic* will admittedly be given a higher marketing budget, but the discrepancy between this marketing campaign and that of other comparable blockbusters, even between the marketing of *Titanic* and of *Blair Witch*, is not so great as their initial production costs might lead one to expect.

Parts of this story are complex, unpredictable and volatile – evidence of emergent patterns from apparently random events. Parts of the story are more predictable and follow a deliberate strategic pattern based upon the positioning of the film in relation to its market. In terms of decision making and emergence, perceptions of value in the film industry are notoriously volatile. Investors, audiences, critics and stakeholders play a cat and mouse game with each other, waiting to see which way the initial decisions will fall. At this point one or two decisions can have an extraordinarily powerful effect on the network as a whole, and initial impressions are reinforced or dampened through individual interactions. What emerges from conversations, bulletin boards and informal contact is a gradual formation of positive or negative 'buzz' about the movie. At this point the emergent pattern is picked up by the film's backers and deliberately reinforced through decisions on marketing budgets which eventually become self-fulfilling. As Björkegren (1996) notes, the commercial strategy of the film industry is to invest heavily in marketing in order to overcome unpredictability of the market. Typically though, this bold intervention is preceded by a moment of indecision when the studio attempts to second guess the market; it is at this point in the process that 'sensitivity to initial conditions' applies and complex patterns can unexpectedly and inexplicably emerge from apparently random information.

Successful films can 'emerge' from random, unplanned interactions ('word of mouth') or from deliberately conceived marketing plans. The reality, as the very different starting points of *Titanic* and *Blair Witch Project* indicate, is that successful films contain elements of both 'emergent' and 'deliberate' approaches in their marketing. The decisions and value judgements of audiences, investors and studios are part of a delicate, complex system of interactions. But as patterns emerge from these interactions, powerful interests exert their influence on the system and subsequent decisions follow a more predictable, conventional route.

In terms of the creative approaches to strategy discussed in this chapter, film marketing demonstrates the complexity of strategy and decision making. Unpredictability and emergence are part of the equation, and the industry has to respond to these with sensitivity and caution. But the industry also capitalizes on emergent opportunities with a decisive commitment of resources. There is space here to accommodate the 'emergent' success of an underground or 'crossover' hit like *Blair Witch*, where marketers and distributors only join the bandwagon after it has established momentum, and the blockbuster approach of *Titanic*, where the top ten status of the movie is established on the opening weekend and subsequent success is prefigured in the initial release strategy. In both cases, marketing is characterized by a combination of deliberate and emergent approaches. Strategy, like creativity, requires different types of thinking for different stages in the process.

The order that emerges in an adhocracy is not quite 'for free'. A number of structural components have to be in place. First, the elements in the system, in this case the people working in the organization, need to be adaptable and to take risks. Secondly, they need to be capable of observing the systems around them in order to adapt. This capacity, described as 'creative listening', is explored in more detail in the second case study later in this chapter. Finally, the system itself requires sufficient internal complexity and diversity to generate the new patterns and relationships through which a complex adaptive system is sustained. In fact, the apparently spontaneous generative system of adhocracy depends upon a deliberately conceived structure around it.

Risk has often been correlated with creativity and innovation. In an adhocracy, risk might simply mean permission giving – allowing people to learn from their mistakes and providing space for operational decisions and actions which deviate from strategic expectations. The British entrepreneur and inventor James Dyson, whose company manufacture innovative products including the bagless vacuum cleaner, cultivated such a risk culture. According to his business partner, 'James lets you run with it and make mistakes. He's the first to say as long as we've learned something it's not disastrous. He gives people vision, the capability to do anything'.[3] Alongside a culture where risk is permissible, there also needs to be a capacity to respond to and capitalize on new ideas and new opportunities. If new ideas are to catch fire, there needs to be a capacity to mobilize resources and people around them, turning individual risks into organizational risks. This requires flexible processes and systems capable of responding to and accommodating new projects, and a capacity to free up 'risk capital' to invest in the first flickering of a new project. Sylvia King, CEO of The Public (formerly Jubilee Arts), a participatory arts project in West Bromwich in the UK, has identified the need for 'adventure capital' in creative organizations. By using overheads and profits from successful projects to cross-subsidize more risky ventures, King argues that creative organizations can mobilize resources around promising new ideas which would not normally attract funding from external investors.

This leads us to the next ingredient in an adhocracy, which is that managers need to be sufficiently alert and self-aware to recognize the new meaningful patterns which emerge from random innovation, risk-takers and individual initiative. For this to happen managers, like the senior strategists at Honda, need to be able to see beyond their own immediate surroundings and priorities and observe the bigger picture which emerges. Managers also need excellent 'horizontal' communication, so that the left hand of the organization really does know what the right hand is doing, rather than having to refer up to the 'head' at the top of the organizational hierarchy. A hierarchical system of communication and resource allocation will inevitably delay decision making and investment and obstruct the consensus-building needed to support innovation.

Finally, in an adhocracy there needs to be a level of complexity and diversity which allows new ideas and new mutations to occur in the first place by reinjecting new variations into the system. If the gene pool for new ideas is restricted by like-mindedness and consensus, the organization loses the capacity to innovate and evolve. As noted in chapter 3, complex adaptive systems depend upon the diversity within the network, not on the grand architectural scheme of a strategist. Without this diversity, adhocracy can degenerate into a recipe for 'groupthink' and cognitive biases, so that the organization becomes trapped inside its own history. Against the new physics of chaos and complexity, we can apply the old physics of Newtonian entropy, which describes irreversible changes in structure and form towards inertia, uniformity and equilibrium. The key point here is that Newton's Second Law of Thermodynamics is describing a *closed* system. If organizations become closed systems, they will cease to be complex or adaptive and will become entropic. Applying this to organizational structures and strategies, as businesses mature they will lose some of their internal complexity and the individual roles within the business will harden into stereotypes. This does not mean that organizations simply need to expand and diversify; however large and diverse the network or system, connections still depend upon the openness of the system, based on a shared tolerance for contradiction and an individual willingness to listen and adapt to each other.

Adhocracy then can deliver order from chaos. But the process of order from chaos is conditional on certain structural conditions. The building blocks of adhocracy are the autonomous individual initiatives which challenge and deviate from centralized strategies. At the same time individually and collectively the organization needs to be capable of adapting to the interactions and emerging patterns within and outside it.

As noted in previous chapters, such a structural pattern well describes the creative and media industries. The boundaries between individuals, organizations and networks are blurred. Organizations crystallize and dissolve in and out of the networks and communities which support them. Individuals and micro-enterprises operating in this shifting network need to maintain their own nucleus of self-identity while responding to the opportunities and relationships around them. One of the paradoxes of such a system is that competitive advantage, the occupation and defence of a uniquely differentiated position for the individual firm, begins to give way to cooperative advantage, based on recognizing and reconfiguring the relationships between one business and another. Strategy, like 'open source' software, is continually being updated and modified by its users, both inside and outside the organization. A strategy based on adhocracy undermines the stability and identity of discrete organizations and strategies. Gernot Grabher (2002) has described this mutual learning between and within individual firms and teams in the 'project ecology' of the advertising industry. Media centres and creative clusters attempt to provide a formal channel for inter-firm cooperation, but more often networks evolve informally through individual contacts and friendships outside the workplace. In an adhocracy, the boundaries around organizations and strategies are arbitrary; strategic choices are patched into multiple networks and patterns emerge from these complex relationships. These patterns might coalesce into a specific organizational form or a specific strategic direction, but the system remains open, not locked into an immutable, final configuration.

Strategy as Continuity in Change

Adhocracy describes a process of strategy formation, not a self-contained strategic blueprint. The approach allows and depends upon interaction and involvement. But might this involvement not also result in stagnation, indecision and complacency? In the previous section, I have argued that the key to avoiding 'death by consensus' is openness and diversity, a willingness to embrace new strategic options. But might not this same diversity and opportunism result in indecision and inertia?

Businesses in the creative industries are often criticized for being opportunistic rather than strategic. The absence of strategy is explained (sometimes justifiably) in terms of lack of resources, unpredictability of the external market, unpredictability of internal processes and a desire for flexibility. But the consequence is a lack of strategic focus and a tendency to make decisions according to implicit values (culture) rather than explicit objectives (strategy). Explicit strategies are open to negotiation and debate, even if only temporarily and by a restricted constituency. Implicit values are more insidious and can be used to impose consensus or reinforce unquestioned habits of thought.

Strong organizational cultures impose subtle constraints on behaviour – as noted in the preceding chapter, the 'stay late' culture in many small creative organizations turns a collective social arrangement ('we're all going for a drink after work') into a coded warning ('nobody goes home before the team leader'). Similar assumptions and values impose coded constraints on decision making. The absence of any explicit strategy or formal strategy process in creative and media organizations can ironically result in inflexible and dictatorial approaches to management. During the 1980s I was briefly involved in a theatre cooperative in Brighton, where a nominally 'democratic' approach to decision making simply allowed the strongest personalities to dominate. This applied especially to artistic decisions, where aesthetic preferences proved less susceptible to rational debate and negotiation than commercial judgements.

Adhocracy allows for endless tinkering around the edges of strategy, but there are few opportunities for visionary leaps forward or radical departures. The lack of any single identifiable source for strategy can lead to a collective inertia. And because strategy in an adhocracy is built out of operational decisions and outcomes, there is always a danger that 'strategic conversations' become hijacked by operational issues, and group members find themselves micro-managing day-to-day problems instead of addressing the underlying strategic causes. This applies especially when the diversity and specialization of the workforce make finding a common language to address strategic issues that much harder. Freeing up time and space to think strategically is especially difficult in small, informal organizations. The fluidity and flexibility of tasks and responsibilities in small creative organizations make it difficult to draw a line under the daily business and adopt a broader strategic perspective.

Many of these criticisms of creative and media businesses are justified. But underlying them is an assumption that strategy needs to involve a bold, radical departure from everyday problems and solutions. In order to be 'strategic' it is assumed that a decision must be deliberately framed by long-term planning and stand outside and above the present situation. In order to be 'creative', a strategy must be innovative. Behind these assumptions is the familiar equation of creativity with individualistic genius, novelty and 'thinking different'. The myth of individual genius licenses business leaders to make far-reaching strategic decisions with minimal consultation or accountability. Strategy becomes associated with a charismatic, 'heroic' leadership style and with bold, visionary decisions which are not bounded by conventional analysis; taken to its extreme, the decision becomes an end in itself, a display of decisiveness and distinctiveness which may be entirely destructive for the organization concerned.

Creativity in strategy does not equate to radical changes in direction. Adhocracy is based on a different model of creativity, an incremental process of 'small steps' rather than a single giant leap. By insisting that strategy is informed by and evolves out of operational realities, the 'innovative' aspects of strategy are reconnected with an emphasis on value and purpose. A gap analysis of organizational competences in relation to new strategy propositions may not appear to be very exciting or 'creative', but it will ensure that new ideas are grounded in the organization's ability to implement them.

From a practical perspective, an incremental and emergent approach to strategy is more likely to build upon the existing capabilities of the organization and is more likely to achieve support from inside the organization. Furthermore, a strategy which has evolved in this way is more likely to continue evolving as circumstances change, whereas a deliberate attempt to establish a differentiated strategy is by definition more likely to remain fixed. Ironically when managers attempt to define, renew or develop such a strategy through an internal review or external consultancy, the resulting strategic deliberation is usually only temporary. When conducted as a one-off event rather than a continuing process, strategy consultation is more often geared towards securing legitimacy and consensus than to generating new options. Pragmatically, the effort and upheaval involved in developing and fixing strategy in this way is a disincentive to further rethinking of the strategy. Once the strategy is in place, its implementation requires escalating commitment from managers, making it much harder to question the premises behind the original decisions. By contrast an evolving or 'emergent' strategy echoes arguments in previous chapters that change and creativity are incremental processes not one-off events. Continuity within change echoes the argument in the previous chapter that creativity takes place within a set of rules and constraints, not outside them. New strategic options emerge from practical activities and processes, not from a one-off strategic planning event.

One method for achieving this 'continuity within change' in strategy is the use of scenario planning as a technique for strategy formation. The idea of scenario planning is to generate rich, complex scenarios of the future, and to apply these to our own organization in the present. Through the process of building, refining and applying the future scenarios, the organization discovers new ways of looking at the present. Unlike forecasting, where the aim is to build an accurate picture of the future, using mathematical models to project current trends, scenario planning is not in the end concerned with projecting a plausible future. Whereas forecasting assumes that the future can be modelled by analysing data in the present and recent past, scenario planning addresses discontinuous change, 'things we do not know we don't know'. At the same time, scenarios are framed by an analysis of current issues and problems. The principal aim is to generate new strategic options in the present. Scenarios thus need to be relevant and they also need to be effective by changing the way we think about our organization now; if the scenario fails to generate alternative strategic options and does not lead to changes in current strategy, the entire exercise has been a waste of time.

The imaginative, fantastical aspects of scenario planning are framed by a more deliberate, analytical approach, with stages of 'preparation' and 'verification' occurring immediately before and after the scenario-building stage. First, participants need to ensure that scenarios are embedded in real organizational challenges and real drivers of change, not on real or imagined changes currently taking place. This starting point not only ensures some continuity and relevance, it also stimulates a more imaginative, less obvious set of future scenarios. Secondly, once the scenarios have been generated, participants need to reapply the emergent future possibilities back to the organizational present. What insights result from the process? What changes might be instigated? By looking at the dialectic between external changes and internal strategic decision making, it is possible to build in further layers of complexity into the scenario, leading to 'second generation scenarios' which incorporate a chain of strategic consequences and modifications.

David Wilson at Warwick Business School recounts the example of Walt Disney using scenario planning to explore future strategic options. One of the scenarios considered the strategic implications of colonizing the moon. The scenario was improbable and outlandish (literally), but it addressed real strategic issues. In particular, the idea of colonizing the moon was a way for managers to talk about the problems of acquiring and developing real estate for the company's theme park business. Continuity in scenario planning is not a continuity of probabilities and projections from present into the future, it is a strategic continuity ensuring that future options are valuable and relevant to current strategy. In terms of creativity theory, the process requires a combination of divergent thinking and convergent thinking, of spontaneous, intuitive guesswork and rational, logical application. Scenario planning may take us into other worlds, but its strategic implications are more down to earth.

The strategy that emerges from a scenario planning exercise may well be radically different from what has gone before, but it will also be rooted in current issues and capabilities. To this extent, the strategic outcome might appear more conservative, less eye-catchingly 'innovative', than the visionary strategy of a charismatic leader. It might also appear disappointingly practical after the imaginative effort invested in the scenarios themselves. But such an approach fits with the definition of creativity as a complex, multidimensional process. An evolutionary, incremental approach to strategic change rather than a totalizing paradigm shift is in these terms a more 'creative' approach to strategy because it combines novelty and usefulness – innovation with a purpose, not as an end in itself. It is also more likely to cope with discontinuous change, because the process of strategy formation engages the hearts and minds of the organization, encouraging participants to think about the future as a complex, adaptive system, rather than pretending that the future is simple.

Scenario planning addresses some of the problems of strategy in an adhocracy, especially in the creative and media industries, shaking up implicit assumptions and challenging unquestioned habits of thought and ingrained organizational cultures. For creative and media organizations, scenarios are a way of engaging creative thinking in the strategy process and involving participants who might shy away from a more conventional approach. By combining imagination with practical application, future possibilities with current capabilities, divergent with convergent thinking, scenario planning is a good example of the 'creative' approach to strategy being advanced in this chapter.

Case Study: Are You Paying Attention? Jazz, Improvisation and Creative Listening in Strategy Formation

Strategic planning requires an ability to listen selectively and identify and construct meaningful patterns from apparently divergent elements. Creative listening – the ability to identify and build upon one's own and other people's creative ideas – is an essential but undervalued element in 'emergent' strategy formation. The technique of creative listening requires an ability to switch focus from one mode of thinking and attention to another. This dual focus is characteristic of creative thinking. In the context of strategy formation, the split focus of creative listening is on present and imaginary actions and strategic consequences.

Strategy theorists have embraced the metaphor of jazz as a way of describing the free association of ideas necessary for innovation and creativity in strategy. The music emerges from the riffs of the soloists, who work without the safety net of a score. Strategy thus seems to be the product not of a plan or blueprint, but of creative individualism. The metaphor reinforces the conventional association between freedom, individualism and creativity.

Jazz musicians and professors of strategy alike have questioned this analogy. Jazz is after all a highly structured, musical form which draws upon formal motifs and themes and which requires discipline and knowledge; these provide the structures and patterns around which the musicians improvise and which are taken apart and reassembled. This fits with the analysis of creativity in the first part of this book as a structured, systematic process, not the product of random innovation and individual genius. Of course, jazz in turn is itself a broad label encompassing many different styles, with varying degrees of structure and formality, but this tension between form and deconstruction is what gives the music its dynamic power. Above all, 'improvisation' is about listening rather than playing. If we want to draw an analogy between jazz and strategy, we should think less about the apparently 'free' association of ideas, and more about the relationship between the players.

Ben Lockwood is a jazz musician who also runs workshops for businesses. Rather than discussing creative thinking and decision making in the abstract, he invites participants to experiment with making music, tapping out rhythms and performing impromptu trios, duets and solos. What emerges from the exercise is first a much greater respect for the discipline and musicianship of the players themselves, but also an understanding that the music is as much about the gaps between the notes as the notes themselves. Even if the participants have no musical knowledge or aptitude, they can start to experiment with the timing of interventions and silences. They also learn to listen to themselves and to others. When they then observe Lockwood's own musicians working together, attentiveness between the performers spreads out into the audience. The quality of attention between performers compels the audience to listen more attentively themselves. Jazz clubs frequently urge patrons to listen silently.[4] This insistence may suggest that listening is not just a matter of politeness or reverence to the musicians, but an integral part of the performance itself.

Theatre improvisation places a similar emphasis on creative listening. Like jazz improvisation, theatre improvisation is not simply a case of 'making it up as you go along', but is based on rules and structures. One of the most important rules is to listen and respond to others. Many improvisation games are geared not so much towards freeing our own minds as opening our minds to what is happening around us. As a tool for business development, theatre improvisation workshops have more to offer in the development of internal communication and relationships than in pure innovation. As noted in the previous chapter, timing in improvisation is critical. Many good ideas fall flat because they are not integrated into the flow of interactions between participants. Experienced improvisers are able to drop their ideas into the slipstream of another performer, or add an imaginative twist to a routine which is beginning to stagnate. Watching an experienced group of performers, it becomes clear that improvisation is an acquired skill which has its own rules and tricks. A major part of this skill consists in timing each intervention, based on a split-second appraisal of the overall performance. Theatre improvisers, like jazz musicians, are attentive listeners.

If we apply this idea of improvisation as creative listening to strategy formation, we can recognize the critical importance of recognizing and reacting to patterns in decision making. Coming up with new ideas is part of the strategy process, but often this is the easy part. Recognizing the value of an idea and how it connects with another is more difficult. This is how strategy adapts and evolves as a creative system. Creative listening is the glue which holds a collection of innovators and innovative ideas together; without it, the system begins to break down into disconnected riffs and solos. It is also the mechanism whereby ideas are picked up and developed by others.

Can creative listening be taught? In the UK, theatre organizations have become increasingly involved in management or 'executive' training. Alongside major players like the Royal Shakespeare Company and London International Festival of Theatre, smaller groups and individual performers are introducing businesses to improvisation, role-play and scenarios. The quality and nature of such training has also developed towards a more reflective practice, inviting participants to reflect on their 'performance' rather than simply delivering outcomes. Actors in Industry is a small company founded in 1992 by Bill Cashmore. To begin with, the group simply 'acted out' everyday problems designed by training providers. Latterly the company has begun to devise more complex scenarios and to explore the group dynamics and communication skills of participants, while Cashmore himself provides one-to-one coaching for executives. Neil Mullarkey is another actor trainer who has combined a successful career as a comedy performer and improviser at the Comedy Store Players with a new business, providing theatre improvisation workshops for business.

Many of the games and techniques used by Mullarkey are designed to get people talking to each other and, more importantly, listening to each other. A different but related training device is the use of 'rehearsal' to build up an awareness of options and group dynamics around a management scenario. Experimenting with students at Warwick, we have found that by reworking a scenario and feeding in suggestions from a professional theatre director, it is possible to develop an understanding of the dynamics of the decision-making process and to understand how apparently arbitrary decisions (who speaks first, the ordering of an agenda) have an impact upon the formal decisions taken by the group.

These theatre games are not simply about brainstorming new ideas or breaking out of conventional habits of thought. New ideas and new strategies are unlikely to emerge in real time during a session. What these exercises can achieve is a capacity for self-observation and creative listening which can in turn contribute to a more creative, interactive group dynamic. Such a capacity fits with a model of creativity based on multiple intelligences and perspectives, and with a strategic approach based on integrating 'small steps' and individual experiments into meaningful patterns.

Are creative strategy formation techniques such as rehearsal, improvisation and scenario planning relevant to real businesses? The answer to that question obviously depends on one's attitude to the future and to complexity. However, there does seem to be something of a shift in the way businesses today are thinking about strategy. The key to strategy formation in an adhocracy, as it is to rehearsal and improvisation, is the ability to recognize and respond to the emergent patterns. Coming up with a brilliant new strategy, like coming up with a new creative idea, is very rarely the product of a single moment of inspiration. But by identifying emergent patterns, we can develop a strategy which continually evolves and accommodates change, both within the organization and in the external market. We also train ourselves, like jazz musicians and theatre improvisers, to play together, learning the rules of interaction and listening, so that as changes occur we can deal with them rather than referring back to a written score or script. As we move into a knowledge-based, creative economy, we need to develop our capacity to adapt and respond to radical, discontinuous change and to complex interdependent systems. 'Creative' approaches to strategy formation can help us do this.

Strategy and Posthocracy: Being Decisive

In this chapter I have considered two versions of 'creative' strategy. On the one hand, there is a 'heroic' model of creative strategy, modelled around the archetype of the visionary leader or entrepreneur. This model is individualistic in its process and outcome, with the individual genius of leaders or strategy specialists generating an individualized personality for the organization, based on originality and 'thinking different'. The aim of the heroic model is to identify and secure a unique competitive position, based on an original, unexpected insight into the market. This approach to strategy corresponds to 'strategy as orientation' – a blueprint which will allow the organization to steer a steady, unhesitating course through a complex, competitive world.

The second model of creative strategy is collective and incremental. Instead of setting up a new paradigm for the organization's future this 'incremental' model is a work in progress. Future strategy emerges from present action. The strategy is an accumulation of small deviations rather than a complete new direction. The strategy is based on an ability to recognize and build upon meaningful patterns in apparently chaotic, disconnected events and practices, not on a singular insight into the market or individual inspiration. Yet the strategy which emerges from this incremental model may in the end be no less novel and extraordinary than the spectacular, acrobatic leap of the heroic model.

There is a third model of strategy, in which the absolute unpredictability of the future becomes so overwhelming that the process of making rational 'planned' decisions, is no longer possible. Instead decisions are driven by emotions, ego and personality. Of course, this chaotic approach to decision making is not openly acknowledged. Once the decision has been made, it may be rationalized and represented to shareholders as a rational, considered move; but this post-hoc rationalization disguises the often personal, emotional and merely arbitrary process through which the original decision was made. Seen in this light, the analytical tools and vocabulary of management are designed to give the appearance of rational decision making rather than to achieve genuinely rational, transparent decisions. This is strategy in a posthocracy – decisions disconnected from analysis or rationality, but subsequently reclaimed as deliberate, logical and far-sighted.

In any decision, there is a moment of choice. This choice is usually framed by several other phases – typically business decisions will be preceded by an analysis of options, risk analysis, analysis of the market and of the business's core competences and objectives, analysis of competitors, and so on. Once the decision is made there will be a second wave of analysis, verification of assumptions, rechecking available data, analysing outcomes and eventually evaluating the success of the decision with the benefit of hindsight. However, the actual moment of choice will be a matter of individual judgement(s) – no matter how hard managers attempt to rationalize that moment of choice by stripping out personal and emotional language and framing it within an analytical context, choice always means taking a leap into the unknown. Even if, especially if, the choice is presented as 'obvious' or a 'no-brainer'.

Postmodern theorists have highlighted the limitations of rational knowledge and scientific analysis. From a postmodern perspective, there is no such thing as absolute truth, only different versions of the truth which are manipulated and deployed by those in power. The analysis of a problem which precedes a decision is not a rational search for knowledge and understanding, it is a 'language game' in which interest groups compete for power and use their skills and influence to present their own positions as inevitable and incontrovertible. In a hierarchical organization, the status of the decision maker takes precedence over the rationality of the decision.

One does not have to be a postmodern theorist to recognize how this war of attrition plays out in management boardrooms. Rational analysis is tactical and selective, and data is always open to interpretation. Rational approaches to decision making are further undermined, first by an appeal to timeliness and deadlines – 'we don't have time for this', 'let's cut to the chase'. Sometimes it is important to respond quickly to a one-off opportunity. On the other hand artificial and arbitrary cut-off points can be used to stifle debate, in the way an agenda is constructed, in the timing of a meeting or the unilateral imposition of a deadline. There is also a relativism in knowledge and data which means that analysis is tainted by what it seeks to prove. Once we start digging out information on a new product, we start to influence the development of that product and the way it is perceived by others in the market, including our competitors and customers. From a postmodern perspective, 'rational' arguments and evidence thus become another tactic in the struggle for power.

Once taken, top-level decisions are difficult to reverse, setting in motion a flow of consequences which ripple downwards through the organization. Even if the original assumptions are wrong, it is difficult to break this momentum. Others who have committed to secondary decisions on the basis of the first one have bought into the original assumptions and now find themselves implicated in the consequences. Of course this in turn influences the way the 'success' of a decision is subsequently evaluated. Once an organization is emotionally committed to a course of action, everybody involved attempts to present that course of action as rational, necessary and ultimately successful. The fall-out from 'wrong' decisions can take many years to materialize. Here the 'moment of choice', often made with little supporting evidence or logical argument, takes on a disproportionate weight, cascading down through the business in waves of secondary decisions which mirror the first. One can observe this effect especially in hierarchical systems, for example in political decision making or in high-level corporate decisions on mergers and acquisitions. In many cases the lack of any clear rationale for the original decision makes it that much harder to develop logical counter-arguments or to evaluate consequences. Those further down the hierarchy are involved in damage limitation rather than questioning the decision which caused the damage in the first place, and gradually become implicated themselves in its success or failure.

Given the limitations and manipulations of 'rational' analysis in business decision making, the temptation is to give up on the more complex process of decision making and focus on making choices. By making choices, even if these are the wrong ones, managers are seen to be taking action. Investors and stakeholders are reassured that the company is not standing still and the announcements of new initiatives paper over a crisis.

When job specifications and training courses identify 'decision making' as a skill, in many cases they are referring to an ability to make choices – and preferably quick choices. The rational analysis which precedes and follows a decision are separated out from the decision-making process and ultimately devalued. There is a parallel here with the deliberate separation of ideas and analysis in brainstorming. As with brainstorming, the quality filter in decision making is being removed in order to speed up the quantity and novelty (not value) of ideas. Decisiveness becomes an end in itself. If all we mean by decision making is making a choice, and preferably without too much time-consuming analysis, it is hardly a skill – being good at making a choice is not the same as making a good choice and requires few attributes or skills beyond a certain bullishness. By equating the intuitive moment of choice with the more complex process of decision making, we elevate choice to a key management discipline. We also push towards innovation and organizational change as ends in themselves.

Decision making in a posthocracy contains several of the 'creative' elements of strategy considered in this chapter, but stripped of their underlying purpose. From adhocracy, posthocracy borrows the assumption of unpredictability and change and the rejection of fixed positions and orientations. Unlike adhocracy, posthocracy does not attempt to adapt to complexity, or to seek continuity in change. It favours decisive action and counters unpredictability with arbitrary certainties. In this respect, posthocracy mimics the visionary confidence of the heroic, differentiated strategy, a model based on charisma, individual insight and bold leaps of faith. The difference is that in a posthocracy, analysis takes place after the decision, not before it. The underlying presumption in a posthocracy is that, to quote Goldman's oft-repeated line about the film industry, 'nobody knows anything'. Strategy becomes another language game, a display of decisiveness as an end in itself, disguising a profound loss of certainty about the future.

The performance of certainty in a posthocracy is essentially nihilistic. Unlike the other models of strategy considered in this chapter, there is no real attempt to make sense of the future, only a desire to be seen to be doing so. This leads to a pursuit of decisiveness for its own sake – change without a purpose, strategy without vision. The suspicion remains that this is how most of us make decisions, most of the time. The best way to appear confident about the future, and to ensure the past never catches up with us, is to insist on a programme of permanent revolution, a succession of radical changes and flamboyantly 'decisive' actions. This animates the organization with a buzz of activity, giving the impression of purposeful energy through what physicists describe as 'constant random motion', but lacks any differentiated vision or emergent strategic pattern.

Posthocracy places a premium on innovation and change for change's sake and removes analysis and verification from the decision-making process. The emphasis on decisiveness as an end in itself is ultimately a form of non-strategy. It is also a radical departure from the two-part definition of creativity (new *and* useful) advanced in psychological theories of creativity.

Strategy as Process

In this chapter I have argued that adhocracy represents a more complex model of creativity in strategy – innovation with a purpose. Creativity in strategy is more demanding and rigorous than what Boden calls 'mere innovation'. The incremental model of creativity in strategy requires a combination of divergent and convergent thinking – an ability to take things apart and to put them back together into a new pattern. It depends upon an open dialogue and self-analysis at all levels of the organization. It combines imagination and risk with an attention to detail and alertness to other people's ideas. New insights emerge from the friction between strategic vision and operational reality, tweaking the boundaries of what is possible and acceptable.

Such an approach to strategy acknowledges that new strategies, like new ideas, are only the beginning – it is in the detail of their application and modification that value is created for the organization. It is also through this process of implementation and adaptation that the original strategy is continually tweaked and updated. Implementation is not a straightforward matter of 'following the plan', it is a process for questioning the plan and for generating new ones.

Creative approaches to strategy require a new emphasis on systems design and organizational complexity. The role of leadership becomes navigating and sustaining complexity by ensuring that strategy remains an open conversation, a dialogue between current capabilities and future possibilities. This does suggest a more open, consultative style of management, but also requires the construction and maintenance of a common language through which strategic conversations can take place across the whole organization. Only if there is a common vocabulary can existing strategies and objectives be cross-examined and new ones introduced, developed and supported.

Creative organizations are complex, adaptive systems in which multiple perspectives and multiple objectives compete for pre-eminence. At any one time, an organization might hold several strategies simultaneously. In the late 1990s, a friend of mine was brought in as a consultant to help a photographers' network adapt to the new market for digital photography and to compete with the new online image banks which were then beginning to replace traditional photography libraries and archives. It became clear that there could be no one-off solution to the group's situation. Strategy in this case became a rolling process, with the group working to one strategy while introducing another and developing a third for the future. Multiple strategies reflected multiple objectives and constituencies. In creative organizations there is a strong relationship between personal and organizational goals, with competing individuals reading their own future plans between the lines of the collective strategy. Faced with such complexity, the role of leadership and strategy becomes devising a system for communication through which future plans can be debated, questioned and tested. Trying to impose order on this complexity would mean stripping out some of the diversity and risk. On the other hand, blind acts of decisiveness would mean ignoring complexity and pretending life is simple. By developing systems for communication and encouraging an exchange of views on the future, managers can tease out emergent strategic patterns from adhocracy and a shared sense of purpose from apparently random processes of individual innovation. Order for free is paid for through tolerance, communication, eclecticism and interaction.

Like creativity, strategy formation is a matter of synthesis. It requires that we see the pattern between apparently unlikely elements and recognize the long-term possibilities contained in short-term opportunities. The future is continually changing and our strategies need to develop with it. This requires that we move away from the idea that strategy is a done deal, a map of the future, or a leap into the unknown. Instead of orientation, strategy can animate us and help us to survive future complexity and unpredictability. The aim is no longer to come up with a perfect strategy but to devise a better system for strategy formation. The result will not be a strategic plan but better strategic planning – a process, not a blueprint.

FURTHER READING

Attempting to classify different approaches to strategy has famously been likened by Mintzberg to a group of blind men trying to identify an elephant. Not content with dividing strategy into five Ps (Plan, Ploy, Pattern, Position, Perspective), Mintzberg himself established nine separate 'strategy schools'. Each of these schools has its advocates and uses for different types of organization at different times. Mintzberg accordingly argued for an 'eclecticism' in strategic planning, advising managers to adopt a combination of approaches to suit their present need (Mintzberg *et al.* 1998). For the 5 Ps, see Mintzberg (1987).

The term 'adhocracy' was introduced by Alvin Toffler in *Future Shock* (1970). Mintzberg used a case study of the National Film Board of Canada to develop his idea of strategy formation in an 'adhocracy' (Mintzberg and McHugh 1985). He and his co-researcher tracked different genres of films in order to identify a series of 'blips' and 'trends' emerging from the individual choices of film makers. Gradually they noticed a pattern emerging, with the overall portfolio of films beginning to develop recognizable strengths in particular areas. The overall direction was not centrally determined, and decisions were devolved to the film makers themselves, but over time a recognizable strategic direction appeared to emerge. The distinction between 'deliberate' and 'emergent' strategy was further explained in another article: see Mintzberg and Waters (1985).

Mintzberg's principal adversary in the strategy debate was H. Igor Ansoff. Ansoff represented the traditional 'design school' approach to strategy, which Mintzberg argued was out of touch with the needs of modern business. The pair exchanged criticisms in a series of articles in *Strategic Management Review* 11 (1990) and 12 (1991). In the end Ansoff's defence of traditional top-down strategic planning provided a soft target and allowed Mintzberg to seize the high ground as innovator and sceptic. See Ansoff (1987).

A more formidable opponent would have been Michael Porter. In *Competitive Advantage: Creating and Sustaining Superior Performance* (1985), Porter defined his three generic strategies – cost leadership, differentiation and focus. According to Porter, every business would need to specialize in one of these areas in order to carve out a distinctive competitive position, and ensure that every aspect of their business was aligned to the core strategy. To achieve this consistency would require a measure of commitment. Porter emphasized that trying to be all things to all people or switching between strategies would be a recipe for failure. Hence there must be 'trade-offs' in order to specialize in the area where the business is most competitive and in order to sustain a clearly differentiated position. Improvisation and 'ad hoc' decision making would obviously be outlawed in this system.

Porter replaced Ansoff as the chief proponent of traditional strategic planning, a corner he continued to fight through the 1990s. When the dot.com boom turned to bust in the early 1990s, Porter was unable to disguise a note of triumph. The Internet was no different from any other market – the dot.coms went bust because they had not followed the golden rules of strategy, as defined by Michael Porter (see Porter 1996 and 2001).

Porter and Mintzberg represent the two opposing views on strategy discussed in this chapter. Mintzberg's emergent strategy approach is perhaps in the ascendancy. See, for example, Richard Pascale's (1984) classic case study of Honda's entry into the American motorcycle market, an article which appeared to cement 'adhocracy' as the dominant paradigm in strategy. But while Mintzberg is perhaps the dominant figure in the management literature, Porter remains a powerful influence on management practice.

For examples of jazz and improvisation as metaphors for strategy formation, see Kao (1996), Hatch (1999), Barrett (1988), and Montuori (2003). For a critical view on the use of creativity theory in management discourse, see Prichard (2002).

My discussion of scenario planning is indebted to Professor David Wilson at Warwick Business School, who introduced me to this approach to strategy formation and has fine-tuned the approach to scenario planning outlined here. For further discussion of scenario planning see Leemhuis (1985), Stout (1998), Heijden (1996) and Wack (1985a and b).

For a discussion of decision making and an accessible literature review on the subject, see 'Process Analysis for Strategic Decision-Making' (chapter 13) in McGee et al. (2005: 503–23). The extent to which management decision-making is actually highly personalized, subjective and irrational has been discussed by many commentators – see, for example, the 'garbage-can model' proposed by Cohen et al. (1972). Duncan Angwin has highlighted the apparently random and ego-driven decision making behind multimillion dollar merger deals in 'Strategy as Exploration and Interconnection' in Cummings and Wilson (2003: 228–65). For a fly-on-the-wall view on management decision making which brings the underlying corridor deals and ego battles to the surface, Roger Graef's fascinating documentary 'Decision: Steel' tracks a controversial investment decision by British Steel in the 1970s. Both Angwin and Graef indicate that what is subsequently sold as an objective, rational business decision was at the time driven by personality and instinct. Major investment decisions, especially merger details, are rarely subject to any 'objective' scrutiny; by the time the real effectiveness and value of the deal can be measured it is generally too late to hold the protagonists to account.

More recently Malcolm Gladwell has elaborated on the 'non-rational' character of decision-making in *Blink: The Power of Thinking without Thinking* (2005), suggesting that most of us most of the time make decisions intuitively. But he also suggests that 'spontaneous' decisions actually conceal a subconscious process of logic, memory and experience. This combination of rational and irrational thought processes is of course very similar to the description of creativity and creative decision making being advanced in this chapter.

For an introduction to complexity theory, see Lewin (1993) and Kauffman (1995). Ralph Stacey has applied complexity theory to management and strategy in several books and articles, including *Complexity and Creativity in Organizations* (1996a); *Strategic Management and Organizational Dynamics* (1996b); and 'The science of complexity: An alternative perspective for the strategic change process' (1995). Stacey is interested in how management adapts to unpredictability and the 'anxiety' provoked when our desire to plan and control the future runs up against uncertainty and unmanageable change. Stacey accordingly locates strategic management at this edge of chaos, the transition point where creative destruction and dynamism meet stable systems and shared assumptions. Management, like creativity, requires us to move out of our comfort zone and confront chaos and uncertainty, but Stacey also acknowledges that our anxiety must be 'contained' or managed. The order of complexity depends upon a dynamic relationship between stability and turbulence. If we are too frightened of the process of change, we are unlikely to achieve this balance and we are unlikely to recognize the new emergent patterns. Creativity in this context is a destructive force but also an integral and dynamic element within strategy and management.

NOTES

1   Defence Secretary Donald Rumsfeld responds to questions on Iraqi weapons of mass destruction, US Department of Defense Briefing, 12 February 2002 (available at http://www.defenselink.mil/transcripts/2002/t02122002_t212sdv2.html).
2   According to Goldman, this is 'the single most important fact, perhaps, of the entire movie industry'.
3   Interview with Fiona Lawrie, *Observer*, 16 January 2000.
4   Displayed prominently on the stage at the Jazz Café in London is a notice with the phrase 'STFU and Listen'. Anglophone readers should be able to decipher the acronym.

6 BUSINESS DEVELOPMENT AND ORGANIZATIONAL CHANGE

> *What is new about the phase of mass culture compared with the late liberal stage is the exclusion of the new. The machine rotates on the same spot. . . . Yet for this very reason there is never-ending talk of ideas, novelty, and surprise, of what is taken for granted but has never existed. Tempo and dynamics serve this trend. Nothing remains as of old; everything has to run incessantly, to keep moving. For only the universal triumph of the rhythm of mechanical production and reproduction promises that nothing changes, and nothing unsuitable will appear.*
>
> (Adorno and Horkheimer 1979: 134)

> *A merely novel idea is one that can be described and / or produced by the same set of generative rules as are other, familiar, ideas. A genuinely original or radically creative idea is one that cannot.*
>
> (Boden 1994: 77)

What Is Organizational Change?

In this chapter I will consider how organizations manage change and some of the implications of creativity theory and practice for this process.

In the previous chapter, strategy and decision making were presented both as a deliberate attempt to change the organization, and as an emergent strategic response to operational change. It is clear that the relationship of strategy to change is double-edged; strategy attempts to change reality, but it must also adapt to changing realities. In the previous chapter I argued for an approach to strategy formation based on experimentation and recognition – a willingness to take risks alongside an ability to recognize strategic patterns emerging from apparently disconnected initiatives and events.

Organizational change can be seen in the same way as a pattern emerging from chaos. What looks from the outside like a sudden radical departure often turns out to be the result of an accumulation of smaller steps taken over time. The great discoveries in science and art have tended to follow this process. When Watson and

Crick discovered DNA, they were one of several teams of researchers all pursuing the same goal, working in separate countries but sharing knowledge through scientific journals and networks. Picasso did not 'discover' Cubism as a fully fledged artistic movement; he moved gradually from a more representational style of painting, experimenting with perspective over many years and exchanging ideas with fellow painters such as Georges Braque as well as drawing on other sources including African tribal art. Organizational change often follows a similar trajectory; new structures, new technologies, radical changes in strategy or rapid business expansion grow out of smaller experimental steps and reflect wider trends in shared knowledge and practice. This idea of collective adaptation has been described as the 'population ecology' model of organizational change; in order to survive, organizations imitate the characteristics of successful peers. Of course there are many other ways of explaining the dynamics of organizational change. But it is worth recognizing that what looks like radical change from the outside is often more gradual and experimental than it first appears, and worth remembering that businesses are likely to overstate the boldness and uniqueness of new initiatives in order to position themselves as progressive and innovative.

The idea that change occurs incrementally and collectively rather than suddenly and individually fits with the model of creativity being advanced in this book. It also suggests an alternative to the separation of deliberate and reactive approaches to organizational change. If organizations are continually experimenting and modifying around the edges of their core business, they are much more likely to adapt to unexpected external changes. Conversely if they are locked into a single strategic vision, it becomes much harder for them to respond to change. Experimental, incremental change is a way of modifying and adapting deliberate, planned strategies; it is also a way of preparing for and adapting to external change. Much of the literature on organizational change and growth describes a stop-go cycle of revolution, crisis and adaptation. In this chapter I will argue that the incremental, evolutionary change which characterizes creativity theory and practice offers a viable alternative. This approach is built upon a combination of deliberate and reactive changes. An organization deliberately releases resources to allow for new projects and initiatives; but the strategic pattern which emerges from these experiments is not fixed and will depend on reacting to change as well as initiating it. Organizational change here is both deliberate *and* reactive.

Organizational change is not the same thing as organizational growth, even if they are both entwined with the commercial imperative of increasing profits. It is possible to expand the commercial scale of the organization while at the same time reducing its strategic scope. A business might increase turnover and profit by concentrating on its core business and cutting back on new initiatives, following Tom Peters' famous injunction to 'stick to your knitting' (Peters and Waterman, 1982). According to Peters, excellent companies focus on their strengths and are not distracted by new opportunities. Such a strategy might consolidate strengths in the present, but leave the business increasingly vulnerable to changes impacting on its core business in the future. Conversely a business which diversifies too rapidly into new products and new markets might be both responding to and exacerbating a failure to grow its core business. Growth does not always correlate to success, and 'change' might not necessarily mean growing the business.

Surveys of small businesses in the creative and media industries indicate a reluctance to grow. Organizational change is more likely to involve development than growth, and profits tend to be reinvested in existing products and services rather than in business expansion. Many smaller creative organizations are project-based and their turnover and cashflow are measured through a succession of peaks and troughs rather than as a steadily rising or falling curve. Consequently investors are reluctant to commit funds to a business which appears unstable and the businesses themselves are often wary of overextending the business after a handful of successful projects. A friend set up an independent television production company in the 1990s, with support from her previous employer. In her first year she turned over approximately £7 million. In her second year turnover was less than £100,000. Production was entirely dependent on commissions from broadcasters. In her first year, she pitched four projects and was commissioned to make three of them. In the second year, having worked flat out in the first year to meet targets, she had very few new or developing projects in the pipeline and she received no commissions. Averaged out over two to three years, the company's turnover, profit and balance sheet were reasonably healthy. But if she had gone out to expand her business at the end of that remarkable first year, she admits that her business might have gone under.

Organizational change describes a process of incremental adaptation to external changes and internal intentions. This process of managed change might pre-empt the crisis management approach to organizational change described in some of the management literature. It might also provide a sustainable basis for developing the business, instead of a too rapid expansion of the business on the one hand or a retreat into core competences on the other. Organizational change encompasses both deliberate and reactive approaches to change, and it includes but is not limited to business expansion and growth. The model of change advanced in this chapter is based on assumptions from creativity theory and examples from the creative and media industries. Before developing this model, it is worth considering how organizations currently manage organizational change and growth.

The Change Cycle

Much of the literature on organizational change describes a stop-go approach to organizational change and growth. Managers adopt a particular style of management based on the needs of the moment, but find that these approaches prevent the business from adapting to the next stage in the firm's life cycle. Subsequently each successful adaptation prompts a new crisis, requiring a new management style – and so the cycle of crisis and consolidation continues. Firms lurch from one crisis to the next, casting off their entrepreneurial skin to emerge as conservative rationalists, only to find at a later stage that they actually need to rediscover some of the qualities they left behind them. The irony is that their success in resolving and addressing one crisis makes the next one inevitable – by attempting to move with the times, the organization gets trapped in its time and can only break free at the next crisis point. Reactive, unplanned organizational change is both the cause as well as the effect of organizational crisis.

It is worth noting that the literature here is descriptive rather than prescriptive – this is organizational change as the authors see it, rather than as they think it ought to be. Most managers would agree that is preferable to anticipate a crisis rather than respond to it. It is also much easier to come up with new ideas for developing the business from a position of strength than it is to innovate one's way out of a crisis. This being the case, why is this cyclical pattern of change such a recognizable and oft-cited feature of organizational change? According to the management literature, one reason is that while it is easy to recognize a crisis after it has happened, it is much more difficult to read the warning signs before the crisis occurs. Consequently managers only know where they stand in the life cycle of the firm after the crisis has struck – by which time only the most drastic of solutions is available to them. I suggest there are two further problems: first the enthusiasm for radical change, and secondly the rise of a 'heroic', entrepreneurial model of leadership.

In the opening chapter I noted that 'creativity' in business is often equated with innovation and change for its own sake. In competitive markets with shrinking margins, operational excellence is no longer a guarantee of success. Even the space for strategic differentiation is diminishing, partly as a result of its widespread adoption; as the entrepreneur John Harvey Jones noted in his preface to Ansoff's book on corporate strategy, if everybody is following the same strategic recipe, 'competitive advantage' becomes another hygiene factor – a minimum requirement, not an opportunity to get ahead.[1] By emphasizing a universal approach to strategy, it is alleged that strategic planners have ensured that differentiation, based on the same rules and methods of analysis, is no longer different. In this context businesses strive to find new ways of competing. The entrepreneur's ability to discover new markets, products, technologies and business models has accordingly become for some businesses the new Holy Grail.

Entrepreneurs are good at identifying new business opportunities but not always so good at developing and exploiting them. Change, discovery and renewal are the essence of entrepreneurial business, but for an established business they may be dangerous. As mainstream business seeks to become more entrepreneurial (or 'intrapreneurial'), managers hope to steal a march on the competition through a singular insight, a moment of daring or an individualistic, unexpected solution to a problem. As noted in the previous chapter, this in turn leads to an emphasis on charismatic, individualist leadership and inventive, counter-intuitive approaches to decision making. The danger here is that in seeking to embrace new businesses and new business models, managers neglect the strengths and competences of the existing business.

There are some parallels here between the myth of individual creative genius and the cult of the individual, entrepreneurial manager. Maverick entrepreneurs share with the creative genius a reputation for volatility, aggression and arrogance. Yet new ideas and individual inspiration in business, as in art, depend upon a context of networks, systems and relationships. Many entrepreneurs depend upon supporting teams or partners who help turn their visions into realities; others receive little credit for their ability to implement business models as well as inventing them. Entrepreneurs like Stelios Haji-Ioannou and Michael Ryan are credited with discovering a new business model for cheap, low cost air travel. Their strengths as old-fashioned managers attending to the details of their business are often overlooked. The success of Easyjet and Ryanair owes as much to operational control (especially cost control) as to the novelty of the business concept; this is why they have continued to thrive as others have copied their original business model.

The pressure to come up with new ideas in business and the emphasis on entrepreneurial leadership is dangerously seductive. New ideas in business must be tested against the existing competences of the organization and the needs of the market. If businesses attempt to expand into new areas where they have no experience, they risk pursuing change for change's sake, failing to locate new developments in organizational and market realities. This leads into the cycle of renewal, crisis and reinvention referred to above in the literature on organizational growth.

The danger of expanding the business too rapidly beyond the organization's core competences was perhaps best illustrated during the dot.com boom of the late 1990s. Here the pressure to grow came primarily from investors, many of whom knew little of the technologies or business models of the emerging online businesses. Given that these businesses were too risky to attract investment from banks, small businesses were largely reliant on venture capital not only to grow their business but to start them. Their investors typically required exponential growth, high returns and an early exit from the business. The combination of fledgling businesses, inexperienced entrepreneurs and impatient investors was a volatile cocktail. Dot.com businesses were encouraged to grow far beyond their capabilities or needs, racking up equity in the business but failing to develop profitable business models or loyal customers. Inevitably many of these businesses crashed because as soon as the inflated share prices started to dip, there was no viable business behind them. The fall-out convinced mainstream investors that intangible assets and knowledge based businesses are inherently risky. In reality the dot.com crash owed as much to the investment strategies of venture capital as to managerial inexperience or the inherent volatility of the knowledge economy.

At the tail end of the dot-com boom, Michael Porter returned with a timely reminder that managers who neglect the strategic core of their business do so at their peril (Porter 2001). Against this, the pressure to expand and to diversify the business is real, and as markets become more fluid and unpredictable Porter's emphasis on consistent, coherent strategy might become a dead weight, blocking off opportunities. Many of today's most successful businesses have been more opportunistic in their strategic approach, expanding aggressively when the time is right. Microsoft is an illustration of this approach, enjoying 'second mover advantage' by exploiting the markets created by the pioneer brand Apple; having capitalized on the personal computer market created by Apple in the 1980s and 1990s, Microsoft looks set to repeat the strategy at the time of writing by taking on Apple in the mobile music market in 2006. The assumption that businesses establish a clear competitive advantage through a distinctive and highly differentiated market position neglects the ease with which businesses can cut and paste business portfolios across market boundaries. This is especially true in the creative and media industries, where technological convergence allows a business to transfer a successful business model from one medium to another (film, music, television and online), exploiting economies of scale and scope and cross-media synergies, despite lacking the accumulated knowledge and reputation of the existing players in the market. So a telecoms provider like British Telecom is set to become a major force in digital film and music distribution, while Apple and Microsoft (even Coca Cola) were quicker into the online music market than the major record labels. With these shifting boundaries, differentiation within a given market becomes increasingly tenuous and businesses must respond rapidly to new opportunities and changing market conditions.

The irony here is that pursuit of change and resistance to change perhaps feed off each other. The 'revolutionary' model of organizational change and growth described in the literature alternates between radical change and stasis. Organizations fix on a business model and stay with it doggedly until it becomes untenable. Then they attempt to innovate their way out of a crisis. To rewrite Tom Peters' prescription, they stick to their knitting until they run out of wool. At any given moment in the life cycle, the organization seems to be either growing too fast or not changing at all. The alternative to the reinvention rollercoaster is to find a more incremental model of organizational change. It is here that theories of creativity can perhaps help develop a more viable approach to organizational change and business development.

Incremental Change

I have suggested that the cult of the heroic entrepreneur and the fetishization of change in business have much in common with the mythical view of individual creative genius discussed in the opening chapter of this book. Conversely creativity theory provides a model of incremental change. According to creativity theory, 'breakthrough thinking' does not result from a moment of sudden insight, since it almost always has an unacknowledged precedent. Instead of seeking a radical break with the past, creative thinking digs deeper into shared resources of experience, memory and knowledge, reconfiguring the existing pattern instead of breaking it.

Applying this model to organizational change, organizational development is achieved not through a revolutionary transformation but through an evolutionary succession of small steps, reconfiguring the business from within rather than searching for a different animal entirely. In this model, change is pre-emptive and continual rather than discontinuous and reactive. Where the entrepreneur and the crisis manager follow an abrupt, sporadic rhythm, with sudden leaps of insight and illumination breaking out of periods of inaction and complacency, the rhythm of incremental change is more fluid and less dramatic. Changes and new ventures build upon current practice through an ongoing process of experimentation and exploration. Change is not disconnected from the questions of value and 'fitness for purpose' which are integral to theories of creativity. The change process at Marks and Spencer was born out of a crisis, but in the end appears to have succeeded by becoming evolutionary rather than revolutionary (see case study).

Case Study: Creativity and Change at Marks and Spencer[2]

By the end of the 1990s, the UK retailer Marks and Spencer experienced dramatic falls in profits and a declining share price. The company's clothing lines, once a byword for quality and reliability, were seen to be old-fashioned and were losing business to trendier high street alternatives. The company's upmarket food business was also suffering new competition from the 'quality' brands launched by many of the major UK supermarket chains. By 2001, the company was forced to close down many of its overseas stores in Europe, North America and the Far East, to widespread criticism from customers. In May 2000, the newly appointed chairman Luc Vandevelde found the company in the grip of a corporate panic, with new initiatives, relaunches, rebrands and rationalizations failing to convince customers or investors that the company was capable of recovery. He gave himself 12 months to turn the business around, promising to resign if he failed. Change was not quite as rapid as he had predicted, and he was forced to extend his self-imposed deadline for another year. Nevertheless, by May 2002, helped in no small part by an increasingly buoyant high street retail sector, Vandevelde was able to announce a dramatic recovery in profits and share price. The battle was not yet over, as retail would suffer another dip in the years which followed and competition continued to escalate, especially in high street fashion. Nevertheless, Vandevelde was able to claim the credit for turning the ship around.

Most observers agreed that the company's initial problems stemmed from its inability to manage change. The company had been a star performer through most of the 1990s, with healthy profits and a rising share price. Yet the company's much loved high street presence and its loyal but ageing customer base concealed underlying problems. Internal changes in the supply chain, changes in fashion, changes in the competition, changes in demographics, changes in the way people bought and wore clothes – all were overlooked while profits remained high. When these changes caught up with the company balance sheet, the company launched into a series of revolutionary changes which seemed to misdiagnose the company's problems, dilute the company's core values and brand and betrayed an increasingly panicky, scatter-gun approach to innovation and change.

The company appeared caught between two opposing and stereotypical approaches to organizational change. A stereotypically 'managerial' approach reacts to external change by reinforcing the internal values, mission and culture of the organization and seeks continuity through a rigorously implemented strategy. A stereotypically 'innovative' approach seeks a radical break with the past, applying 'blue sky thinking' and brainstorming to 'think the unthinkable' and transform the company. Both of these approaches were applied at Marks and Spencer – sometimes simultaneously. Yet neither of these versions fits with the more complex definition of creativity advanced in this book that requires linking continuity and change, new elements and old, to achieve particular purposes or solve context specific problems. In a web chat and focus group with students from the MA in Creative and Media Enterprises at University of Warwick in summer 2001, we discussed the relationship between change, innovation and creativity at Marks and Spencer.

> 12:33:45 pm chris
> *What do you think managers and consultants mean when they talk about creativity?*
> 12:34:09 pm Gonzalo
> *They refer more to 'innovation' than to 'creativity'. Do you think this implies any differences?*
> 12:34:33 pm Ruth
> *There is little mention of aptness or relevance for purpose in their definition of creativity and we've talked a lot about how value is implicit in a definition of creativity.*
> 12:34:52 pm Gonzalo
> *I mean, usually I feel a kind of rigid/recipe approach to creativity among managers.*
> 12:35:54 pm Ruth
> *Edward de Bono focuses on problem solving – you need to identify you have a problem before you set out to solve it – M&S were slow to realise they had one.*

The management 'recipe' for innovation was equated with radical innovation and 'thinking outside the box'. Much emphasis was placed on doing things differently, breaking norms and solving problems. Little attention was paid to more incremental models of change advanced in this chapter, to establishing what the norms and boundaries are in order to challenge them. Here, there was a sense that managers had underestimated the need for preparation and research as an integral part of the creative process and confused 'creativity' with 'innovation'.

> 12:41:35 pm joy2
> *Know norms and boundaries in order to break. Yes, but sometimes, if you know too much, you will be trapped. So, your own judgement and evaluation is crucial in order to break them.*
> 12:43:39 pm Ruth
> *For judgement and evaluation you need lots of the right information and perhaps M&S was not well informed enough to exercise these effectively.*
> 12:44:19 pm joy2
> *Don't translate research data directly . . . think in different way!*

Marks and Spencer responded to the decline in its existing business by attempting to innovate its way out of trouble. New franchises were launched in store, including underwear by Agent Provocateur, Per Uno 'designer' clothing by George Davis (the star clothing designer and retailer behind Next and

George at Asda). New products and services were also introduced, for example financial services. Yet many of these innovations jarred with existing customers and with the company's established identity.

Creativity does not consist only in introducing new, innovative elements, it may also require reconfiguring the existing elements – a new recipe perhaps, but not a new set of ingredients. Artistic innovation typically revisits themes and motifs from existing work rather than starting from scratch. This is how, for example, a painter like Picasso, or a performer like Madonna builds a body of work which continually changes yet remains identifiably theirs. This may be the secret of those black polo necks and tailored white shirts: an incremental, contextual approach to change which builds upon but subtly reinvents a tradition. This reinvention of 'classic' items represented a more creative solution to the company's dowdy image than the eye-catchingly unfamiliar innovations.

Artists who change direction are often ridiculed for 'selling out' or losing their artistic integrity. Students identified a similar problem with many of the more 'radical' changes adopted by M&S at the time. Attempting to take on Gap and Next on their own terms, selling sexy underwear or youth fashion failed to convince members of our focus group, or their teenage daughters. Random innovation or diversification in this context simply meant diluting the identity or the brand.

M&S lost track of this core identity (and its 'norms and boundaries' to use Ruth and Joy's words). This made it difficult to direct and develop its body of work effectively. 'Quality', for example, might once have referred to workmanship or longevity. But today's consumers may not want their clothes to last forever, just a season or two. Other aspects of 'quality' have simply become hygiene factors, notably in the food department. M&S has been part of this transformation, gradually extending what consumers mean and understand by 'quality'. Unfortunately, they have not allowed space for a similar evolution in the way their own managers address the brand; quality needs to be re-imagined – repetition with a twist. It is in the attention to detail (another traditional creative strength, of course) that the important changes take place, not in major re-branding exercises or radical overhauls.

Creativity, according to our discussion, is about incremental change and continually adjusting to shifting boundaries – reconfiguring existing elements into a new pattern. Creativity, according to many managers still means 'thinking outside the box' and radical change. This is perhaps the final lesson – when it comes to creativity, like that black polo-neck, less is often more.

12:30:29 pm elli
yes . . . I would say that you need to push the boundaries
12:30:52 pm chris
i.e. change inside the box, not 'thinking outside the box' . . .

12:30:53 pm elli
This is really important to any creative organisation
12:31:02 pm Ruth
yes they should have concentrated on boundary tweaking in the first place rather than exploring new territories altogether
12:32:17 pm Jen
it's the attention to detail that gave them a [creative] edge in the first place. like the measuring tapes around the neck as a symbol
12:47:58 pm joy2
only one thing will never change is: keep changing. i think M&S forgot this common sense.

This less drastic approach to organizational change has two benefits for the organization. First, by pre-empting the crisis-revolution model of organizational change, new initiatives are more closely harmonized with the existing business. Instead of equating creativity and change with a drastic, destructive attempt at total renewal, organizational change is gradual, logical and planned. The revolutionary model pits the agents of change against the agents of continuity and perpetuates a fear of change and creativity as something inherently painful and destructive; the resulting tensions and mistrust become self-perpetuating and self-fulfilling. The evolutionary, incremental model of creativity theory embeds change in the organizational culture and allows the agents of change and the agents of continuity to work together. Instead of setting creative entrepreneurs and conservative rationalists against each other, creativity theory encourages them to work together. In terms of creative thinking, moments of inspiration and 'divergent thinking' are integrated with deliberate, rational processes of re-examination and project implementation.

The second benefit of this proactive, incremental approach to organizational change is that instead of avoiding change until it is too late, the organization is continually investing in new ideas and new ventures from a position of strength. Incremental change aims to pre-empt the need for crisis management. By investing in new ideas and new ventures at the point when their existing business is still successful, managers can achieve a smoother transition between one phase of development and the next. In this more controlled environment, change and innovation can be pursued through myriad experiments rather than a single imaginative leap. Equally importantly, the resources (financial, human, emotional and temporal) are still available to support new initiatives. Typically most organizations recognize the need to change only after they hit crisis point. The solution is to build continual incremental change and development into the organization's strategy.

The idea of incremental change and planned progression is less extreme and less obviously innovative than the totalizing changes of the revolutionary model. In order to plan sustainable organizational change, a manager has to take into account the organization's resources, including its human resources, as well as its markets, both real and potential. These boundaries provide a reality check and reference point which stimulates rather than inhibits new initiatives. A *creative* approach to organizational change (as opposed to 'mere innovation') will look for points of contact between continuity and change and explore ways of combining old and new elements in order to address a specific problem. This combination of continuity and continual experiment is characteristic of the theories of creativity considered in chapter 1, including Weisberg's theory of incremental creativity and Boden's 'boundary-tweaking' model. It also reflects artistic practice. Artists generally achieve 'originality' not by a moment of divine madness, but by locating their work within an internal and external context, with ideas continually evolving through successive drafts, versions, sketches and improvisations. They also retain their own distinctive identity through successive phases of a career, building upon and at the same time subtly reinventing their own tradition. Their creativity consists in the modifications they make to an evolving body of work, not in any drastic departure from their own self-imposed boundaries.

Organizations like artists are more likely to develop something of value by building on strengths than by attempting to deny their own history. Without some sense of a core identity and the norms and boundaries around that identity, there is little scope to evaluate the meaning and purpose of organizational change. Incremental change allows the organization, like the artist, to bring their customers and their internal stakeholders along with them. By gradually extending perceptions of the meaning and value of the business, incremental organizational change extends and deepens the meaning of brands instead of diluting them or denying them. When British Airways attempted to rebrand itself overnight by painting a series of multiethnic 'world art' logos on the tailfins of its planes, customers reacted to the new corporate identity with confusion and disbelief. In the end the company was forced to abandon the attempt and reverted to an updated version of its traditional red, white and blue livery. Rebranding is only convincing as an outcome of organizational change, not as a substitute. British Airways has had to reposition itself in relation to a drastically changing competitive environment, but the 1997 rebrand was too much too soon. BA's current strategy is more incremental, using brand extensions, joint ventures and equity investments to extend its business without sacrificing its core identity and values. Through a succession of smaller steps, rather than a single giant leap, BA's heritage of past performance, products, relationships with customers and existing competences is gradually being reconfigured into a new pattern.

The Aesthetics of Organizational Change: Organizational Integrity

In the previous section I explored the parallels between models of organizational change and creativity theory. In this section I will consider organizational change in the light of artistic practice, in particular the expectation that a work of art should have an integrity or unity in its form and content. Can this idea of artistic integrity be applied to organizations and organizational change?

First, artistic integrity describes an internal consistency both in the individual artistic career and in the work of art itself. This does not simply mean that artists are bound to repeat the same pattern. After all, many successful artists from Mozart to David Bowie and Madonna, have been eclectic in crossing boundaries between genres and reinvented themselves at different stages in their career. Such artists still have an integrity because these changes in direction nevertheless appear to be part of a continuing journey and an evolving body of work. Applying this logic to organizations, diversification and change are unlikely to be convincing if undertaken opportunistically. There needs to be an underlying strategic logic. Organizations that attempt to deny their own history will find it difficult to convince their customers and stakeholders. Change can work provided the underlying rationale for change is consistent and clear. When Bob Dylan started to play electric guitar his fans at the time were unhappy, but at the same time the move made sense in terms of Dylan's own musical career, his personality and his subversive intentions. Despite the initial shock, the change was absolutely consistent with Dylan's artistic integrity.

Second, artistic integrity describes not only an internal consistency but an external relationship with the field of art. From an audience's perspective, integrity describes a continuity of values and expectations around a work of art. Bourdieu describes the rules of art resulting from a complex relationship between a work of art and a field of cultural production comprising other art works and institutions. Aesthetic innovation occurs within a field of cultural production where different influences and conventions push and pull the meaning of the work and generate rules, conventions, genres and structures – as well as other art works and institutions. The relationships within this field shape the meaning of each work of art. These relationships can be manipulated or reconfigured in order to generate new forms which might in turn redefine the field. From the perspective of creativity theory, Margaret Boden describes a similar relationship between artistic creativity and the 'generative system' which lies behind it. Innovations both play upon and challenge our expectations. Screenwriters describe this effect as 'jeopardy'. By building towards an expected outcome, then providing something slightly different the writer both satisfies and subverts the audiences' expectations. Narrative jeopardy describes the cat that leaps from the cupboard or the key change in a chorus. As well as surprising our expectations of narrative, jeopardy also plays with expectations of genre. Horror movies exploit the fact that audiences have increasingly sophisticated expectations of genre which writers and directors are able to subvert. Conventional motifs and plots are repeated, but with an unfamiliar twist.

Applying this framework of expectations to the dynamics of organizational change, it is clear that organizations can reinvent themselves through quite subtle realignments of their existing relationships within 'the field' which challenge and subvert the perceptions of customers and stakeholders. Increasingly perceptions of organizations and of brands are influenced by their relationships with other businesses and brands. So when businesses enter new strategic partnerships or associations they may not be radically changing their organization or strategy, but they do challenge customer expectations. Microsoft has forged partnerships with some of its former rivals, including Apple and Linux, revitalizing the company's reputation for innovation and perhaps projecting a less conservative, more enterprising corporate identity. More recently Microsoft has announced a partnership with Nokia to develop mobile music software and hardware, challenging the market dominance of Apple. All of these moves are consistent with Microsoft's history of developing software applications which become indispensable to other manufacturers and to consumers and eventually become the industry standard. Yet the choice of partners allows this approach to be presented as entrepreneurial, independent and alternative – not corporate, monopolistic and mainstream. It is of course ironic that in the mobile music market, the Microsoft-Nokia partnership can even present itself as the underdog to Apple.

These arguments draw upon postmodern and symbolic perspectives on organization, recognizing that organizational change is in large measure a matter of internal and external perceptions as much as 'real' change. By manipulating these perceptions, managers can reframe an organization's values and missions around relatively small 'symbolic' changes. This adds a creative function to management, recognizing the importance of myth and storytelling to organizational culture and acknowledging that organizations can take on an aesthetic quality beyond their functional, structural components. In other words by reconfiguring the interpretative context through which members and stakeholders perceive the organization, it is possible to effect a change in perceptions about the organization with only minimal changes to the organization itself.

For small creative organizations, changes in perception can provide an alternative to real organizational change. Many of the tensions which are both the cause and effect of organizational change result from the way in which change is perceived by members, customers, competitors and collaborators. In the creative and media industries, small independent organizations have become extremely adept at reinventing themselves to suit different audiences and partners. The possibility for organizations to reinvent themselves simply by reconfiguring their relationships with other organizations is most apparent in the online marketplace. For a dot.com business, it is no longer the size of the dot that counts, but the connections which radiate outwards from it. Through an astute choice of partners and inventive branding, it is possible to construct a virtual organization, a portal to an expanding range of project partners. Because of the project-based nature of their work, many small creative businesses take on the quality of hubs within networks or portals to a loose aggregate of partner firms. Many individual entrepreneurs trade under more than one name, and several job titles within each business. A film production company with an address in London's Soho and an impressive letterhead and website may actually be run by two entrepreneurs in southern Europe, using the business to broker their own and others' collective talents.

Given the unpredictability of markets in the creative and media industries, 'virtual' expansion becomes an attractive alternative to real growth. Paradoxically these cosmetic changes allow the business to retain its organizational integrity. For small creative businesses, dependent on a stream of one-off projects rather than an expanding business portfolio, growing the business is unusually risky. Instead of using profits from a successful project to accumulate staff and other assets which might turn into expensive liabilities, creative businesses invest in the quality of their products. If they want to 'grow' the business, a combination of branding and networking allows them to expand virtually, changing people's perceptions of the business without over-stretching the business. This may frustrate business advisers who still measure success in terms of turnover and employment, but for small creative firms this is one possible response to the challenges of organizational change.

The aesthetics of organizational change and the concept of organizational integrity suggest that organizational change can be achieved through what are in effect quite small, real changes. By building upon a shared history and especially by building upon and challenging the perceptions of customers, competitors and internal stakeholders, organizations can reinvent themselves, not through a drastic make-over, but simply by reconfiguring their existing elements and relationships within the field.

Aligning Individual and Collective Change

I have considered artistic integrity as an internal consistency or continuity between past, present and future, and more broadly as an external relationship between elements and expectations within a field. The final definition of artistic integrity which relates to organizational change is the relationship between the parts and the whole. For a work of art, this might be a question of formal coherence. For an organization it is likely to mean the relationship between the organization as a whole and its individual members.

Commenting on the relentless sameness of mass culture in the 1940s, Adorno and Horkheimer argued that 'innovation' in the products of the culture industry had become disconnected from their meaning and value as 'whole' works of art. Specifically, 'the development of the culture industry has led to the predominance of the effect, the obvious touch, and the technical detail over the work itself' (Adorno and Horkheimer 1979: 125). This fetishization of novelty and special effects in film, music and literature proceeded alongside the formulaic, prearranged harmony of the twentieth-century culture industry. Whereas in the previous century there had been a dynamic tension between the 'rebellious' detail and the formal unity of a work of art, now no such tension existed. The rebellious details no longer connected with the whole, their 'insubordination' was crushed and made to 'subserve the formula, which replaced the work'. The 'idea' or meaning of the work had become a formula, a method of ensuring 'order but not coherence' (1979: 125).

Adorno's cultural pessimism, especially his pessimistic view of audiences, has become unfashionable in contemporary cultural studies. It has also been argued that his perspective on the culture industry was distorted by his experiences of Nazi propaganda in Germany, leading him to be unduly suspicious of mass media. While his social and cultural critique remains controversial, Adorno's aesthetic critique is sometimes overlooked, especially his criticisms of film and music (Adorno was himself a practising musician). Adorno's critique of the structure of the culture industry as a system of exploitation and mass deception is nevertheless closely related to his critique of the aesthetics of mass culture. The core of the argument is a distinction between the novelty of 'effects' or details and the significance of the whole. According to Adorno, the novelties of the culture industry have no meaningful connection with the overall meaning and value of the work of art, and actually reinforce its meaninglessness. The culture industry's promise of novelty is likewise never consummated – deviance is tolerated and encouraged precisely because it does not threaten the sameness of the formula. In the business of culture, 'well-planned originality' thus becomes another way of fitting in and 'realistic dissidence is the trademark of anyone who has a new idea in business' (Adorno and Horkheimer 1979: 132). Novelty is fetishized as a surrogate for change – everything appears new, but nothing ever changes.

The problem with novelty, according to Adorno, is that the change it proffers is concerned with details – with parts, not with the whole. Novelty tinkers with insignificant details but the bigger picture remains regimented, predictable and unchanging. The disengagement between parts and whole is a kind of trade-off; random innovation distracts us from the sameness of the formula. The hyping of innovation and novelty is directly proportional to the predictability of the underlying pattern.

What has this got to do with organizational change? First, Adorno's analysis of the fetishization of novelty in our culture helps to explain the tendency for business leaders to embrace 'change for change's sake'. Secondly, Adorno highlights the pointlessness of 'innovation without a purpose'. This is the 'innovation' of the Innovations catalogue – a world where we can find products such as bedroom slippers with headlights or talking alarm clocks, a world of inventiveness where nobody seems to have asked the inventors the question 'why?'. Applied in an organizational context, such an approach results in more of the same, disguised beneath a superficial layer of new initiatives and details which have little or no impact on the organization's underlying strategy and structure. Finally, Adorno highlights the disengagement between the parts and the whole. Piecemeal innovations do not in the end change anything. Similarly individual initiatives and projects which are not informed by and acting upon the overall direction of the business are a distraction from real organizational change, not a part of it.

For organizations, the relationship between parts and the whole can be considered from a strategic perspective in terms of strategic business units or structurally as divisions within a hierarchy. But in the end the principal drivers of change inside the organization are likely to be individuals, not least in the creative and media sector. For organizations to change, there needs to be an alignment between individual members and the overall identity and direction of the business. If the parts become too disconnected from the whole, the organization starts to drift apart; on the other hand if the parts are too tightly integrated and controlled, the dynamic tension of the 'rebellious detail' is lost and the organization starts to stagnate. Too much individual initiative or too little, both eventually lead to a crisis, following the familiar pattern of explosive change, crisis and recovery/consolidation already described in this chapter.

The alternative is to allow individuals to challenge organizational norms without ignoring them entirely – to march just out of step without breaking into a run. If individuals run too far ahead of the rest of the organization, they will become frustrated and eventually break away entirely. If the organizational expansion outpaces individual personal and professional development, the changes will not be sustainable. And if the whole system is perfectly aligned and individuals and organization march forward together, the result is death by consensus. The friction between individual abilities and ambitions and organizational needs and imperatives is what drives the organization forward and forces it to evolve.

Applying the aesthetics of artistic integrity to organizational change, it is clear that there needs to be a continual realignment between the organization and its members. Organizational change is achieved by a succession of slight deviations from the script, accumulating into a gradual change of direction. This incremental model of organizational change fits with the theories of creativity as a gradual extension of the rules of the game, rethinking the box rather than thinking outside it. There is accordingly a tension between individual aspirations and the overall capacity of the organization, a slight but deliberate misalignment between the individual and the collective. Achieving this balance depends upon trust between individuals and organizations, and on that same balance between release and control described in chapter 4.

There is a fine line here between success and failure. An online media company set up by a friend with two colleagues in the mid 1990s appeared at first to contain the perfect balance between creative tension and collective impetus. The three individuals were very different. The first was the managing director and had conceived the business at precisely the right time to catch the mix of fascination and mystery surrounding digital media. He astutely recognized the opportunities for providing creative solutions to corporate clients, designing websites and corporate products, using emerging technologies and skills. He recruited two colleagues, one a writer and the other a designer. His two colleagues were more interested in the creative possibilities of new media, in designing games and developing interactivity. The business aimed to make its money from corporate clients and use the profits to fund more experimental, creative, interactive projects. Of course, this 'edgy' creative profile would also attract the corporate clients, who felt a frisson of expectation as they visited the company's crumbling offices in a run-down part of town.

The business expanded rapidly, and soon the three friends found themselves with 50 employees on the payroll and a multimillion pound turnover. The company's main business, designing corporate websites, was booming. The creative work had also been successful, winning industry awards despite failing to generate any profits. Of the original triumvirate, the writer and designer felt marginalized, taking on personnel management responsibilities which did not interest them, and feeling that their own creative work was increasingly resented by their colleagues as self-indulgent and irrelevant. At the point when the company appeared to be at its most successful, the original partnership split up. The writer and designer left to set up their own creative company, which after a shaky start established itself as a pioneering interactive media business, developing a succession of award-winning products and attracting funding from Internet service providers, broadcasters and educational companies. The managing director successfully built up the original business, eventually securing an equity buy-out by a major advertising company which made him a millionaire.

There were several reasons for the partnership to break up. First, the business expanded too rapidly for the individuals to adjust their own individual roles to the new organizational reality. The writer and designer in particular found themselves marginalized as a result. Secondly, there was a power imbalance from the outset, with the managing director owning the majority of the equity in the business; what appeared to be a triumvirate was in reality an unequal partnership. This became a crucial factor as the three debated the company's future direction and questions of trust and ownership were highlighted. Thirdly, there was perhaps a lack of candour from the outset about the contradictions within the business and the conflicting aims of the founders; splitting the business between 'creative' and 'commercial' directions (despite the possible synergies and trade-offs) was perhaps inevitably going to stretch the business to breaking point. Certainly, the 'alignment' between organizational and individual development was too far out of joint for the business to be sustainable.

The other twist in the tale is that the break up of the original partnership resulted in success, not failure, for all concerned. In the creative and media industries, this kind of split is not unusual. Organizations are loose affiliations of individual talents which eventually pull apart. The organization may not survive, but the individual talents do. These talents might perhaps be absorbed into the gene pool for new organizations, as in this case. But, with a little less luck and ability, it would be equally possible for the protagonists to watch their talents and ideas wither away in bitterness and regret. As a metaphor for organizational change, this is not encouraging; organizations disintegrate, at best composted down to provide talent and ideas for successors and former competitors, at worst left to languish on the stony ground of isolation and indifference. It is possible to imagine an alternative future for this business in which the original partnership could have survived in some form, but this would have required a much greater degree of trust at the individual level and a more deliberate and planned approach to organizational change.

Evolutionary Change

Organizational change depends upon a relationship between individual and collective development, and on the integration of individual initiatives and experiments into an ongoing dynamic pattern. As in the discussion of creative strategy in the previous chapter, managing change requires an ability to recognize and respond to emerging patterns. The possibility of change thus depends not just on a willingness to take risks and experiment, but on the capacity of the organization to absorb and act upon individual initiatives and projects. Just as innovation depends on the capacity to respond to ideas as much as the capacity to generate them (c.f. chapter 2), so for organizations the capacity to perceive change, or to see the organization in a new light is as important as diversifying or expanding the business.

The capacity to absorb and build upon innovative ideas will require an ability to make connections between the new and the old. The model of organizational change being proposed in this chapter is essentially evolutionary. Ideas mutate and some of the mutations thrive as a result of changing conditions – these mutations are absorbed into the future strategy and structure of the organization. As with the discussion of strategy formation in the previous chapter, new ideas emerge out of slight deviations from the existing knowledge base, and an accumulation of apparently minor changes adds up to a much more complete transformation than a clean break with the past.

For this to happen, organizations need to allow sufficient autonomy and independence for individuals to challenge existing strategies and structures. At the same time, they need to be able to absorb new proposals and shape these into collective decisions about allocating resources and redirecting strategy. In Darwinian evolution, when new mutations occur, they are absorbed by the species as a result of similarities as well as differences. Changes occur within the same generative system and the differences from one generation to the next are relatively small, even apparently insignificant. Common characteristics are encoded in the DNA of organisms and organizations – without these similarities, successful mutations could not be reabsorbed back into the gene pool and eventually become part of the genetic code of the species. So although the mutations themselves may be random, the evolution of the species is integrated and organized. This combination of continual experiment alongside a capacity to absorb and integrate change shows how individual development and organizational change can evolve together.

When individual and collective development fall out of alignment, organizational change is likely to lead back into the revolution-crisis model described earlier in this chapter. Hierarchical organizations which allow little scope for individual autonomy are essentially centripetal and entropic, turning in on themselves and refusing to change course until it is too late. On the other hand, individuals who feel they are not being listened to and whose proposals for new developments are repeatedly blocked may become frustrated or branch out on their own. This leads to the opposite of over-centralization and entropy, a centrifugal model of organizational change and an individualistic culture with individuals pursuing personal goals at the expense of the organization as a whole. Small innovative organizations, while apparently 'creative' in terms of their personnel and products, are not always very adaptable. They may have an excess of ideas and initiatives, but lack the capacity to absorb these ideas into a coherent direction or to put ideas into action. We tend to think of hierarchies and bureaucracies as being resistant to change, but actually a loose affiliation of individuals can prove equally brittle. Organizations in the creative and media industries often fail to adapt to new situations, not because they have no idea how to respond to new situations, but because they have too many ideas and no consensus can be reached.

Managing the process of change requires that managers identify 'centrifugal' and 'centripetal' tendencies in their organization and attempt to address them. For organizations with strong collective cultures and a tendency towards consensus, management interventions will involve disrupting routine procedures and spinning out new initiatives and new trajectories from the overall strategic direction of the business. For smaller, more innovative organizations, interventions will aim not to disrupt and diversify but to improve communication and to consolidate individual projects and pursuits within a coherent plan.

Evolutionary organizational change requires first a capacity for experiment and deviation, but equally importantly a capacity to reabsorb experiments back into the system. Organizational change is achieved through an endless cycle of minor deviations and experiments, continually stretching the genetic make-up of the species and continually being absorbed and reincorporated into the system. Of course this is much easier to achieve if change and development are proactive and continual, as an accepted part of organizational routines and procedures, rather than reactive, erupting in a panicked response to a crisis.

The management style required to achieve incremental, ongoing change is a mix of release and control. Release means first accepting that other people will change and challenge current policies and systems, even if for now these appear to be working satisfactorily, and secondly delegating the resources and responsibilities which will allow them to develop alternatives. Control means monitoring and modifying the alliances and relationships between different teams, individuals and divisions in the organization, and reinjecting diversity or reconnecting peripheral groups back into the system. Rather than directing change, managers provide a climate within which change can occur.

Once this balance is established, the second stage is to delegate power and resources to those who are championing new ideas and new directions. Not all of these will succeed, but diversifying the business leaves it less vulnerable to external change and better equipped to generate change internally. The key lesson emerging from the 'crisis-resolution' model of organizational change described in the literature on organizational growth is that change needs to be pre-emptive, working from a position of strength, not responding to failure as a last resort. In the brutal language of Hollywood script development, this is called 'killing your babies' – accepting that in order to release new ideas it is sometimes necessary to kill pet projects, surrendering the ideas in which we have invested our energy and commitment (and to which we have perhaps become overly attached).

If 'killing babies' and devolving power represent the point of release, this is succeeded by a moment of recollection and regrouping. Managers need to be alert to the patterns and directions which emerge from innovative processes and reconnect these back into the organization, building new constituencies around them and supporting them with new resources and people. Recognizing the value of innovation is as important as initiating it.

This three-part process – balance, releasing, recollecting – follows a similar pattern to the alternations of preparation, incubation, illumination and verification in creativity theory and requires a similarly complex mix of thinking styles and capabilities. Managers, like artists, need to be able to switch roles and inhabit apparently opposing perspectives in order to take an innovative idea to fruition. This is very different from the stereotype of the visionary inventor or entrepreneur referred to earlier in this chapter. Entrepreneurs have great ideas but they are not so good at letting go of them. Visionaries are not best placed to recognize the vision of others. Managing creativity, or managing creatively, is a complex, multifunctional task and is carried out under the surface of an apparently spontaneous, continual process of incremental change. The process of change is managed in small steps, successively releasing and regathering other people's ideas, not in spectacular interventions and initiatives.

Creativity and Change

In the preceding chapters I have argued for a systematic approach to creativity in business, based on incremental change rather than flashes of insight and genius. Culturally, especially in Western cultures, we tend to equate creativity with novelty and with individual genius. But if these moments of novelty and individualism are not reabsorbed into an evolving system, they are unlikely to be productive.

Innovation has been fetishized as the source of competitive advantage and the catalyst for organizational change and growth. In fact, innovation only becomes valuable alongside continuity, coherence and integrity – and Porter's arguments about sustainable competitive advantage remain as relevant as they ever have been. In the end what matters is maintaining a balance between change and continuity, between diversity and coherence, between novelty and purpose. And when it comes to organizational change and organizational growth, a pattern of ongoing miniature experiments is going to be more useful than searching for a fresh start. Innovation, like creativity, requires more than a moment of inspiration. The detailed working out and presentation of an idea are at least as important as its originality or novelty.

The fetishization of novelty – the cult of the new – is part of the fetishization of genius. As Adorno and Horkheimer indicate, this approach to innovation, the idolization of the maverick individualist and the delight in novelty for its own sake, do not in fact change anything. New ideas crackle like fireworks, but they provide only a temporary spectacle, distracting us from the underlying monotony. The real work of innovation and change is more laborious and less spectacular, based on gradual, almost imperceptible shifts in perception and on the reconfiguring of the existing elements into new patterns. Such an approach is less eye-catching, and harder to pin down. But in the end it is much more likely to result in a 'radical transformation' of the system. It also requires intervention from management, providing points of continuity between present and future, and seeking a balance between diversity and coherence.

Some of the metaphors applied to creativity in business draw upon the language of art and music, but fail to grasp the real complexity of artistic creation. The creativity of jazz or Picasso is not spontaneous and 'free'. Artistic innovation follows its own internally generated rules and is the result of a deliberate, self-conscious, process which encompasses different thinking styles, different points of contact with others, different aspects of the self. Above all the creative process is complex, multidimensional and this process is 'managed' by the artist (occasionally with some outside help). Organizational change can follow an analogous process of adaptation, complexity and incremental change. Or it can pursue novelty and innovation. But if managers choose the latter route, they are not engaging in a creative process, and they are not in the end going to achieve the 'radical transformation' they claim to aspire to.

FURTHER READING

The discussion of innovation in this chapter as an incremental, evolutionary process derives from the theories of Robert Weisberg and Margaret Boden. Weisberg (1993) deconstructs the apparently spontaneous, explosive nature of artistic inspiration and scientific discovery, demonstrating that many of these new ideas have unacknowledged sources in preceding works and in the innovator's internal resources of experience, knowledge, memory, logic and domain-specific expertise. He also emphasizes the deliberate, rational nature of innovation over intuitive and subconscious mental processes; creativity is described in terms of 'convergent' rather than 'divergent' thinking. Weisberg describes his model as 'incremental creativity', with new ideas developing cumulatively, driven by deliberate intellectual effort and consciously directed. The 'incubation' and 'illumination' phases in creative thinking are not, according to Weisberg, evidence of dreamy inspiration or undirected, spontaneous thought processes. Rather they are the result of an accumulation of experience, memory and knowledge within the individual's domain of expertise, and during the period of incubation, creative thinkers dip into this resource to solve their problem.

Margaret Boden's definition of creativity places similar emphasis on incremental change. As noted in chapter 4, Boden locates creative thinking within a 'bounded conceptual space'. By challenging the rules which govern this framework from within, creative thinking achieves a 'transformation of the generative system'. This transformation challenges our existing assumptions and values and forces us to reconfigure the way we see the world. The eventual outcome may be a radical innovation, but the methodology is less spectacular than 'thinking outside the box', requiring us to attack the problem from within, according to its own set of values and assumptions. As with Adorno's comments on aesthetic innovation, there is a strong implicit connection in Boden's model between the parts and the whole; it is by attending to the details within an interconnected system of assumptions and values that we will eventually transform the total system (Boden 1992: 75–9).

The chapter argues that organizational change tends to be associated with crisis management, especially in the classic models based on 'stages' in development – see Greiner (1972) and Churchill and Lewis (1983). The crisis-adaptation model is to some extent self-fulfilling. As Danny Miller (1993) notes, organizations have a tendency to pursue 'simplicity', homing in on their core competences and perceived competitive advantages. According to Miller this traps them in an increasingly narrow perception of themselves and makes it difficult for them to adapt. It also encourages them to strip out or 'simplify' some of the complexity and internal resistance which might have held their more extreme and self-destructive tendencies in check. This inevitably pushes them into more extreme positions and combined with the growing rigidity of their processes and self-perceptions, makes a crisis inevitable.

The crisis model of organizational change resembles a sigmoid curve, with a succession of dips and peaks in performance as the organization lurches from one stage in development to another. Identifying this pattern in *The Empty Raincoat* (1994), Charles Handy argues that we find it difficult to recognize the need for change until it is too late – we seek change after the downturn instead of just before it. Asking for directions to 'Davey's Bar' during a trip to Ireland, Handy is told that if he sees a turning to the left, it means he will have gone too far – he should have taken the turning before. Applying this story to organizational change,

Handy argues that even though we know that the time to change is before the crisis and not when the crisis is upon us, we only recognize the turning after we have passed it.

Building on this paradox, Nigel Sykes has created an elegant 'organic' model for organizational change in smaller businesses, based upon a series of incremental additions to the organization's membership which diversify individual and organizational strengths. Like Handy, Sykes recognizes the need to pre-empt a crisis by investing in change from a position of strength. His model, based on Edith Penrose's analogy, compares the evolution of the firm to the life cycle from egg to butterfly and presents an incremental and person-centred approach to organizational change (Sykes 2003).

The references to Bourdieu come from 'The Field of Cultural Production' in *The Field of Cultural Production* (1993: 29–74). This is an English compilation of Bourdieu's writings – for a more comprehensive discussion, see Bourdieu's *The Rules of Art* (1996).

The symbolic aspects of organizational structures are referred to in the article by Meyer and Rowan (1977). Other postmodern perspectives on the symbolic and aesthetic aspects of organization are included in the collection edited by Reed and Hughes (1992).

For an application of evolutionary theory to the life cycle of ideas and institutions, see Richard Dawkins' discussion of 'memes' in 'Memes: The new replicators' (1989). There are several applications of Darwinian theory to creativity, for example, Perkins (1994). Some of Dawkins' ideas about memes recur in Gladwell (2000).

For an introduction to Adorno's theories, I recommend J.M. Bernstein's introduction to his edited collection of Adorno's writings (Adorno 1991).

NOTES

1   'Superficially at least, the corporate strategy could be drawn up by an unintelligent computer. As many of us know, that is unlikely to produce competitive advantages, since what one computer can do another can do with equal ease' – John Harvey Jones, writing in the introduction to the revised 1987 edition of *Corporate Strategy* by H. Igor Ansoff.
2   This case study has been adapted from a case originally prepared for Cummings and Wilson (2003). Participants in the web chat were: Chris Bilton, Gonzalo Enriquez-Soltero, Ruth Leary, Joy Li, Elli Reynai and Jennifer Heim.

7 FROM CREATIVE MARKETING TO CREATIVE CONSUMPTION

By the time you have my address, my marital status, my age, my income, my car brand, my purchases, my drinking habits, and my taxes, you have me – a demographic unit of one.

(Negroponte 1995: 184)

Symbolic Goods

The distinguishing feature of the creative industries is that they deal in 'symbolic goods'. Symbolic goods describe products, such as films or music, whose value is contained not in physical properties or even in intangible qualities but in symbolic meanings – ideas, images, emotions and experiences. The value of products and services in the creative industries is thus determined wholly or primarily by the interpretation of symbolic meanings by individual consumers. This of course makes the value of symbolic goods highly unpredictable and subjective. It also places an emphasis on cultural consumption as the site where meaning and hence value is created – or recreated.

The idea that consumption is a creative act has influenced approaches to marketing, production and investment in the creative industries. But the implications of creative consumption extend into other industries as well. As the symbolic aspects of branding, packaging and marketing become progressively more important, it becomes increasingly difficult to separate out the material, functional aspects of products and services from their symbolic content. When we buy a car or a pair of trainers, we are doing so in part because of the product's symbolic associations. The weighting we give to this symbolic content will vary for different products and different consumers, but is almost never entirely absent. Consequently creative consumption plays some part in the way almost all products are experienced and valued.

At best we can argue that the products of the creative industries are 'more symbolic' than the products of manufacturing industry. A film, for example, contains a residual material component, but its value is almost entirely contained in the symbolic meanings we extract from sound, colour, emotion and narrative. A pair of Nike trainers on the other hand may be sold on the strength of brand value and associations with youth, street culture and sports stars – but they still have to function as footwear, and in the end if the boot doesn't fit, we won't wear it.

The growing emphasis on symbolic meaning over material function is a reflection of a society whose basic needs have been met. In rich countries, where food, shelter and security are increasingly taken for granted, citizens become more concerned with satisfying what Maslow called 'higher needs', in particular the need for 'self-actualization'. Consumption, especially cultural consumption, thus becomes a method for shaping our sense of identity, rather than a means of obtaining the basic goods we need to survive. Again it is possible to make a distinction here between types of product and types of consumer. In poorer countries, 'basic needs' such as food, shelter and safety are not so easily taken for granted. Aspirational branding messages about Coca Cola or Nike trainers are less likely to convince somebody who is thirsty or shoeless. But even here, advertising attempts to play with the consumer's sense of identity – the global success of Coca Cola may partly reflect a monopolistic grip on distribution, but it also demonstrates the triumph of symbolic aspirations over material poverty.

In this chapter I will focus on the 'creativity of consumption' and its implications for management. Inevitably some of the arguments will apply more strongly to the 'creative' industries than to other forms of industry, and to the markets of the developed world rather than the developing world. But the implications for the value chain, for marketing and for production can be interpreted more broadly. Before considering these managerial implications, I will outline two theoretical arguments for creative consumption, the first from the point of view of 'postmodern marketing', the second from the perspective of cultural studies, 'sub-culture theory' and 'audience theory'.

Postmodern Marketing

Marketing has been described as the quintessentially postmodern management discipline. As marketers have started to question the scientific certainties and predictions of modern marketing, marketing theorists have begun to explore other ways of explaining the value of products, in terms of perceptions, aspirations and shifting identities. This may be a case of theory belatedly catching up with practice – marketing practitioners have always demonstrated a healthy scepticism regarding the tools of their trade and many consider their work an art, not a science. Postmodern theory gives a theoretical basis for some of these sceptical, non-scientific practices, and suggests a new way of thinking about products, customers, needs and benefits.

Postmodern marketing can be seen first as a response to postmodern theories of identity. Our sense of self is no longer bound up in stable attachments to place, ethnicity, gender, class and work. Demographics (postcodes, social classifications by occupation) are thus unreliable bases for market segmentation. Nor does previous purchasing behaviour offer a reliable guide to future intentions, especially in the case of cultural consumption. Here consumers are attracted to unprecedented experiences, or at least seek an element of surprise or novelty within an otherwise familiar product. Even psychographic approaches to market segmentation (based on emotional or psychological factors) underestimate the complexity of consumer self-image. No sooner has a tendency been identified than consumers reject the label and seek a new way of differentiating themselves. Underlying all these theories is the postmodern idea of 'reflexivity' – a self-conscious awareness among consumers of how they are being 'read' by the marketer prompting a deliberately subversive or playful attempt to rewrite the script. None of us likes to admit to our own predictability.

As the stable bases of identity collapse under the weight of these subversions and reflections, postmodern theories of identity steer us towards more complex, hybridized concepts of the self, 'hyphenate' identities, postcolonial identities, sub-selves, communities of choice replacing communities of attachment. At the same time personal identity becomes more customized and individualized and more 'subjective'.

Postmodern marketing responds to this complexity in one of two ways. One solution is to give up on any predictable pattern of collective identity and focus on the individual. Through increasingly sophisticated data collection, it is possible to map individual preferences and address the customer as a 'market of one'. This leads into an emphasis on relationship marketing or CRM (Customer Relationship Management), using technology to mine personal data and build a predictive portrait of the individual customer. The individual's personal data thus becomes the ultimate commodity. But even here assumptions are being made about the stability and continuity of individual identity. At its crudest, predictive personal profiling leads to an assumption that if a customer likes one thing, she or he will probably like another similar product just as well. This is the blunt logic behind 'My Amazon', which uses previous purchases to make future recommendations, to the irritation of some customers.[1] The appearance of a personal relationship with the customer is often no more than that – despite the sophistication of technologies and the possibility of individualized, 'addressable' advertising, marketers still seek the economies of scale and scope of traditional market segmentation, clustering individuals according to shared characteristics or preferences. Real customization requires a more flexible and responsive approach to the individual – a theme to which I will return in this chapter.

The other 'postmodern' response to complex, hybridized identity is based on what Bernard Cova calls the 'retribalization' of identity (Cova 1996). Individuals reject familiar patterns of identity, only to regroup into new 'tribes' based around shared rituals and icons created through consumption. Instead of the atomization of the market of one, 'retribalization' describes new forms of collective identity, often based around shared cultural consumption. These identity tribes might be ephemeral and transient, but for the alert postmodern marketer they offer an alternative target in place of the fixed categories of traditional market segments. This attempt to play catch-up with shifting trends is manifest in the practice of 'cool hunting', with marketers attempting to track sub-cultural style and sell it back to the customer. It also leads to 'affinity branding' with one product attempting to ride on the coat tails of another brand's collective associations. Markets are no longer segmented along predictable lines. Instead they become 'self-segmenting' with new patterns forming around specific products.

Alongside the questioning of consumer identities, postmodern marketing's second contribution to marketing theory is to question the nature of customer benefits. One of the core assumptions of modern strategic marketing is that customers are not interested in products, they are interested in benefits. Marketing students are thus taught to quantify the benefits of a product, to sell 'holes not drill bits', the sizzle not the steak, to see not what the product is but what it can do for the customer. At the theoretical level this is supported by the distinction between 'product' and 'product surround', and with reference to 'levels of the product' and Maslow's hierarchy of needs. All of these models emphasize that marketing is concerned with the meaning and value of the product, not the thing itself.

Postmodern marketing takes this logic a step further. If the product is less important than what the customer chooses to do with it, our attention shifts away from the product to the customer, in particular to the 'customer experience'. The customer experience is a subjective projection of the objective benefits identified by the marketer. Crucially, the subjective experience of the product may be entirely unpredictable from the marketer's point of view. Here, postmodern theory picks up on literary and textual theory to argue that meanings are created at the point of consumption, not at the point of production. Tragedies become comedies and vice versa. In marketing terms, brands are appropriated by customers and made their own, absorbed into sub-cultures, subverted, retribalized. When the iconic 1950s American singer Tony Bennett played at the Glastonbury Festival in 1998, the enjoyment came not so much from the music or even Bennett's old-fashioned showmanship, but from the anomaly of seeing an old school entertainer in a white suit amid the mud and grunge of a rock festival. The crowd celebrated their adoption and ownership of a 'brand' more familiar to their grandparents.

Postmodern theory projects us into a new 'economy of signs', where meanings are disconnected from objective realities, and where nothing is what it appears to be. Reality is filtered through 'language games' and there is no objective truth, only subjective versions of truth contested by those with money and power. In this postmodern hall of mirrors, marketing ceases to be a science designed to uncover truths about products and consumers and becomes an art, telling stories and creating new meanings. Advertising, according to this logic, is no longer designed to sell products or to communicate key messages about the brand – it *is* the product. The trailer has replaced the film. The aim of marketing and advertising in a postmodern world is to construct a symbolic web of associations around the product, allowing consumers to create their own meaningful experiences. Consumers thus become active participants, not passive recipients, making their own sense out of the building blocks of narrative laid out by the marketer. Contemporary advertising has become increasingly detached from the product, emphasizing story-telling and image-building as an end in itself. A recent cinema trailer for a non-existent road movie, featuring Benicio Del Toro driving through a desert landscape, was actually an advertisement for Mercedes but contained no branding or sales information. Nike and Adidas produced their own 'non-branded' advertising during the 2004 Olympics, in which short films presented images and stories with no mention of what was being sold. Customer involvement has become the primary objective; the sale is a by-product of this relationship and transactions become less important than customer experiences and customer attention as the basis of the new economy.

Postmodern marketing is controversial among management theorists, not least because it appears to delight in its own iconoclasm while recycling questions and complexities with which most marketers are already familiar. It might be no more than the latest fashion in academic theorizing, part of a more general takeover bid by postmodern theory seeking to colonize other academic disciplines. Marketers have always recognized the need to improvise beyond textbook models – in this sense marketing has perhaps been modernist in theory but postmodern in practice. It may be that postmodern marketing simply takes certain tendencies already present in modern marketing to their logical conclusion, much as postmodernism itself is sometimes described as 'late modernism'. These postmodern tendencies are also likely to be more convincing in relation to certain types of consumer and certain types of product, operating in saturated, mature markets where there are limited opportunities for differentiation. Far from signalling the death of market segmentation, postmodern marketing may itself be subject to a segmentation of marketing theories and an adaptation of marketing practice to particular market segments (see the 'Arts Marketing' case study).

Case Study: Arts Marketing – From Products to Experiences

The recent history of arts marketing in the subsidized arts sector exemplifies the changing approaches to marketing outlined in this chapter. At first, 'the arts' were seen to be exempt from the market, defined as public goods in the public domain, not private commodities, and treated as 'exceptional' to the rules of the market. One of the recurring aims of post-1945 European cultural policy has been to protect the arts from market failure.

The introduction of mainstream marketing techniques into the arts during the 1980s and 1990s was thus politically contentious. The political argument over the value of culture as a public good was reproduced in a managerial argument between product-led and customer-led approaches to marketing. Many arts marketing texts emphasize the integrity of the product and resist attempts to make art and artists subject to consumer demand. Despite the changes in cultural policy through the 1980s and 1990s, many of those working in the arts retained an idealist faith in the transcendent power of art and the absolute integrity of artistic products and individual artists. At the same time, reductions in subsidy through the 1990s forced arts organizations to behave like commercial businesses and to adopt the classic marketing tools.

The emergent solution to this controversy in arts marketing was a compromise, in which marketing techniques focused on reconfiguring the product surround while leaving the product itself intact. Arts marketing thus focused on the total package of the customer experience, the comfort of the seats, the car parking and transport, pricing policies, the friendly smile on the face of the box office staff, while attempting to protect the integrity of the artistic director's vision and the individual freedom of artistic expression. If audiences did not initially accept the product, they needed to be educated into accepting it. Arts marketing became entangled with arts education in the new practice of 'audience development'. Meanwhile marketing's traditional 'four Ps' of product, place, price and promotion became arts marketing's 'three Ps'; while managers developed increasingly ingenious solutions to price, place and promotion, the product was sacrosanct. When UK museums and galleries attempted to reach out to excluded audiences in the late 1990s, the argument centred on the need to cut admission fees, not on the value and relevance of the collections themselves. However ingeniously they tweaked the product surround, arts marketers were excluded from tampering with the product.

As an approach to marketing the arts, this was not very satisfactory. The rows between the idealists and the modernizers rumbled on. One consequence of the internal debate within arts organizations was to perpetuate the 'great divide' between creatives and suits, with artists shielded from their audiences and arts marketers kept at arm's length from the creative process. The divide was both spatial, with separate departments and offices, and temporal, with the creative process happening first and the marketing process coming in afterwards, closer to the point of sale.

Yet art is a collective experience. Most performers and writers want to engage with an audience and incorporate some understanding of the experience of viewers, readers and listeners back into their own creative process. Most marketers are prepared to contribute ideas and information throughout the process, not just to layer in crass promotional gimmicks after the fact. Above all, the great divide excludes the audience, whose needs and wants are conceived almost entirely in terms of the peripheral benefits rather than in relation to the core aesthetic experience.

More recently, arts marketers have begun to research this aesthetic experience more carefully. Some of this research suggests that audiences want to be challenged by their experience of art. They are not seeking reassurance, nor do they simply want to reproduce and reassert their own tastes. They value an experience which makes them think, where they are not sure what something means or what will happen next. These findings fly in the face of a conventional 'customer-led' approach to marketing and challenge the sociological analysis of artistic taste pioneered by Pierre Bourdieu. If artists are attempting to redefine themselves and to challenge their own thinking by their experience of art, they are not going to fit comfortably into predefined socio-demographic categories and behave according to the expectations of marketers and sociologists.

One of the leading figures in this new approach to audience research and arts marketing, Miranda Boorsma, argues that arts marketing needs to take into account the aesthetic experience of the audience. If audiences do indeed value art that is difficult, that makes them think, then artists and arts marketers need to find ways of involving them in the creative process. This means leaving gaps, allowing audiences to fill in the blanks, to complete the story in their own heads. It also means that 'arts marketing', meaning the way in which a work is presented to an audience, becomes an integral part of the creative process, not a reluctant afterthought or a Philistine enemy within. Audiences are co-creators of meaning and the pleasure of the audience comes from actively recreating the artistic process, not simply reproducing the artistic product – from opening up new questions, not decoding pre-digested answers. This move towards

Table 7.1   A short history of arts marketing: three models

	Product led	Customer led	Experience led
When?	Pre-1980	1980s, 1990s	The future?
Product	Art for everyone	Customer benefits	Aesthetic experiences
Customer	Everybody	Specific groups	Individuals
Market segments and tools	Attenders and non-attenders; overcoming barriers, arts education	Demographic approach: stable market segments; strategic marketing	Psychographic approach; unstable segments; customisation, co-creation
Marketing activity	Promotion and sales	Strategy and segmentation	Personal relationships
Marketing objective	Bring the maximum number of people into contact with the work of art	Identify specific needs and wants and provide products to meet those needs	Facilitate creative consumption by providing 'symbolic resources'
Centre of power	The artist	The marketer	The customer
Theory	19th century Romanticism, cultural idealism Arnold/Schiller Liberalism Access	Modernity Sociology of culture Gans/Bourdieu Rationalism Control	Postmodernity Aesthetics, media theory, psychology John Dewey Experiential goods Participation

'bringing the audience back in' as co-creators, towards a genuine interaction between artistic creativity and creative consumption, may represent an alternative future for arts marketing. Boorsma argues that arts marketing should 'support the co-creation of artistic experiences', both in the way the work is presented and in the seeking out of new and unfamiliar audiences. It is perhaps ironic that arts marketing, having initially remained trapped in a wilfully old-fashioned 'product-led' approach to marketing, is here perhaps moving towards a model of 'postmodern marketing' (see table 7.1).

These trends in arts marketing are part of a broader shift towards 'experiential marketing', defined by Rifkin (2000) as the staging of 'branded customer experiences'. As described in this chapter, marketing and branding have become increasingly centred on the aesthetic experience of the customer, not just the selling of products. The history of arts marketing shows a shift, from marketing grudgingly accepted as a necessary evil in the production of art and culture, to a growing recognition that art and aesthetics are integral to the practice of marketing. The tensions and mutual suspicions between 'arts' and 'marketing' are perhaps finally beginning to ease.

Despite these caveats, what is undeniable in postmodern marketing is a shift towards the primacy of subjectivity and the unpredictability of the customer experience. Customers are no longer malleable consumers who can be manipulated into recognizing core benefits. They are, increasingly, calling the shots as active co-creators of meaning and value. This echoes the sophistication of audiences and consumers of cultural products according to contemporary theories of cultural consumption.

From Segments to Sub-cultures: Bringing the Audience Back in

'Audience theory' and 'sub-culture' theory emerged in the late 1970s and 1980s to describe a more complex model of cultural consumption than the old model of corporate domination and control. The so-called 'hypodermic' model of media effects, in which the audiences passively absorb whatever the producer chooses to inject them with, was replaced by a new interest in the 'symbolic work' of audiences in decoding media messages, and in the extent to which this decoding was in turn embedded in localized structures of feeling. Academic cultural and media studies became more concerned with modes of consumption than models of production. In the process a Marxist emphasis on the structures of power in the creative and media industries was gradually replaced by a relativist, sociological interest in audiences and audience response. This can be seen in part as a backlash against increasingly simplistic, abstract models of media dominance towards a more audience-centred approach. It also allowed for a more optimistic reading of audience behaviour, through which audiences were 'empowered' or 'resistant' against media manipulations. Audiences no longer 'absorbed', they reflected and interpreted, becoming active co-creators in the production of meaning.

Some of the 'subversive' re-readings of popular culture picked out by sub-culture theorists and media academics in the 1980s betrayed an underlying cynicism – ironic celebrations of the kitsch and the camp rather than a critical, sceptical rejection of dominant norms and values. As the media and entertainment industries caught up with the game, the sub-cultural subversions were themselves reappropriated, repackaged and sold back to the customer. Rebellion has always been a marketable commodity in the entertainment industry. Sub-cultures, from punks to skaters and riot girls, found themselves tidied up and pasted into advertisements and music videos. Street fashion, conceived as a rebellion against the fashion industry, was reflected back from the catwalk and the shop windows of the high street. The attempt to escape from the cycle of commodification only served to accelerate the cycle, with edgy trends and Next Big Things hurriedly dragged from the fringe to the mainstream before the paint had dried on their alternative credentials. Sub-cultural studies and audience theory thus played into the hands of the cool-hunters and the talent scouts, who made a quick killing before spitting out the dregs. Cultural commentators doubled up as brand consultants. The new market populism was fuelled by dreams of rebellion.

In the 1990s the academic celebration of 'empowered' audiences and creative consumption received a new technological impetus. The development of new interactive technologies again seemed to place the individual consumer centre-stage. Academic commentators like Nicholas Negroponte at MIT and new media publications like *Wired* magazine, celebrated the potential of the Internet to place the consumer at the centre of the new information infrastructure, pulling in ideas and products to fuel their own creativity instead of accepting the information 'push' from the mass media. With the availability of cheap and free content reaching saturation point and with the Internet's non-hierarchical structure making it apparently ungovernable, the gatekeepers who controlled the media and entertainment industries were no longer in control. The old mass market was fragmenting into a postmodern playground where meaning and value were a matter of individual taste.

Whereas in the 1980s consumer creativity had been virtual – a reworking of the raw material thrown up by the culture industry – in the 1990s affordable and sophisticated technology appeared to allow consumers to literally create their own music, films and radio programmes. Peer-to-peer distribution and the new era of media abundance allowed them to distribute their work and to bypass the old restrictive channels. The availability of content encouraged them to create, customize and manipulate the raw material offered by the copyright industries, whether legally or illegally. Not only were they replaying and reinventing the products of the cultural industries, they were making new products of their own, from quirky podcasts to grainy news footage shot on their video phones. Consumers had, it seemed, become the new producers.

The reality is of course more complex. Consumer creativity still depends upon the tools and resources which the media and entertainment industries choose to make available. The fragmentation of markets into sub-cultures and communities has proceeded even more rapidly in the opposite direction, with DIY culture absorbed back into the aesthetics and branding of mainstream cultural products. The structural consolidation and concentration of the media and entertainment industries around a handful of cross-media conglomerates has continued apace, untroubled by the peripheral subversiveness of active audiences and new technologies. Consumer creativity has been actively promoted by brands like Sony, Microsoft, 3G and Apple, who are the chief beneficiaries of our new desire to burn CDs, edit photographs, compose music and make 'professional' home movies.

Viewed from the perspective of cultural studies, the question of creative consumption is politically controversial. The extent to which the new economy genuinely empowers consumers or simply engages them in a more subtle form of manipulation and exploitation is linked to the extent and nature of the customer's 'creativity'. What is clear from the theoretical literature is a growing emphasis on consumption as a creative act, and a view of consumers as active collaborators in the creation of meaning and value. What is also apparent is that this consumer creativity is tolerated and encouraged by a media and entertainment industry which has grown adept at absorbing this creativity and selling it back to the consumer. This book does not set out to review the politics of cultural populism. My main concern is to consider the mythology of consumer creativity in relation to creativity theory and management practice.

The New Value Chain

As companies begin to outsource production and marketing, and as new channels of communication between producers and consumers open up, value chains in all areas of business have been reconfigured. The initial move towards disintermediation appeared to allow producers to address consumers directly, without submitting to traditional channels of marketing and communication. This was followed by a recognition of the need to organize and channel the glut of information and choice flowing from producers to consumers through a new generation of intermediaries. Old intermediaries (retailers, distributors) were thus replaced by new infomediaries (websites, search engines, aggregators of both content and information about content). Much of the discussion of reconfiguring value chains has focused on the inter-firm rivalries between producers and intermediaries of one kind or another.

At the same time, the new value chain identifies the end user as the crucial link where value and meaning are ultimately created. To some extent, this recognition of consumer creativity is nothing new, especially in the context of culture and art. Aesthetic theories have always emphasized the experience of receiving or viewing art and culture as dynamic. We do not simply absorb, we also reflect and reinterpret, even if we do so from starting points and within limits which are not of our own choosing. John Dewey in the 1930s argued that the experience of art was essentially creative, with the aesthetic process of looking at a painting requiring the same combination of analysis, imagination and reflection as the artistic process of painting it.

What is different in today's creative and media industries is the extent to which Dewey's aesthetic process has been incorporated into the product and turned into a marketable commodity. Reality television shows like *Big Brother* provide a structure for consumers to intervene in the programme both on and off the screen, through websites, chat rooms and message boards, phone-ins and on-screen text messages, spin-off programmes and voting. The popularity of these shows has very little to do with the onscreen content and everything to do with a format which acknowledges and celebrates viewer participation. It is the intellectual and emotional investments made by viewers (and by other media, especially the popular press) which build up the stories and personalities from what often appears rather unpromising raw material. 'Interactivity' in this case consists of incorporating consumer creativity back into the product and selling it back to the customer.

The other variable in creative consumption is the extent to which the consumer's interpretation or adaptation deviates from the original. Obviously no two people will see any product, especially a cultural product, in quite the same way. Nevertheless, Dewey's aesthetic theory expects some correspondence between the viewer's response and the artist's intention. As noted, contemporary aesthetic and literary theory assumes no such correlation. Similarly, today's cultural products are capable of accommodating a range of apparently contradictory responses, without apparently devaluing the integrity of the author or the work itself. Indeed it has been suggested that today's most successful cultural products are 'open texts' allowing a variety of localized responses to a single global narrative. Liebes and Katz (1990) developed this theory in relation to the 1980s television soap, *Dallas*. Basing their study on the different interpretations of the programme's characters and plot among Jewish and Arabic viewers in Israel, they argued that *Dallas* was successful precisely because its archetypal characters and primordial themes (good and bad brothers, treacherous women, wise parents, love and greed) drew upon religious or mythical iconography, allowing the viewers to interpret these stories in terms of their own culture and experience.

If cultural producers and marketers want to create successful cultural products, according to this logic they must allow space for audiences to negotiate their own personal, 'alternative' or 'resistant' readings and misunderstandings. This is an argument for framing multimedia experiences which provide the raw materials for creative consumption rather than finished products. Quality and content will only become valuable when filtered and reinterpreted by the customer. The author becomes an enabler of other people's creativity rather than the visionary creator. In terms of the value chain, the focus shifts from the primary creativity of the producer towards the secondary creativity of the consumer.

Yet many interactive media experiences or 'open' texts are actually highly manipulative, curtailing consumer creativity within the limits of the format. Reality television shows offer multiple opportunities for participation, but little active control, and the plotlines and character studies played out in chat rooms and websites are quite predictable. Consumer creativity, if it is to be transformative rather than simply imitative, needs to challenge the boundaries within which it operates. Applying this to interactive media, the consumer needs to be given an opportunity to challenge the rules of the game, rather than simply working within predefined parameters and tools. Only then does interactivity become truly creative. Many computer games allow the user to customize options; taking this further, composers of electronic music distinguish between software which allows them to sample a huge number of sounds and notes (however extensive) to software which allows them to actually make up or sample their own sounds and use these as building blocks in their compositions. Here, the line between composer and software engineer, between electronic music and 'live' music, starts to blur. True interactivity, like open source software, allows participants to reinvent the operating system, not just to use the existing tools.

Consumer creativity also requires a concession of authorial authority and control. Tim Wright, founder and partner of XPT, an interactive media company specializing in online games, discovered midway through the company's Online Caroline project that some of his players were taking his stories much more seriously than he was. This led on to a recognition that participants enjoyed playing their own creative games within the scenarios that XPT was making, and these self-generated games were much more valuable to them than any self-contained narrative created by XPT. From here he became interested in using interactive media not just as a vehicle for his own creativity but as a means for framing and facilitating the creativity of other people. The result was the 'Oldton' project – see the case study.

Case Study: In Search of Oldton

> When I was six years old, my father killed himself and we had to leave the old town where I was very happy. Now I go back to look for it, it isn't there.

So begins Tim Wright's vast digital archive of postings, images, artefacts and stories, 'In Search of Oldton'. Wright began the project by inviting web users to contribute their own memories and stories of this lost town to the Oldton website in order to recreate (or reinvent) the past. The response was extraordinary, ranging from the waggishly postmodern (pictures of the author in Lapp national costume) to the poignant ('Dear Grandma, I love you and I always will').

The themes of the site (memory, death, loss, nostalgia, British seaside towns) lent themselves to a range of responses and offered an accessible entry point for contributors. People sent e-mails, postcards, photographs and objects. Themes included childhood memories, relationships with loved ones, the nature of history. As with much of Wright's work, the lines between reality and fiction, between the heartfelt and the flippant were loosely drawn. Throughout the site there is a sense of playfulness and invention, yet real emotions crack through the artful surface.

'In Search for Oldton' was in fact a creative writing project, designed to explore the possibilities of writing in digital media and stimulate 'writers of the future' across the UK. Wright created an elaborate architecture which gave the individual contributions a context (a physical map of Oldton) and connected threads of commentary and elaboration from one posting to the next. The detective story element encouraged users to pick up and cross refer between random names, images and artefacts, creating an elaborate web of memory and fiction. At the same time Wright encouraged an element of randomness – anything was possible on the site, and nobody knew quite what would happen next. He toured the country showing people how the site worked and handing out postcards which allowed non-digital contributions to be incorporated into the project.

Consequently the site evolved into a community of story-tellers, with Wright weaving their narrative threads into an elaborate topography of Oldton. The completed project was collated into two anthologies or artefacts, first as 'Our Oldton', which comprised a grid map of the town laid out in 52 sections, each containing a set or memories and reflections which connected to each other and to a specific location on the map. By flipping the map section over, it was possible to experience another version of Oldton, 'My Oldton' in which Wright's structured his own version of Oldton as a set of 52 playing cards, comprising reflections and memories of his own real/fictional past as well as a running commentary on the site itself.

While there is no doubt that Wright was the driving force behind the Oldton project, he was not the author in the conventional sense. Oldton was a compendium of many authors. Wright was the architect who provided the structure and context which connected individuals into an imaginative (and imaginary) community. He was also the orchestrator who stimulated other people's creativity. But he was not the author.

The Oldton project shows how new forms of ownership and authorship are possible, particularly as a result of digital and interactive media. By delegating ownership of the project to its users, Wright produced a sense of communal identity and unleashed a collective energy and dynamism which was more than the sum of its parts. The loyalty and engagement users felt for Oldton went well beyond the conventional relationship between readers and writers or consumers and products.

Oldton was a non-profit project, supported by public institutions in order to stimulate new writing. Nevertheless, there are lessons here for marketing commercial products and services. Indeed most of Wright's work takes place within a semi-commercial context, with interactive projects and online communities being used to drive web traffic, advertising and e-commerce. Commercial investors in Wright's work recognize the value added of a loyal, engaged community to their own businesses. Wright is alert to the commercial opportunities of his work, especially the customer profiling and data mining possibilities which grow out of his detailed interactions with project participants.

Advertisers are keen to turn markets into communities, especially through the use of online media. There are obvious benefits for marketers in nurturing a committed, loyal and active constituency of users/customers. Yet for these communities to thrive, the members need to build relationships with each other, not just with the product or the brand. Sifting through the postings on Oldton, it is clear that many feel a close personal connection to Wright, but many more are responding to another user or posting, not following any narrative line conceived by Wright. For this to happen, Wright himself had to take a step back, allowing users to play with his creation and take it in directions not of his devising. Indeed one of Oldton's many attractions is precisely this feeling of unpredictability and quirkiness – according to one posting, 'the whole point of most online adventures is to *not* know what the next link will bring; to be unable to guess the next card in the pack'.

From a marketer's perspective this loss of control, allowing the customer to rewrite the meaning of the brand, is potentially risky. Yet as marketers try to build relationships with contemporary consumers, something more than transactional marketing is needed. By allowing the customer to reshuffle the pack, a more engaged relationship is possible and in an economy where customer attention is the scarce commodity, customer relationships drive transactions, not vice versa.

Along with this community building approach to brand development, the other marketing lesson from Oldton is the consumer's search for authentic forms of experience which are not mediated or manipulated. This can be seen as a reaction against a highly intrusive and pervasive online market which has bred a new generation of media-savvy consumers who refuse to be manipulated. As predicted by Negroponte, today's consumers, especially in the digital domain, are not convinced by clumsy attempts towards personalization or by intrusive attempts to sell them things they have not asked for. Oldton is constructed as a game, but the players are allowed to rewrite the rules. Wright is not pushing the narrative in any direction, he is allowing himself to be pulled along by the rest of the Oldton community. This loss of control may not amount to genuine authenticity or empowerment of the consumer, but it does avoid the feeling of manipulation and exploitation present in many interactive or participatory products, whether in the commercial or non-commercial context.

Finally, despite the emphasis on collective ownership and the author's deliberate surrender of control, Wright is not a passive observer in all of this. The site is artfully constructed and conceived to shape apparently random and disconnected individual postings into a coherent whole. That unity and coherence is Wright's principal contribution to Oldton – without it, the site would be interesting but ultimately dissatisfying. Marketers who involve consumers in reinterpreting and repositioning their brands must eventually make sense of the revised proposition and shape it into a meaningful and coherent brand. Finding the right moment to do this, deciding when to rein the project back in again and shape it into a final product is a difficult but necessary decision in the evolution of the project, product or brand.

In interactive media, the value chain has shifted and the consumer is king. But there is a choice to be made as to the meaning and extent of that consumer sovereignty. At one level, 'interactivity' becomes another form or manipulation, in which the consumer's choices, responses and preferences are absorbed back into the product and sold back to him as a commodity. Opportunities for such interaction are rife, but do not in the end allow for 'transformative' creativity by the consumer, only the possibility to play within a set of prescribed rules and choices. Alternatively, interactivity can allow a greater depth of involvement in which there is a genuine concession of authorship and creativity to the consumer. Such models of interactivity are rarer but in the end more satisfying and more genuinely transformative. For this to happen, producers themselves need to be prepared to equip consumers with a critical and conceptual apparatus to play the game on their own terms. There is a genuine transfer of symbolic resources here, from producer to consumer – a release of control. For the author, this surrender of authority places individual creativity at the service of systems creativity, where the parts played by individuals add up to a greater whole.

Towards the Social Product

Creative consumption emphasizes the extent to which individual consumers add value and meaning to products and services through an investment of their own 'symbolic resources'. According to this argument, consumers are becoming the new producers. They are also increasingly using cultural consumption to construct a collective identity or to signal their membership of an existing group or sub-culture.

On the other hand, the same technologies used by consumers to appropriate and reinvent cultural products are also available to producers. Addressable technologies and flexible production methods allow producers to target their products to the market of one and to offer an apparently customized, unique experience. Just as consumers can take mass media products and reinvent them in their own image, producers can pick up on consumer trends, repackage them and sell them back to paying customers. Creative consumption becomes a meaningless concession, allowing consumers the illusion of control while continuing to exploit their desire to be different.

Faced with this relentless commodification, contemporary culture, especially youth culture, has become a battle between the cool hunters and the cool hunted. Consumers fight back by continually reinventing themselves, distancing themselves from new labels and seeking out a defiant sense of community. One important weapon in the fight for authenticity is the tribalism of contemporary youth culture. Clubs, websites and illegal parties exist just off the radar of mainstream media but provide a strong affirmation of collective identity. As soon as mainstream recognition beckons, this group identity begins to break up and rebuild itself around a new set of venues, icons, rituals and rules. The rules of membership are enforced through a mix of peer group recognition and more formal regulations, such as the door policy in clubs, or through guest lists, back-stage passes, mailing lists. Some of these rules, notably the 'dress code' applied by door staff, may appear confusing or arbitrary, but the important message here is that only the like-minded need apply. The rules are constantly updated. At its most spontaneous, the community or 'tribe' becomes self-regulating and self-fulfilling. Outdoor raves and parties announced through word of mouth and 'secret' gigs become a rallying point for a shared sense of community, even if this is short-lived.

For the club promoter, this sense of community is both the source of 'value added' which brings in the punters but also a source of frustration when the same punters suddenly decide to move on. Traditional approaches to relationship marketing designed to build a sense of loyalty to the club have limited effectiveness; the crowd's real loyalty is to each other. The brand of a successful club night is owned by the clubbers, who pay for the privilege of acting out a certain aspirational image of themselves and of having that aspirational self-image reinforced by like-minded others. Once that delicate ecology is broken, as when a brand becomes too successful and expands too quickly, the collective identity starts to fall apart and the 'sub-cultural capital' is abruptly devalued. As the manager of one highly successful London club[2] noted, once the club began to diversify its activities and to exploit the brand, it lost its credibility: the people who bought the T-shirts were precisely the people who would not have been allowed into the club. The club's brand in the end was not really in its own possession – it belonged to the hardcore clubbers who simply took their custom elsewhere.

Night clubs are a form of 'social product'. The value of a club night is not inherent in the music, the ambience or the DJs, however impressive and important these might be in attracting customers, but in the clubbers themselves. Their participation in the club, for which they are prepared to pay, is a kind of 'creative consumption', but the value and meaning of their experience, the result of their creativity, is collective not individual. Witnessing this collective self-affirmation among television audiences, clubbers or gig-goers can be a humbling experience for promoters, performers and producers. The audience takes centre stage and those responsible for the event find their role downgraded from star attractions to conductors and facilitators.

Clubs and sub-cultures indicate an alternative way of understanding 'creative consumption', not in terms of individual self-expression but in terms of collective identity and 'retribalization'. This in turn leads us away from customization and the market of one and towards an appreciation of 'social products'. Social products are the result of a more complex form of creativity than mere self-expression, reflecting a purposeful search for meaning and value, not random deviation from a cultural producer's script. The 'value added' here is not just in the mind's eye of the individual consumer, but in a shared sense of identity and authenticity. If creative consumption leads us towards an appreciation of 'social products', what then are the implications of this for marketing and production, not just in the creative industries, but for management as a whole?

Letting Go

The techniques used to produce and market 'symbolic goods' can be applied to any product or service where brand value and customer relationships are at the core of the customer experience. As ordinary manufacturing and service industries start to behave more like the so-called 'creative industries', it is worth considering some specific implications of cultural approaches to marketing.

I have argued that cultural products are increasingly valued on the consumer's own terms. The shift in the value chain towards the consumer as the site where value is ultimately determined is supported by theoretical arguments from postmodern marketing, cultural studies and sub-culture theory, as well as by practical experience in the creative industries. I have further argued that as consumers make their own sense out of the products of the creative industries, they participate in a collective creative process, seeking out shared sources of value, identity and meaning from the raw materials presented to them. In doing so they create temporary communities or clubs based around a collective response to a given product or service. This in turn generates new rules, rituals and experiences which may be at several removes from anything conceived by the product's originators.

Applying these arguments to other types of industry, it is clear that creative consumption assumes a release of control and authority by the producer. The value of the brand is no longer determined by the producer. Instead, producers need to find ways of involving customers in the brand and allowing space for new interpretations and uses of their products and brands to take shape. This involvement in the brand has become increasingly important as the value of advertising is being measured in qualitative rather than quantitative terms. In an increasingly subdivided marketplace, and with sophisticated consumers reacting against 'mass' or 'push' media, campaigns which build a depth of involvement within a narrow niche market are more plausible than campaigns which aim for breadth.

The lesson from the creative industries, and in particular from interactive media, is that customer loyalty is more likely to accrue around a collective sense of ownership and involvement among customers than through individual relationships. Authenticity and involvement derives from the relationships between customers, not the relationship between customer and brand. Providing opportunities for these communities and clubs to develop, through forums, user groups, social projects and sponsorships is a more plausible approach to relationship marketing than a pseudo-personal approach targeting individuals through call centres and 'personal' recommendations. Again this requires a light touch. Allowing and encouraging users to take ownership of the brand, even if this means straying off message, will create a richer and more involving interactivity and allow new forms of 'social product' to evolve.

Today's marketers are constructing 'social products' within which consumers discover shared meanings and values through a process of interaction with like-minded consumers. The value does not come from the product, it comes from the product's users. Today's successful brands are open texts within which customers co-create their own meanings, through a process of story-telling, interaction and self-projection. All of this requires that creative producers defer to the creativity of consumption, allowing the customers to call the shots. By letting go of their products and brands, producers free them to be reinvented and reinhabited by consumers. By providing a framework within which this collective creativity can take place, producers become the orchestrators and architects of a collective creative system which can grow into greater complexity. Successful brands are nightclubs we want to join, not because of the music or the décor, but because of the people we might meet and the people we might become if we are invited inside.

Granting more space for creative consumption inevitably means a loss of authority for the producer. This surrender of authority is not without risks. When Nike introduced a new programme allowing consumers to 'customize' their shoes with their own individual logo, Jonah Peretti, a graduate student at MIT, requested the word 'sweatshop' be sewn into his trainers as his personal ID. The company was not amused and refused his request. Peretti persevered in a gently mocking series of e-mails which he then published on the Internet. The confrontation highlighted the distance between 'creative consumption' of brands in the West and the realities of material production in the developing world. It also showed that if companies are serious about co-authoring products and brands with their customers, they need to deliver on their promise, and this entails a genuine concession of control to the consumer – even if that consumer then holds them up to ridicule.

The Nike 'sweatshop' case demonstrates how creative consumption reconfigures the value chain. The companies closest to the customer are responsible for branding and marketing and this is where value is added and profits are made. Production becomes a necessary evil, poorly paid and remote from the point of delivery, both geographically and culturally. In the context of the creative industries this changing value chain has led to a power shift from companies traditionally involved in content generation towards the intermediaries who stand between content and the consumer. At the time of writing, approximately 70 per cent of the legitimate music download industry in the US and Europe belongs not to a record label but to a technology company, Apple's i-Tunes. For Apple, music is a cheap and attractive form of software being used as a loss-leader in order to drive sales of hardware (the i-Pod). There is little scope in this new creative economy for romantic theories of individual authorship. The creativity of the product is only part of its value – total value is only realized through creative consumption. Content is the grit in the oyster, but the real work of today's creative and media industries centres on the forms and technologies through which that content is delivered, and real creativity is needed to engage the mind of the consumer in the work of creative consumption.

Theories of creative consumption connect with the *realpolitik* of today's creative industries. They are also allied to the theories of creativity being developed through this book. 'Creativity' is not the possession of a handful of gifted individuals at the point of origination, it is passed along the value chain to include managers, marketers and customers. Creativity encompasses not only novelty, originality and product origination, but the whole process which turns ideas and content into a valuable and valued experience for customers. From this perspective the real creative work of the creative industries lies not in the origination of new content, but in the selection, filtering, delivery and interpretation of that content by consumers and their collaborators.

The Aesthetics of Marketing

In this chapter I have argued that theoretical developments in marketing and cultural theory place the customer experience at the core of the value chain. Creative consumption becomes the process through which customer value is generated. Creative consumption is interactive, but the key interaction here is not the relationship between customer and product or brand, but the relationship between customers themselves.

The arts and creative industries have long recognized the value of creative consumption as a shared aesthetic experience. New digital media, while appearing to replace this shared aesthetic with atomized individuals, have actually enriched the collective experience by opening access to virtual communities and alternative realities. Through these interactions between audiences and consumers, new forms of value, community and identity are created.

Transferring the notion of creative consumption to other forms of industry, marketing becomes the core business function. If businesses want to tap into consumer creativity, they need to use marketing not just as a method for communicating brand values to customers, but as a medium in its own right, through which customers can interact with each other and reinvent the meaning of the product. The creativity of marketing lies not in the talent of individual copywriters and art directors nor the genius of a specific campaign or promotion, but in the ability of marketers to facilitate and orchestrate the imaginations and creativity of consumers. Marketing provides 'open texts' which allow space for viewers, readers and listeners to negotiate their own personal readings, even if (especially if) these readings seem to deviate from or 'resist' the encoded messages of the advertiser.

In the mid-1990s, I visited NikeTown, Nike's newly opened flagship store in Manhattan. The store was pure theatre: pumping sound system, orchestrated excitement as the clock counted down to the next video screening, artfully arranged trainers framed in illuminated glass boxes, like pictures in a gallery. Caught up in the razzmatazz, I naively asked about trying a pair of trainers. The assistant appeared bemused. These shoes were not for sale. If I wanted to buy something, she suggested I try one of the bargain basements downtown in Canal Street. She was not selling me trainers, she was selling me a brand. NikeTown was many things – a sporting showcase, brand emporium, entertainment experience, tourist attraction – but not, emphatically, a retailer.

Ten years on, NikeTown's brand experience seems old-fashioned and clumsy. Today's brands are less brash, artfully concealing their identities instead of emblazoning them on the big screen, inviting the viewer to construct their own messages instead of shouting out their own. As marketers seek out more oblique and open-ended approaches to selling products, marketing has become an aesthetic project in its own right. Rather than working through conventional media such as television or press advertising, advertisers are using the full armoury of popular culture, from festivals and art galleries to short films and club nights. Matt Hardisty at Naked Communications describes a 'blurring' between subsidized cultural institutions and commercial marketing agencies. Much of his own work at Naked seems more akin to a freelance cultural promoter than a conventional advertising agency.

Such an approach to marketing might appear chaotic. If users are allowed to take ownership of brands, to reinvent them in their own image, they will inevitably take the brand in unexpected directions. But this unexpectedness will not only cement the relationship between brand and customers, it will also allow the brand's meaning and value to evolve and grow in response to its users. Rather than providing a recipe for chaos, 'consumer-led' branding leads to complexity – towards a self-generating, adaptive system which develops its own rules and boundaries. Markets become self-segmenting, products and brands accumulate new meanings and new customers. Whether we view this process as empowering or manipulative, the brand has become an aesthetic experience, and marketers and consumers have turned consumption in general, and cultural consumption in particular, into a creative act. New approaches to marketing and branding might represent the corporate takeover of cultural expression, or the aestheticization of commerce. But there are signs that in the field of marketing at least, the historic divide between 'creatives' and 'suits' is beginning to disappear.

FURTHER READING

For an accessible introduction to postmodern marketing, see Firat *et al.* (1995) and Cova (1996). Stephen Brown's approach is more provocative, challenging the assumptions of traditional marketing and identifying the non-rational, imaginative aspects of marketing in a postmodern world (see Brown 1996, 1998).

These postmodern theories have been used by Jeremy Rifkin to describe a new economy based on consumer attention, not production. According to Rifkin (2000), economic competition now centres on the attempt to build a relationship with the customer, not to sell them something. Over time, the 'life-time value' of the customer will be worth far more than a single transaction.

The chief proponents of audience theory are John Fiske and Paul Willis. Fiske (1989) showed how television audiences reconstruct the meaning of television programmes in relation to their own experiences. Paul Willis (1990) showed how teenagers in the 1980s made up their own narratives and meanings out of the music and television they absorbed from the mass media. Popular culture simply provided raw material for young people to engage in their own creative play or 'symbolic work'. Willis described this as a form of empowerment, working 'through, not against the market'. He acknowledged that this empowerment was at best only partial, allowing consumers to select from a menu not of their own choosing. Yet even this limited empowerment seemed to Willis preferable to reliving yesterday's lost battles.

Willis and Fiske drew on an older heritage of 'sub-culture theory' developed by British researchers during the 1970s and 1980s. Historically this can be seen as an attempt to continue a political argument about the relative power of individuals, especially young people, in a mass media age, transferring a debate about culture and authority from the political sphere into the sphere of consumption. Academic cultural studies argued that young people were fighting back, admittedly in subtle ways, by 'reappropriating' the products of fashion, music, television and film and reinventing them in their own rebellious self-image (see Hall and Jefferson 1976; Hebdige 1979). For an updated and more cynical take on the same topic, see Matthews and Wacker (2002).

The argument that new technologies have extended the empowerment of the customer was predicted by Nicholas Negroponte in *Being Digital* (1995), with his claim that in the future consumers will 'pull' information from the mass media and his prediction that new technologies open up a new 'market of one'. For further discussion of this topic, see Tapscott *et al.* (1998) and Kelly (1998). Kelly was the editor of *Wired*, while Negroponte was a researcher at the Massachusetts Institute of Technology (MIT) – two institutions at the forefront of the new media revolution. For a more sceptical perspective on the transforming effects of technology, see Webster (1995).

The meaning and extent of empowerment through the market is of course part of a larger political debate. Several academic commentators, including Graham Murdock, Frank Webster and Jim McGuigan have analysed the political implications of the new cultural populism, arguing that 'empowerment' of consumers has disempowered them as citizens and that the rhetoric of creative consumption disguises a drift towards marketization and neoliberalism. For an overview of these debates see McGuigan (1992) and Leys (2001).

Activists and protesters have attempted to turn the promise of 'consumer empowerment' into a reality through 'culture jamming' – a reappropriation of brands and products by consumers for their own subversive ends which recalls Dick Hebdige and the subcultural activism of the 1970s. The Nike sweatshop case cited in this chapter is one such example – the full correspondence can be found on http://shey.net/niked.html. Culture jamming features in Naomi Klein's *No Logo* (2000) – for more examples, visit www.adbusters.org. One of the problems for the culture jammers is that their inventive distortions and countercultural subversions are all too often themselves reappropriated by the very corporations they seek to undermine and reincorporated into mainstream advertising campaigns – see Frank (1997).

On the restructuring of the value chain, the literature falls into three related areas. First, post-Fordism describes a disintegration of traditional value chains and the emergence of specialist firms connected through networks. Ash Amin's edited collection, *Postfordism: A Reader* (1994) provides a useful introductory collection of articles and perspectives on this theme. Secondly, there is a literature on the effects of globalization on the value chain – see, for example, Gereffi and Korzeniewicz (1994) and Dicken (2003). Finally there is a growing literature on the effects of new technolologies and digital distribution on the value chain, particularly in the creative and media industries: see, for example, Tapscott *et al.* (1998); Rifkin (2000). These trends have been particularly pronounced in the music industry – see Brindley (2000).

Miranda Boorsma's arguments on arts marketing are summarized in a recent article, 'A strategic logic for arts marketing: Integrating customer value and artistic objectives' (2006). Boorsma draws upon research by Hirschmann and Holbrook into the emotional or 'hedonic' satisfaction of aesthetic experiences, and on Prahalad's concept of 'experiential goods' – see Hirschman and Holbrook (1982) and Pine and Gilmour (1999). For a product-led view of arts marketing, see Diggle (1994); for an application of mainstream 'customer-led' marketing to the arts, see Kotler and Scheff (1997). The argument that marketing should focus on the product surround rather than the product is still the default setting for most arts marketing textbooks, including Colbert (1994) and Hill *et al.* (1995).

NOTES

1   Michael Wolff found Amazon's 'familiar depersonalized personalized greeting' so irritating that he predicted that Amazon would become 'the Atari of the Internet' (Michael Wolff, *Guardian New Media*, 10 January 2000). In fact the 'recommendations' only work properly if the customer takes the time to customize their preferences; this is another example of creative consumption, with the customer effectively taking over the job of customer profiling and market research. ·

2   For commercial reasons this club, and the manager, must remain anonymous.

8 THE POLITICS OF CREATIVITY

Converge 05 is New Zealand's first ever celebration of creative industries, it will be held in Christchurch and show the creative technologies that benefit our own and the world's economy. Creative technologies bring design, software, engineering and sometimes visual arts together to meet the practical needs of commerce and industry.

Creative technologies are, for example, the world-beating Britten motorcycle, the kiwifruit, Black Magic, the Formway Chair, New Zealand Fashion week, the Hamilton Jet Unit, the tranquilliser dart gun, Swanndri, the animation for Lord of the Rings and frozen meat for export.

(Converge05 Brochure, Creative
Industries New Zealand Conference,
29 May 2005)

When I worked at Faber, we published a book called Creative Britain which was pilloried. If you look at the back it includes many statistics. They were made up by me and the copy editor at Faber to get the book published. How can you identify an important area which you want government to support when there are no statistics?

(Matthew Evans, UK Government
Chief Whip, House of Lords)[1]

Promoting the Creative Economy

This book began with an observation that 'creativity' has become a buzz word in politics and management, even if its meaning and value are rarely discussed. Much of this interest centres on the economic consequences of creativity; as Howkins observes, creativity is not in itself an economic good, but in its applications it can become so.[2] The rhetoric of the creative economy highlights individual talent and innovation as the productive elements in the creative process and the magic ingredients in the creative economy. The social processes and systems which precede and follow flashes of individual inspiration and inventiveness are relegated to the background.

This one-sided account is consistent with the Western 'genius' model of creativity. The creative economy is concerned with differentiation and originality, not continuity and context, and sees creativity in terms of individual talents not a collective social process.

The idea of a thriving creative economy rests on two related definitions. First, there is a long-standing tendency to see culture and creativity in economic terms, which can be traced back to political efforts to 'justify' investment in the arts in terms of its economic outcomes through the 1980s and 1990s in the UK, Europe and the US. The restructuring of the economies of many Asian countries including Taiwan, Singapore and China since the late 1990s placed a similar emphasis on the economics of culture and stimulated government interest in the 'creative industries' as a new form of economic development. This has led to the definition of the creative industries as a narrowly defined list of media, entertainment and arts-related activities capable of generating wealth through intellectual property (mostly in the form of copyrights).

The second version of the creative economy is a relatively new attempt to identify the 'creative' elements of industry much more broadly across the economy as a whole. Here creativity is defined as a tendency within all industries to develop and depend upon individual talent and intellectual property – framed much more generally to include a range of intangible assets, from 'know-how' to branding. This shift from looking at the economic outcomes of creativity ('the creative industries') towards considering the creative inputs into the economy as a whole ('the creative economy') opens up a vast range of applications. As 'intellectual property' in the forms of patents, trademarks and design rights becomes an integral part of mainstream products and services, the creative economy has become virtually synonymous with the economy as a whole.

These two definitions of creative economic activity, the economy of the creative industries themselves and the creativity of the economy as a whole, are connected through a third policy strand, the branding of creativity as a national or regional asset. As 'creativity' becomes the key to economic success in all aspects of industry, governments at every level are keen to highlight their creative credentials. This is where the more narrowly defined creative industries come back into the picture, since creative excellence in the arts, media and entertainment industries can be used as a powerful symbol of the creativity and dynamism of the economy as a whole. Governments highlight the creative industries not as an end in themselves, but as an indicator of industrial creativity.

This might explain the disproportionate emphasis by policy makers on the economic success of the creative industries. Despite the impressive performance of the creative and media industries in terms of growth and employment, it is still far too early to consider them as a straight substitute for declining manufacturing industry. The copyright industries depend on an infrastructure of more traditional industries for logistics and support, from transport, manufacturing and reproduction to legal and financial services and computer hardware. This in turn leads to a blurring of the definition of creative industries. The so-called 'creative industries' are embedded in a much broader range of activities, some of which can lay little claim to being 'creative'. So, for example, it is difficult to measure employment in the creative industries, because many apparently 'creative' occupations lie outside the so-called creative industries, and many 'non-creative' jobs exist inside the creative industries. Is an accountant or driver who happens to work for a film production company part of the creative industries? Is a designer employed by a car manufacturer part of the manufacturing sector? Such problems are exacerbated by a lack of consistency in the way statistics are collated and interpreted at national and international level, and a tendency to rely on data sets which were designed to deal with older, more stable patterns of employment.

Statistical inconsistencies are compounded by the commissioning of research for purposes of advocacy and policy making, with researchers customizing their data and definitions to a predetermined research agenda. Consequently data and definitions vary widely, and we still lack clear and objective information on the scale and scope of the so-called creative industries. In these circumstances it is very difficult to develop a clear and convincing picture of the creative industries, still less a coherent creative industries policy, not least when those responsible for policy are tending to monopolize the research agenda. Amid the confusion it is very easy and very tempting to manipulate the figures to match the political vision of the moment (as evidenced by the quotation at the head of this chapter). Far from enjoying 'evidence-based policy', the creative industries are characterized by 'policy-based evidence'.

The creative industries themselves, if we mean those industries concerned with the production and exploitation of copyright material, may or may not be a significant or important element in the global economy. The definitions are too contested to allow anything like an objective assessment. However, when we open out the definition of the creative economy to take in a broader input-based definition, encompassing a creative 'tendency' or component in industry generally, the prospects become much more enticing. For example, if we accept Howkins' definition of the creative economy to include intellectual property in the form of patents, trademarks and design rights in areas such as automobile design, GM foods and biotechnology, healthcare and home computing, science and technology, research and development, the category threatens to engulf most of the world's economy. Seen in this context, the so-called 'creative' industries are merely the tip of a very extensive creativity iceberg.

From the perspective of government, creativity matters not because politicians believe that the music industry is going to replace car manufacture as a provider of mass employment. Even if this proposition contains a germ of truth, there are ethical and political questions to be asked of such a position, and the evidence base for such a projection simply does not exist. From a political perspective, creativity and the creative industries matter because they provide a kind of branding statement for the new economy – a brand for an economy which is based on brands, insubstantial and marginal in themselves perhaps, but nevertheless important as a statement of intent by governments and marketers.

Flagship cultural projects in areas of mass unemployment may perhaps lead to social and economic regeneration, generating secondary employment in related industries as well as providing a source of micro-employment in the creative industries themselves. But until we can unravel objective data and analysis from the interest groups which are driving these projects and policies, we cannot be certain whether this is a real justification for investing in arts facilities as opposed to education, hospitals, or other forms of local infrastructure. Measured purely in visitor numbers and impact on the local economy, shopping centres, theme parks or sports stadia may be at least as successful as galleries, museums and concert halls. It is sometimes argued that cultural facilities provide a reason for rich professionals to relocate to a particular town or region. But cultural facilities actually feature well down a list of relocation factors which includes education provision, transport facilities, open space and, above all (of course), real estate prices. Even the so-called 'creative class', credited as the driving force in the creative economy, is as likely to be impressed by the quality of its cappuccinos or cheap Internet access as it is to be drawn in by the local cultural scene.

One possible reason for the continuing popularity of arts-led approaches to economic regeneration rests not on their immediate economic and social outcomes but on the secondary economic impact achieved by rebranding a district, town or region as 'creative'. The standing of cutting edge contemporary art centres like Tate Modern in London or the Guggenheim in Bilbao is measured according to their prestige and profile rather than their size and turnover, signalling that a region or country contains a modern, creative, entrepreneurial energy. The symbolism suggests that the 'creativity' to be found in the design or content of a single building represents something at large in the city. Visitor attractions like Disneyland or Legoland or out of town shopping centres may compete with high profile arts projects in terms of visitor numbers, but they cannot compete in terms of this symbolic value. By locating high profile art projects in former industrial buildings (electrical turbines, warehouses and factories) or in former industrial districts (docklands, textile towns) the symbolic meaning of these projects is thrown into relief. Never mind the statistics, feel the creative buzz.

All of this explains why the creative industries and the creative economy have become politically fashionable, regardless of the statistical evidence for or against their quantifiable impacts on employment, export earnings and GDP. Rather than considering creativity narrowly in terms of outputs in the form of intellectual property and copyrights, governments see creativity as a more general indicator of dynamism and innovation in the economy. Statistical data on the creative industries needs to be seen in this context, not as a precise measurement of the economic outcomes of creative work, but as a symbolic statement about the creativity of the economy in general (see case study).

What follows from this is a particularly loaded definition not only of the creative industries themselves but of creativity. From being something capable of generating economic outcomes, creativity has now become an industrial asset in its own right. This has influenced approaches to the creative industries in cultural policy, and has also influenced managerial approaches to creativity.

Case Study: Creative New Zealand – The Branding of Creativity
New Zealand's eclectic collection of 'creative technologies' at the start of this chapter is typical of the broadening definition of creativity and the creative economy. Whereas the UK government's definition of the creative industries is still wedded to the old idea of 'cultural industries' and still refers to a shortlist of core arts and entertainment industries, New Zealand has taken the rhetoric of the creative economy to its logical conclusion. Why cannot creative technologies in areas as diverse as meat-packing, engineering and manufacturing take their rightful place in the creative economy?

New Zealand's creative economy strategy in 2005 is based on two related approaches. The first approach is to invest in its traditionally defined 'creative industries', building on the success of Peter Jackson's 2002–4 *Lord of the Rings* film trilogy in order to kick start the country's resources and reputation as 'the second Hollywood'. The second approach is to identify and support 'creativity' across the economy as a whole, as demonstrated by the list of creative technologies at the start of this chapter. In particular the government has highlighted design and packaging as a key competitive factor for New Zealand's manufacturing economy. Here the emphasis is not on defining certain industries as 'creative', but on identifying a creative element which can be propagated across all industries.

New Zealand's dual strategy, represented by its support for its film post-production houses and for its designers, points to the ambivalence of the 'creative economy' concept. On the one hand, the creative industries themselves represent a specific branch of the knowledge economy, where ideas, images and individual talent form the raw material for a burgeoning media and entertainment industry which is outperforming the rest of the economy – for example, film special effects and post-production facilities. On the other hand, creativity reflects a tendency within all businesses to place a premium on creative design and delivery of products, since this is where value is being added to even the most unpromising of raw materials – for example, the packaging of frozen meat. In promoting this broader definition of creativity, government representatives argue that for a small country like New Zealand, one of its greatest assets is a certain individual inventiveness or offbeat quirkiness, the product of a rugged individualism rooted in their way of life. This eccentric inventiveness will provide the country with a creative edge when competing in the global economy.

Of course, these two approaches – promoting the economics of creativity and the creativity of the economy – are related. By hitching the creativity bandwagon to *Lord of the Rings*, the New Zealand government is using the film industry as a symbol of the creativity of the Zealand economy and the New Zealand people. The idea that New Zealand will overtake other global competitors as a major sub-Hollywood player in the film industry is highly debatable. If we focus solely on the indigenous film industry and its related post-production, animation and CGI spin-offs, the government's massive investment in Peter Jackson's film, principally in terms of tax breaks, will take many years to pay

> back. But as an iconic brand of native imagination and inventiveness, the
> investment is more than justified.
>
> How many non-New Zealanders are familiar with the creative technologies
> of the Britten motorcycle, the Formway chair, Swanndri? How many are not
> familiar with *Lord of the Rings*? In government marketing videos and inter-
> national conferences, the *Lord of the Rings* imagery is the hook, but the real
> content is likely to be more diverse and more surprising.
>
> The example of New Zealand shows how the creative industries are being
> represented by government, not only as an economic success story based
> around a specific cluster of arts- and media-related industries, but also as an
> iconic statement of the significance of creativity in the national economy.

From 'Cultural' to 'Creative' Industries

As noted in chapter 4, the individualistic model of creativity based on individual
skill and originality is supported by neo-liberal assumptions about motivation and
individual talent. The creative economy concept takes this tendency a step further,
grafting the individualism of Western theories of creativity onto neo-liberal market
economics. The idea of the creative economy and the creative industries is thus a
politicized concept. This politicization can be traced through the gradual introduction of the term 'creative industries' into the discourse of cultural policy.

The UK was one of the first countries to introduce the term 'creative industries'
in 1997, replacing the older term 'cultural industries' which continues to be the
standard in other European countries. The change in terminology indicates some
of the changing political and economic associations of creativity noted above. It also
signals some of the policy imperatives which follow on from these assumptions. The
term 'cultural industries' indicates that creativity grows out of a specific cultural
context and emphasizes the cultural content of ideas, values and traditions. The term
'creative industries' emphasizes the novelty of ideas and products and places creativity
in a context of individual talent, innovation and productivity.

The category of 'creative industries' has gradually replaced 'cultural industries'
as the flag of convenience for arts and cultural organizations in the UK, Taiwan,
Singapore and China. Australia, Canada, New Zealand and Korea have adopted
the rhetoric of 'creativity' even if they have not consistently adopted the 'creative
industries' label. Meanwhile other European countries, notably France, have preferred
the older term 'cultural industries', as does UNESCO. The Council of Europe is still
more cautious, using the term 'audiovisual industries' to describe broadcasting, film,
music and web-based media, a much more limited 'industrial' application of arts
and culture. It is interesting to note that Europe, especially France, has resisted the
attempt to treat culture as a commodity like any other (the 'exception culturelle')
and resisted neo-liberal efforts to remove subsidies, quotas and other instruments
designed to shield cultural products from the market.

The emergence of the 'creative industries' is by no means universal, and reflects Anglo-American traditions in cultural policy and a tendency to see intellectual property rights in terms of tradable economic goods. Historically, the Anglo-American interpretation of copyright as a primarily economic right differs from the French and European emphasis on moral rights of artists and authors. This has led to a recurrent argument in World Trade Organization (WTO) negotiations, with France and Europe opposing the US in talks on GATT (General Agreement on Tariffs and Trade) and GATS (General Agreement on Trade in Services) on the grounds that cultural goods such as films and television programmes are public goods, not tradable commodities. As the creative economy concept spreads to new WTO member countries including China, this is a battle France is unlikely to win. In this context, the transition from 'cultural' to 'creative' industries thus represents a significant political step, based on a reading of creativity as a privately owned individual asset.

In Europe, two distinctive cultural policy traditions have formed around the cultural / creative industries. During the 1980s, the cultural industries were at first associated with popular culture and cultural diversity. Policy makers and activists urged greater investment in the cultural industries as part of a more democratic, inclusive approach to culture and cultural policy. 'New' art forms like video, popular music and local publishers were set against the alleged elitism of traditional 'high' arts such as theatre, opera, ballet and classical music. The populist embrace of the cultural industries was associated with an attempt to engage with new audiences and communities and to develop a more participatory culture. Cultural industries policies thus spilled over into community arts, urban socio-cultural development and the European 'cultural democracy' project. From one perspective then, the cultural / creative industries were associated with a politicized, populist, inclusive approach to cultural policy. By appropriating the term 'cultural industries' as part of this movement, the cultural activists and administrators of the 1980s were reclaiming television, popular music, film and the mass media from the negative connotations of Adorno's 'culture industry' in the 1940s.

At the same time, the cultural industries also appealed to those on the neo-liberal right. The cultural industries fitted with an ideological conviction that all social and cultural life could be framed in terms of economic transactions. At a time when the traditional high arts were demanding state subsidies and against a background of economic recession and ideological economic liberalism, the cultural industries represented an entrepreneurial, market-driven alternative. In the UK the European emphasis on the democratic, empowering aspects of the cultural industries struck a chord with the right-wing government of Margaret Thatcher. For those on the political right, the traditional arts institutions were the spoiled children of the 1960s, catering to a middle class, liberal elite whose self-regarding pleasures were being subsidized by the state. The cultural industries were a meritocratic alternative, unsubsidized, accessible and undemanding, representing the populist, demotic, entrepreneurial spirit of the new Europe.

These two tendencies have been inherited by contemporary cultural policy in Europe. Cultural policy through the 1990s continued to be torn between the social democratic idealism of the late 1970s and the economic pragmatism of the 1980s. The differing policy strands have often become entwined together, as with the deregulation and privatization of European broadcasting, driven by an unlikely alliance of anti-establishment activists and opportunistic entrepreneurs like Silvio Berlusconi. The cultural/creative industries encapsulate these contradictions. On the one hand they represent a source of economic good, measured in export earnings, employment statistics and Gross National Product. On the other hand, they are described as a mechanism for social inclusion, through training and development, youth employment, community regeneration and participatory arts projects.

Given these inherited contradictions, the gradual shift from the cultural industries to a definition of the creative industries in terms of individual talent and the generation of wealth and employment is significant. Despite paying lip-service to the inclusive, social aspects of the arts and media sectors, the hard-nosed rhetoric of the creative industries highlights individualism and economic outcomes over collectivism and social values. As noted at the start of this book, in terms of creativity theory, the 'creative industries' concept highlights certain aspects of the creative process at the expense of others. In particular, by emphasizing individualism and the generation of new ideas, the collective processes and traditions through which individual talents and innovative ideas acquire value and meaning are underplayed. Of course, these collective values and systems are precisely what would have been highlighted in the old rhetoric of 'cultural industries'.

The contradictions between social democracy and neo-liberalism contained in the cultural/creative industries debate are evident in the various policies towards the creative industries to which we now turn. They are also indicative of the contradictions and complexity inherent in the notion of creativity. The rhetoric of the creative industries underplays this complexity, suggesting a simple equation linking individual talent, creativity, intellectual property and profit. While this reading of creativity may not be convincing in terms of creativity theory, it fits conveniently with the political interests and arguments of government and arts advocacy.

Creative Industries and Cultural Policy: Assumptions and Models

Opposing definitions of creativity result in opposing policies towards the creative industries. If we believe in the primacy of individual talent and the spontaneous inventiveness of the creative genius, the first political response is one of 'laissez-faire'. At one end of the policy spectrum, a pure *neo-liberal cultural policy* is not merely passive and would typically include an active attempt to roll back state involvement in the creative sector through deregulation, removal of subsidies and tariffs, and the embrace of free trade and market economics. In order to remove all constraints which might inhibit the release of innate talents and individual creative excellence, neo-liberal cultural policy thus merges with liberal economics. The logic behind such measures would be, to cite a senior record industry executive attending a DCMS consultation on UK music industry policy, 'cream always rises'; intervening in the music industry, or in any aspect of the creative economy, would merely obstruct the spontaneous rise of natural talent.

Such a pure neo-liberal policy is rare. A modified response to the genius model of individual creativity is a policy based on identifying and supporting individual talent. A *talent-based cultural policy* would allow for some minor corrections of market failures, focusing on the development and support of individual talent as the key to a successful creative economy. New ideas and new talents are a public good which will not initially reward private investors. Rather than assuming that individual talent is self-sustaining and self-generating, a talent-oriented cultural policy might accordingly attempt to stimulate the market by identifying, developing and supporting individual talent in its formative stages through education and training, targeted investment (based on an assessment of 'creative potential') and special economic privileges and exemptions accorded to the creative individual. This investment in youth can be seen in the Singapore government's attempts to develop a creative curriculum for schools, or in privately funded schemes to support 'gifted children' by taking them out of state education. Once the ingredients for the perfect market are in place, the talent-oriented policy would nevertheless still assume that the market for creativity will reward excellence and that the creative economy will eventually become self-regulating. Thus in the UK, creative businesses are offered considerable assistance at start-up, but support for developing or expanding businesses is limited.

Moving further away from the pure neo-liberal model, a talent-oriented policy might also merge with a *national development-oriented cultural policy*. In order to develop a strong national creative economy, the national development-oriented cultural policy attempts to protect creative individuals from the vicissitudes and short life cycles of the open market through subsidies and import quotas. It might also offer tax breaks and other discriminatory incentives designed to build up a national stock of talented individuals and individual businesses (even if this influx of creative talent comes from outside the home country). These deviations from pure neo-liberalism are justified in relation to national economic self-interest. Protectionism and special measures are designed to support native talents and national centres of excellence as the best guarantee of a competitive creative economy. An example of this approach would be the Irish government's attempt to attract inward investment into its film and music industries by offering tax breaks to film makers and musicians resident in the country and to offer grants and subsidies to film makers using home-grown talent, facilities and locations.

All of the above policy approaches are premised on the primacy of individual talent and define creativity in terms of individual skill, innovation and productivity. This inevitably leads towards an emphasis on cultural production and cultural products or outcomes, rather than process.

Set against the neo-liberal, national economic and talent-oriented models of creativity and cultural policy, a systems view of creativity leads to an appreciation of the infrastructure, networks and collaborations which underpin the visible peaks of creative output. This logically leads away from a policy based on cultural production towards a policy encompassing the developmental phases which precede and follow cultural production, including cultural distribution. There is also likely to be greater attention paid to process, especially the invisible or 'non-creative' elements in cultural production, and to non-quantifiable social outcomes as well as economic products.

A cultural policy for the creative industries which is based upon a systems view of creativity would include most of the measures already referred to. But in addition it would take in a broader range of interventions designed to support the social networks of exchange and collaboration and the industry connections up and down the value chain through which creative individuals can thrive. Furthermore, rather than intervening directly in cultural production, a *systems-based cultural policy* would tend towards a more oblique approach, designed to develop a framework of opportunity and communication which can connect separate individuals into a broader 'project ecology'. Some of these measures have already been considered in chapter 3. The central assumptions of the systems approach to creativity are the primacy of networks over individuals and the idea that creative ideas are always rooted in a specific cultural context. The investments by Swedish local government in building a local infrastructure for fledgling musicians and local bands are examples of such an approach. France's emphasis on supporting not only film makers but film distribution and exhibition provides another (mirrored by recent developments in the UK).

A systems approach to cultural policy can of course tilt over into bureaucratic interventionism, stifling individual flair and difference. If neo-liberal cultural policy pursues innovation and change without regard to value and meaning, a statist approach to cultural policy holds creativity accountable to the traditions, institutions and objectives of the state – novelty takes second place to politically correct value judgements. If neo-liberalism aims to minimize state intervention, an emphasis on systems, networks and infrastructure can lead policy in the opposite direction, locking creative enterprises into the iron cage of state bureaucracy and upholding the values and ideals of the state and state institutions. Creativity in this system is indeed purposeful, but its purposes, values and objectives may be upheld at the expense of innovation. At its most extreme this was the role of cultural policy in the Eastern European countries under communism, with film makers, writers and musicians integrated into the state machinery as party members and loyal citizens.

In practice, most contemporary national cultural policies are likely to include a range of measures from across the spectrum of neo-liberalism and state interventionism. However, national governments with their distinctive cultural policy traditions are becoming increasingly marginal to the structure and direction of the creative industries. Today's creative industries are dominated not by government but by a handful of global corporations. As these transnational corporations seek economies of scale and scope, national markets and national cultural traditions are merged into global flows of ideas and information. The inevitable tendency is towards a model based not on national or regional cultural policy, but on the free flow of cultural commodities across borders. The shift from cultural to creative industries needs to be seen in this context. Culture reinforces national borders, while individual creativity and talent transcend them.

The shift towards a Western model of creativity based on genius and pure innovation and a definition of the creative industries based on talented individuals is therefore politically significant. These assumptions are etched across the rhetoric of the creative industries and manifest in a continued emphasis on creative talent as a national asset which can be measured and exploited. These arguments are especially dominant in the emergent cultural policies of Taiwan, China, Singapore and Hong Kong, driven no doubt by the prize of WTO membership and the promise of global competitiveness. As national creative industries are absorbed into a global creative economy, neo-liberal assumptions begin to drive out the old ideologies. Seen in this context, France's 'exception culturelle' appears as a defiant anachronism threatened by a gathering consensus.

Korea is poised between these policy traditions and thus represents an interesting barometer for creative industries policy in the future. In the past Korea aggressively defended its indigenous film industry from competition, using quotas and subsidies to protect national film makers. More recently Korea has begun to open its markets and open up trade agreements with some of its neighbours, even making tentative overtures towards Japan, its old political enemy and now its chief economic competitor in the region. Korea's gradual adjustment to the global rules of free trade has been reciprocated by access to new markets, notably the US. A succession of Korean films has broken through into Western cinemas, while in the Asian region Korea is the dominant force in film and popular music. The unanswered question is how much of Korea's current success is a result of its new policy of embracing the market and how far it is a legacy of its protectionist past. It might be that it is currently enjoying the best of both worlds, having used a protectionist policy to build up a strong domestic industry and market which is now reaping the benefits in a global marketplace; if this is the case, the current 'Korean wave' (*han-ryu*) may not be sustainable. As a further indicator of underlying policy trends, it is also interesting to note that Korea's policy makers still prefer to speak of 'cultural' rather than 'creative' industries.

In general it seems that neo-liberal cultural policies towards the creative industries are in the ascendant. Those who support this approach can point to the apparent success story of the creative industries, backed by impressive statistics charting export earnings, employment and contribution to Gross Domestic Product. However, the sustainability of this new creative economy remains unproven. As global competition increases, some of the former heavyweights in the creative economy, and the neo-liberal assumptions which lie behind them, may be under threat. Hollywood's film dominance may in the long run be challenged by India or China – India already has the largest domestic film audience in the world but has failed to compete internationally while China has yet to mobilize its own domestic market or to capitalize on its global competitive position. The suspicion remains that by failing to invest in the underlying infrastructure which supports individual creativity, today's leading creative economies may be banking on past successes instead of building for the future. Neo-liberalism chooses to neglect this invisible infrastructure at its peril. If a country like China were to invest in its creative infrastructure and encourage cultural participation and dissemination among its youthful population, the global creative economy might experience a significant shift in the balance of power.

The UK, as one of the most enthusiastic adopters of the creative industries concept makes an interesting test case in this context. Nearly ten years on from the UK government's adoption of the creative industries as a major theme in cultural policy, some of the gloss on Cool Britannia is beginning to fade. Television export earnings have proved disappointing despite the UK's obvious advantages resulting from English language content and strategic proximity to both US and European markets. In other sub-sectors, such as music, encouraging statistics disguise the extent to which the industry is actually living off past glories rather than from a burgeoning of new talent. During the 1990s, the major export earners in the UK music industry were the back catalogues of successful rock acts from the 1960s and 1970s. In terms of current popular chart success, the UK's music industry was frequently overtaken by several of the Scandinavian countries, notably Sweden, where there has been a much more concerted attempt to invest in the grassroots infrastructure.

The UK's faith in individual talent has likewise proved misplaced. Colin Welland's celebrated announcement that 'The British are coming!' when *Chariots of Fire* won its Best Film Oscar in 1981 marked a historical moment when individual talent was equated with industrial success. The British have continued to come to the Oscars, winning more than their share of Academy Awards, but this has been largely irrelevant to the success or failure of the UK film industry. Individual artists, in spite of the European 'auteur theory' of the late 1960s and the way in which individual directors and stars are marketed and branded today, are not the sole or primary creators of films. Successful artists and award-winning films do not make a successful industry. Attempts to define a particular film's identity according to the national identity of its individual talents may be an effective way of securing tax breaks or co-production deals, but it is of limited relevance to the development of a national film industry. British film talents have continued to cross the Atlantic, leaving the UK film industry behind them.

UK employment and growth projections for the creative industries have also proved optimistic, overlooking the extent to which the sector is characterized by self-employment and micro-enterprise. Across the small business sector as a whole, business expansion is the exception rather than the rule; in the creative industries, additional reasons for entrepreneurs to be cautious about growing their business were noted in chapter 6. The creative sector is further characterized by high levels of 'churn', partly as a result of informal patterns of organization and employment, partly reflecting the project-based nature of much creative enterprise. The tacit assumption that the creative industries might 'replace' traditional manufacturing industries as a provider of mass employment now appears naive. The UK's endorsement of its creative industries has largely been to claim the credit retrospectively for its success stories, and to claim kinship with the individual talents who have succeeded in global markets, ignoring the systems and networks on which these talents and successes depend. Only very recently has the UK begun to invest more seriously in this underlying infrastructure, for example in its support for distribution, exhibition and training and development through the UK Film Council.

The neo-liberal trends in cultural policies outlined in this section are closely allied to Western assumptions about creativity and the creative industries. By defining creativity in relation to its economic outcomes, and by identifying individual talent as the basis of the creative industries, cultural policy makers have moved towards a neo-liberal model which favours deregulation of markets, and an emphasis on global brands at the expense of national and local cultural content. The experience of the UK indicates that while this is being promoted as a route to a thriving national creative economy, its sustainability, even as a purely economic strategy, is open to question. Creativity and the creative industries are locked into complex social interactions and embedded in local cultures and communities which the neo-liberal model does its best to ignore. Ideas and products in the creative industries are not simply the spontaneous outpourings of gifted individuals; they follow a complex evolution through interaction, diversity and adaptation. If we place our faith in individual talents and open markets, our policies will inevitably be ineffective and one-sided. A creative economy can only thrive if policy makers, firms and individuals invest in the processes and systems which lie behind it.

The Politics of Management

Neo-liberal cultural policies are locked into certain assumptions about creativity and creative business which I have attempted to challenge in writing this book. The same assumptions continue to predominate in management, both in the creative industries and beyond. In this final section, I hope to consider why and how these assumptions have become so dominant.

First of all, the adoption of the discourse of creativity associates traditional businesses with individualism, unpredictability and iconoclasm. Dressed up in the language of creativity, management is the new rock and roll – invested with a hip, bohemian anti-authoritarianism not normally available to the corporate world. More specifically the individualistic model of creativity reinforces a humanistic, individualized model of organization. The rhetoric of creativity is thus attuned to the new management orthodoxy which opposes the hierarchical, mechanistic models of classical management theory with the flexible entrepreneurialism of 'post-Fordist' organizations and postmodern theories. In practice, this anti-hierarchical rhetoric is associated with the brutal 'delayering' of the traditional organization, stripping out the apparently unproductive intermediate levels of middle management in order to free up front-line entrepreneurs and to release the creative potential of individual employees. Yet a more complex theory of creativity would acknowledge that creativity consists not only in individual innovation but in the capacity to capture and act upon new ideas, to manage relationships within teams and redeploy resources. By focusing on innovation at the individual level, this collective capacity to add value to innovation is compromised.

Secondly, creativity in business is associated with risk and entrepreneurship. Again, what this means in practice is a compromise between strategic centralization and operational decentralization. Risk is delegated unevenly across the industry supply chain. Risk is outsourced to smaller organizations and to subcontractors, allowing the core organization to concentrate on exploiting ideas instead of discovering and developing them. As noted in chapter 4, deviance can be tolerated at the fringes of the organization, precisely because it does not threaten strategic control at the centre. By allowing greater autonomy to those on the periphery, risk is kept at arm's length. The appearance of an apparently informal, devolved approach to operational decision making restricts the margin of risk and legitimizes the centre's authority over the strategic decisions that matter.

Thirdly, creativity in business is equated with innovation and change. In an intensification of traditional competence-based competition, innovation has become the one remaining source of competitive advantage. The desperate search for novelty and difference gets in the way of a more incremental approach to innovation and change, both at the level of new product development and at the macro-level of strategy development and organizational change. The pursuit of novelty and difference as ends in themselves encourages a destructive, self-indulgent approach to change and innovation which does not acknowledge how new products and changes in strategy and structure affect the wider ecology of the organization and does not build on existing competences. The onward rush of innovation can deliver the appearance of energy and dynamism without addressing the important issues where change is necessary rather than merely fanciful.

Finally, the pursuit of innovation in business results in a polarization of the creative and the uncreative. Individualism in one part of the business legitimizes corporatism in another. Risk and entrepreneurship at the periphery are traded off against a conservative strategy at the centre. The promise of originality and difference prevents incremental change. Instead of exploring, expanding and eventually transforming core competences, values and strategies, maverick individuals pursue novelty without value, disconnected from the context and systems which would give their random innovations meaning and purpose. All of this in the end perpetuates a mutual suspicion between the innovators and those who have to clear up after them, and the familiar stereotypes of unmanageable 'creatives' and uncreative 'suits'.

Neo-liberalism in management embraces the rhetoric of creativity, but the creativity on offer is paradoxical. Behind the appearance of change, innovation, individualism and iconoclasm, the consequences of creativity are not followed through and converted into something of value and meaning. The appearance of change does not really change the organization's values or ideals. According to creativity theory, novelty without value or purpose is not the same thing as creativity – this is the difference between child's play and radical transformation. By thinking outside the box, today's business innovators and change-masters are failing to challenge the systematic and conceptual boundaries around their businesses. Ignoring the rules bypasses the need to change them.

Creativity Is Difficult

The creative industries find themselves at the leading edge of a new creative economy, where the exchange of goods and services has been superseded by an economy based on ideas, knowledge and information. From a theoretical perspective, the creative industries appear to represent a new economic and organizational model, characterized by self-employment, autonomy and flexibility, a highly skilled workforce of highly motivated freelance individuals, clustered into communities and networks of specialist knowledge and expertise. From an empirical perspective they represent one of the fastest-growing sectors of the global economy (meaning the economy of the rich industrialized countries), measured in statistics on employment, export earnings and growth potential. The creative economy is accordingly attractive to governments and to industrialists, not least because it seems to have abolished some of the limitations of traditional capitalism: raw materials are (theoretically) inexhaustible, labour is securely embedded in a highly skilled culture of expertise, markets are (potentially) global in scope, albeit rather unpredictable, and consumer demand is not tied to specific, finite needs. Furthermore, while ideas remain a relatively cheap commodity to be exploited, the barriers to entry at the top of the food chain, in the global management and exploitation of intellectual property rights, remain reassuringly high.

Creativity, meanwhile, is claimed as the source code for the new management theory, encompassing everything from individual empowerment to innovation and flexible specialization. Creativity is the magic solution to the problems of business, but also to the problems of the economy, knocking down outdated structures and systems.

I believe that creativity has been misunderstood not just by business but by many policy makers and managers in the creative industries. Creativity is not a simple capacity to think differently or to generate new ideas, nor can it be disconnected from the systems and social structures which give it meaning and value. The capacity to be creative depends upon a contradictory capacity to encompass different ways of thinking. It does not lend itself to new solutions but to the unearthing of new problems. It is not a simple asset to be bottled and exported from one industry to another.

If managers want to become more creative, I believe the answer lies not in dressing up in the borrowed clothes of the creative artist or the romantic individualist. Creativity is actually to be found closer to home in a process of managed change. The difficulty comes in the contradictory nature of the creative process, which requires that we can encompass both an inward focus on our own ideas and questions while also keeping in mind the context in which those ideas and questions will be tested. According to this argument artists are not free spirits or irresponsible individualists but people with a capacity to tolerate contradictions and to move between apparently opposing perspectives. Creative management requires a similar split focus, between present realities and future possibilities, between individuals and teams, between organizations and systems. Nobody should pretend that this dualism is easy – it is much more difficult than mere innovation, which may plunge us into the unexpected and unpredictable but does not require us to make sense of what we find there.

Complexity and contradiction come at a price – the engagement with other realities and ways of thinking requires a chameleon ability to absorb and manipulate ideas and experiences both from the outside and internally. This in turn requires what Barron (1968) calls 'ego strength'. Inhabiting other realities, our own and other people's, is stressful. The correlation between psychological illness and artistic creativity is more plausibly explained through this strain on the ego than in the 'divine madness' of artistic genius. Along with ego strength, living with contradictions requires a measure of humility and an acceptance of uncertainty. Keats used the term 'negative capability' to describe Shakespeare's genius, a willingness to embrace uncertainty 'without any irritable reaching after fact and reason'. What is being described here is not mere indecisiveness or vacillation, but a recognition of the limits of one's own certainties and a willingness to pursue half-truths at the risk of personal failure. In a business context, negative capability might be applied by creative teams, allowing individuals to interact with each other and with each others' ideas. It might also extend to a managerial ability to trust others and to hand over control. The personal qualities associated with creativity in art or in business, based on a tolerance for risk and uncertainty, take us a long way from prescriptions of individual skill and talent. Far more important than any checklist of competences and skills is the ability to understand the limits of our own abilities and to press up against them.

In the end then, creativity is difficult. My own belief is that creativity matters not because of its symbolic importance in a 'creative economy', but as a social process which has implications for the processes of change in organizations, management and society. Creativity might not make us richer, but it will help us to adapt to the real complexity of organizations and to handle uncertainty and discontinuity. By embracing these complexities, managers and artists might find they have a good deal in common. Management is a creative process and creativity is a managed process. If managers and artists wish to pursue creativity they have much to learn from each other.

The first chapter of this book began with 'creatives' and 'suits' at opposite ends of a long corridor, separated by centuries of traditions, assumptions and institutionalized routines. I hope this book has opened a door between the worlds of management and creativity. Walking the corridor between them will mean leaving behind some old habits and taking some new risks.

FURTHER READING

John Howkins and Richard E. Caves have both written excellent accounts of the creative economy, showing how a global economy built on the trade in intellectual property and intangible assets is replacing the old industrial order (see Howkins 2001 and Caves 2000). Rifkin's *The Age of Access* (2000), cited in earlier chapters, also addresses the same subject matter, albeit from a slightly different perspective. Howkins' account is based primarily on the UK, as is Charles Leadbeater's *Living on Thin Air: The New Economy* (2000) and *The Independents: Britain's New Cultural Entrepreneurs* (1999), the latter co-authored with Kate Oakey. Leadbeater and Oakey describe the creative economy from the perspective of freelance individuals and small enterprises in the UK, observing the shift towards new business models and structures and alternative measures of value. Michael Wolff's (1999) description of the 'entertainment economy' centres on the larger media and entertainment corporations, capturing the excitement and hype surrounding the 'new economy', particularly in Hollywood and Silicon Valley.

Many governments have produced their own policy documents and baseline studies of the creative industries, including New Zealand, Canada, the UK, Australia, Taiwan,

Singapore, Korea among many others. It is significant that much of this policy activity is now generated by departments of trade or economic affairs rather than by departments of culture. For an account of the creative industries in the Far East, see Keane (2004).

For an account of the difficulties in measuring employment in the cultural sector, see Feist (2000). Those attempting to measure employment in the creative industries must decide whether to classify work according to the employer or the employee, in terms of occupation or area of business, or a combination of both. Inevitably this results in distortions and a tendency to inflate the statistics by expanding the categories. So 'publishing', for example, always scores highly in employment statistics on the creative industries, partly because the category normally includes those involved in printing and other logistical operations.

Much of the literature on cultural policy towards the creative industries is nationally based rather than looking at global trends. A special issue of *The International Journal of Cultural Policy* (Vol. 11, No. 1, March 2005) edited by Andy Pratt and David Hesmondhalgh recently brought together a range of perspectives on the cultural industries from an international selection of scholars. Pratt and Jeffcutt (2002) have criticized the tendency to treat creativity as a kind of 'magic dust' to be sprinkled across every component of the global economy. John Hartley's edited collection *Creative Industries* (2005) brings together several key articles and international perspectives on the creative industries. The book's overall theme addresses the politics of the creative industries as well as the industries themselves. Within the UK the most comprehensive exploration of cultural policies towards the creative industries is David Hesmondhalgh's *The Cultural Industries* (2002).

For a critical perspective on neo-liberal cultural policies, see McGuigan (2004: chapter 2; and 2005).

NOTES

1   From 'Capitalising on Creativity', special supplement in *New Statesman*, 5 October 2005, pp. vii–viii. The book in question was a collection of speeches by the then UK Secretary of State for Culture, Media and Sport, the Right Hon. Chris Smith MP.
2   'Creativity is not necessarily an economic activity but may become so when it produces an idea with economic implications or a tradeable product' (Howkins 2001: x).

BIBLIOGRAPHY

Adams, J. L. (2001) *Conceptual Blockbusting: A Guide to Better Ideas*. Perseus Books, Cambridge, MA [1974].

Adorno, T. W. (1991) On the fetish character in music and the regression of listening. In T. W. Adorno, *The Culture Industry: Selected Essays on Mass Culture*, edited with an introduction by J. M. Bernstein. Routledge, London, pp. 26–52.

Adorno, T. W. and Horkheimer, M. (1979) The culture industry: Enlightenment as mass deception. In *Dialectic of Enlightenment*, tr. John Cumming. Verso, London [1944]), pp. 120–67.

Amabile, T. M. (1988) A model of creativity and innovation in organizations. *Research in Organizational Behaviour* 10, pp. 123–67.

Amabile, T. M. (1990) Within you, without me: The social psychology of creativity. In M. A. Runco and R. S. Albert (eds.), *Theories of Creativity*. Sage, Newbury Park/London.

Amabile, T. M. (1998) How to kill creativity. *Harvard Business Review* 76 (5), pp. 76–87.

Amin, A. (ed.) (1994) *Postfordism: A Reader*. Oxford University Press, Oxford.

Ang, I. (1991) *Desperately Seeking the Audience*. Routledge, London.

Angwin, D. (2003) Strategy as exploration and interconnection. In S. Cummings and D. Wilson (eds.), *Images of Strategy*. Blackwell Publishing, Oxford, pp. 228–65.

Ansoff, H. I. (1987) *Corporate Strategy*, revised edn. Penguin, London.

Banks, M., Calvey, D., Owen, J. and Russell, D. (2002) Where the art is: Defining and managing creativity in new media SMEs. *Creativity and Innovation Management* 11 (4), pp. 255–64.

Barlow, J. P. (1992) *Selling Wine without Bottles: The Economy of Mind on the Global Net* (available online at <www.eff.org/IP??f=idea_economy.article.txt>).

Barrett, F. J. (1988) Creativity and improvisation in jazz and organizations: Implications for organizational learning. *Organization Science* 9 (5), pp. 605–22.

Barron, F. (1958) The psychology of imagination. *Scientific American* 199 (3), pp. 251–66.

Barron, F. (1968) *Creativity and Personal Freedom*. Van Nostrand, Princeton, NJ.

Barthes, R. (1977) The death of the artist. In R. Barthes, *Image-Music-Text*. Fontana, London.

Barwise, P. and Ehrenberg, A. (1988) *Television and its Audience*. Sage, London.

Becker, H. (1982) *Art Worlds*. UCLA Press, Los Angeles.

Beer, J. (1959) *Coleridge the Visionary*. London: Chatto & Windus.

Belbin, R. M. (1993) *Team Roles at Work*. Butterworth-Heinemann, Oxford.

Benjamin, W. (1979) The work of art in the age of mechanical reproduction. In W. Benjamin, *Illuminations*, tr. H. Zohn. Fontana, London, pp. 219–53.

Bilton, C. (1999) Risky business: The independent production sector in Britain's creative industries. *International Journal of Cultural Policy* 6 (1), pp. 17–39.

Bilton, C. (2000) Disorganised creativity: The challenge for British cultural policy for the creative industries. *Boekmancahier* 45, pp. 273–86.

Bilton, C. and Leary, R. (2002) What can managers do for creativity? Brokering creativity in the creative industries. *International Journal of Cultural Policy* 8 (1), pp. 49–64.

Björkegren, D. (1993) Arts management. *Journal of Socio-Economics* 22 (4), pp. 379–95.

Björkegren, D. (1996) *The Culture Business: Management Strategies for the Arts-Related Business.* Routledge, London.

Blair, H. and Rainnie, A. (2000) Flexible films? *Media Culture and Society* 22 (2), pp. 187–204.

Boden, M. (1992) *The Creative Mind: Myths and Mechanisms.* Abacus, London.

Boden, M. (ed.) (1994) *Dimensions of Creativity.* MIT Press / Bradford Books, Cambridge, MA / London.

Bollier, D. (2002) *Silent Theft: The Private Plunder of Our Common Wealth.* Routledge, London.

Boorsma, M. (2006) A strategic logic for arts marketing: Integrating customer value and artistic objectives. *International Journal of Cultural Policy* 12 (1), pp. 73–92.

Bourdieu, P. (1984) *Distinction: A Social Critique of the Judgement of Taste.* Routledge, London.

Bourdieu, P. (1993) *The Field of Cultural Production: Essays on Art and Literature.* Polity Press, Cambridge.

Bourdieu, P. (1996) *The Rules of Art: Genesis and Structure of the Literary Field,* tr. Susan Emanuel. Polity Press, Cambridge [1992].

Brindley, P. (2000) *New Musical Entrepreneurs.* Institute for Public Policy Research, London.

Brown, S. (1996) Art or science? Fifty years of marketing debate. *Journal of Marketing Management* 12, pp. 243–67.

Brown, S. (1998) *Postmodern Marketing 2: Telling Tales.* International Thomson Business Press, London.

Burnett, R. (1996) *The Global Jukebox: The International Music Industry.* Routledge, London.

Burns, P. and Dewhurst, J. (eds.) (1996) *Small Business and Entrepreneurship,* 2nd edn. Macmillan Business, Basingstoke.

Carson, D., Cromie, S., McGowan, P. and Hill, J. (1995) *Marketing and Entrepreneurship in SMEs: An Innovative Approach.* Prentice Hall, London.

Caves, R. E. (2000) *Creative Industries: Contracts between Art and Commerce.* Harvard University Press, Cambridge, MA / London.

Chandler, A. (1977) *The Visible Hand: The Managerial Revolution in American Business.* Harvard University Press, Cambridge, MA / London.

Churchill, N. C. and Lewis, V. L. (1983) The five stages of small business growth. *Harvard Business Review* 61 (3), pp. 30–50.

Cohen, M., March, J. and Olsen, J. (1972) A garbage can model of organizational choice. *Administrative Science Quarterly* 17, pp. 1–25.

Colbert, F. (1994) *Marketing Culture and the Arts.* Morin, Boucherville.

Cova, B. (1996) The postmodern explained to managers: Implications for marketing. *Business Horizons* (November–December), pp. 15–23.

Cowan, T. (1998) *In Praise of Commercial Culture.* Harvard University Press, Cambridge, MA / London.

Csikszentmihalyi, M. (1988) Society, culture, and person: A systems view of creativity. In R. J. Sternberg (ed.), *The Nature of Creativity: Contemporary Psychological Perspectives.* Cambridge University Press, Cambridge, pp. 325–39.

Csikszentmihalyi, M. (1999) Implications of a systems perspective for the study of creativity. In R. J. Sternberg (ed.), *Handbook of Creativity*. Cambridge University Press, Cambridge.

Cummings, S. and Wilson, D. (eds.) (2003) *Images of Strategy*. Blackwell Publishing, Oxford.

Davis, H. and Scase, R. (2000) *Managing Creativity: The Dynamics of Work and Organization*. Open University Press, London.

Dawkins, R. (1989) Memes: The new replicators. In *The Selfish Gene*. Oxford University Press, Oxford/New York [1976].

De Bono, E. (1982) *Lateral Thinking for Management: A Handbook*. Penguin, Harmondsworth.

De Bono, E. (1993) *Serious Creativity: Using the Power of Lateral Thinking to Create New Ideas*. HarperCollins Business, London.

Department of Culture, Media and Sport (1998) *Creative Industries Mapping Document*. DCMS, London.

Dewey, J. (1958) *Art as Experience*. Capricorn Books, New York [1934].

Dicken, P. (1998) *Global Shift: Transforming the World Economy*. Paul Chapman Publishing, London.

Dicken, P. (2003) *Global Shift: Reshaping the Global Economic Map in the 21st Century*. Sage, London.

Diggle, K. (1994) *Arts Marketing*. Rheingold, London.

DiMaggio, P. and Powell, W. W. (eds.) (1991) *The New Institutionalism in Organizational Analysis*. University of Chicago Press, Chicago.

Du Gay, P. and Pryke, M. (eds.) (2002) *Cultural Economy: Cultural Analysis and Commercial Life*. Sage, London.

Feist, A. (2000) *Cultural Employment in Europe*. Council of Europe, Strasbourg.

Feist, A. and O'Brien, J. (1996) *Employment in the Arts and Cultural Industries: An Analysis of the 1991 Census*. Arts Council of England, London.

Firat, A. F., Dholakia, N. and Venkatesh, A. (1995) Marketing in a postmodern world. *European Journal of Marketing* 29 (1), pp. 40–56.

Fiske, J. (1989) *Television Culture*. Routledge, London.

Fletcher, W. (1999) *Tantrums and Talent: How to Get the Best from Creative People*. Admap, Henley-on-Thames.

Florida, R. (2002) *The Rise of the Creative Class: And How It's Transforming Work, Leisure, Community and Everyday Life*. Basic Books, New York.

Florida, R. (2004) America's looming creativity crisis. *Harvard Business Review* 82 (10), pp. 122–30.

Frank, T. (1997) *The Conquest of Cool: Business Culture, Counterculture and the Rise of Hip Consumerism*. University of Chicago Press, Chicago.

Frank, T. (2001) *One Market under God: Extreme Capitalism, Market Populism, and the End of Economic Democracy*. Secker & Warburg, London.

Freud, S. (1985) Creative writers and daydreaming. In S. Freud, *Art and Literature: Jensen's Gradiva, Leonardo da Vinci and other Works*. Penguin, Harmondsworth, pp. 131–41.

Gablik, S. (1984) *Has Modernism Failed?* Thames & Hudson, London.

Gardner, H. (1982) *Art, Mind, and Brain: A Cognitive Approach to Creativity*. Basic Books, New York.

Gardner, H. (1984) *Frames of Mind: The Theory of Multiple Intelligences*. Heinemann, London.

Gardner, H. (1993) *Creating Minds: An Anatomy of Creativity Seen through the Lives of Freud, Einstein, Picasso, Stravinsky, Eliot, Graham, and Ghandi*. Basic Books, New York.

Garnham, N. (2005) From cultural to creative industries: An analysis of the implications of the 'creative industries' approach to arts and media policy making in the United Kingdom. *International Journal of Cultural Policy* 11 (1), pp. 15–29.

Garrison, D. (1979) *Apostles of Culture: The Public Librarian and American Society 1876–1920*. The Free Press, New York.

Gereffi, G. (1994) The organization of buyer-driven global commodity chains: How US retailers shape overseas production networks. In G. Gereffi and M. Korzeniewicz (eds.), *Commodity Chains and Global Capitalism*. Praeger, Westport, CT/London, pp. 95–122.

Gereffi, G. and Korzeniewicz, M. (eds.) (1994) *Commodity Chains and Global Capitalism*. Praeger, Westport, CT/London.

Ghiselin, B. (ed.) (1985) *The Creative Process: A Symposium*. University of California Press, Berkeley/London [1958].

Ghoshal, S. and Bartlett, C. A. (1997) *The Individualized Corporation*. Heinemann, London.

Gladwell, M. (2000) *The Tipping Point: How Little Things Can Make a Big Difference*. Little, Brown, London.

Gladwell, M. (2005) *Blink: The Power of Thinking without Thinking*. Allen Lane, London.

Goldman, W. (1983) *Adventures in the Screen Trade: A Personal View of Hollywood and Screenwriting*. MacDonald, London/Sydney.

Goss, T., Pacale, R. and Athos, A. (1993) The reinvention roller coaster: Risking the present for a powerful future. *Harvard Business Review* 71 (6), pp. 97–108.

Grabher, G. (2001) Ecologies of creativity: The village, the group, and the heterarchic organisation of the British advertising industry. *Environment and Planning A* 33, pp. 351–74.

Grabher, G. (2002) The project ecology of advertising: Tasks, talents and teams. *Regional Studies* 36, pp. 245–62.

Grabher, G. (2004) Learning in projects, remembering in networks? Communality, sociality and connectivity in project ecologies. *European Urban and Regional Studies* 11 (2), pp. 99–119.

Granovetter, M. S. (1973) The strength of weak ties. *American Journal of Sociology* 78, pp. 1360–80.

Greiner, L. E. (1972) Evolution and revolution as organizations grow. *Harvard Business Review* 50 (4), pp. 37–46.

Hall, S. (1980) Encoding/decoding. In S. Hall, D. Hobson, A. Love and P. Willis (eds.), *Culture, Media Language: Working Papers in Cultural Studies 1972–1979*. Hutchinson, London, pp. 128–38.

Hall, S. and Jefferson, T. (eds.) (1976) *Resistance through Rituals*. Hutchinson, London.

Handy, C. (1984) *The Future of Work*. Basil Blackwell, Oxford.

Handy, C. (1985) *Understanding Organizations*, 3rd edn. Penguin, Harmondsworth.

Handy, C. (1991) *The Age of Unreason*. Arrow Business Books, London.

Handy, C. (1994) *The Empty Raincoat: Making Sense of the Future*. Hutchinson, London.

Harrington, D. (1990) The ecology of human creativity: A psychological perspective. In M. A. Runco and R. S. Albert (eds.), *Theories of Creativity*. Sage, Newbury Park/London, pp. 143–69.

Hartley, J. (ed.) (2005) *Creative Industries*. Blackwell Publishing, Oxford.

Hatch, M. J. (1997) *Organization Theory: Modern, Symbolic, and Postmodern Perspectives*. Oxford University Press, Oxford.

Hatch, M. J. (1999) Exploring the empty spaces of organizing: How improvisational jazz helps redescribe organizational structure. *Organizational Studies* 20 (1), pp. 75–100.

Heartfield, J. (1998) *Need and Desire in the Post-material Economy*. Sheffield Hallam University, Sheffield.

Heartfield, J. (2000) *Great Expectations: The Creative Industries in the New Economy*. Design Agenda, London.

Hebdige, D. (1979) *Subculture: The Meaning of Style*. Routledge, London.

Hedberg, B., Dahlgren, G., Hansson, J. and Olve, N. G. (1997) *Virtual Organizations and Beyond: Discover Imaginary Systems*. Wiley, Chichester.

Heijden, K. A. van der (1996) *Scenarios: The Art of Strategic Conversation*. Wiley, Chichester.

Hennessy, B. A. and Amabile, T. M. (1988) The conditions of creativity. In R. J. Sternberg (ed.), *The Nature of Creativity: Contemporary Psychological Perspectives*. Cambridge University Press, Cambridge, pp. 11–38.

Hesmondhalgh, D. (1996) Flexibility, post-Fordism and the music industries. *Media, Culture and Society*, July, pp. 469–88.

Hesmondhalgh, D. (2002) *The Cultural Industries*. Sage, London.

Hill, E., O'Sullivan, C. and O'Sullivan, T. (1995) *Creative Arts Marketing*. Butterworth Heinemann, Oxford.

Hirsch, P. M. (1972) Processing fads and fashions: An organization-set analysis of cultural industry systems. *American Journal of Sociology* 77 (4), pp. 639–59.

Hirschman, E. C. and Holbrook, M. B. (1982) Hedonic consumption: Emerging concepts, methods and propositions. *Journal of Marketing* 46 (summer), pp. 92–101.

Hoppe, K. D. (1994) Affect, hemispheric specialisation and creativity. In M. P. Shaw and M. A. Runco (eds.), *Creativity and Affect*. Ablex, Norwood, NJ, pp. 213–24.

Howe, M. J. A. (1999) Prodigies and creativity. In R. J. Sternberg (ed.) *Handbook of Creativity*. Cambridge University Press, Cambridge.

Howe, M. J. A., Davidson, J. W. and Sloboda, J. A. (1998) Innate talents: Reality or myth? *Behavioural and Brain Sciences* 21, pp. 399–442.

Howkins, J. (2001) *The Creative Economy: How People Make Money from Ideas*. Penguin, London.

Jamison, K. R. (1996) *Touched with Fire: Manic Depressive Illness and the Artistic Temperament*. Free Press, New York.

Jarausch, K. A. (ed.) (1983) *The Transformation of Higher Learning 1860–1930: Expansion, Diversification, Social Opening, and Professionalization in England, Germany, Russia and the United States*. University of Chicago Press, Chicago/Stuttgart.

Jeffcutt, P. and Pratt, A. C. (2002) Managing Creativity in the Cultural Industries. *Creativity and Innovation Management* 11 (4), pp. 225–33.

Kantor, R. M. (1988) When a thousand flowers bloom. *Research in Organizational Behaviour* 10, pp. 123–67.

Kao, J. (1996) *Jamming: The Art and Discipline of Business Creativity*. Harper Business, New York.

Kauffman, S. (1995) *At Home in the Universe: The Search for Laws of Self-organization and Complexity*. Viking, London.

Keane, M. (2004) Brave new world: Understanding China's creative vision. *International Journal of Cultural Policy* 10 (3), pp. 265–79.

Keat, R. and Abercrombie, N. (eds.) (1991) *Enterprise Culture*. Routledge, London.

Kelly, K. (1995) *Out of Control: The New Biology of Machines, Social Systems, and the Economic World*. Addison-Wesley, London.

Kelly, K. (1998) *New Rules for the New Economy: 10 Ways the Network Economy Is Changing Everything*. Fourth Estate, London.

Kelly, T. A. (1970) *A History of Adult Education in Great Britain*, 2nd edn. Liverpool University Press, Liverpool.

Kirton, M. J. (1984) Adapters and innovators – why new initiatives get blocked. *Long Range Planning* 17 (2), pp. 137–43.

Klein, N. (2000) *No Logo: Taking Aim at the Brand Bullies*. Flamingo, London.

Koestler, A. (1976) *The Act of Creation*. Hutchinson, London [1964].

Kotler, P. and Scheff, J. (1997) *Standing Room Only: Strategies for Marketing the Performing Arts*. Harvard Business School Press, Boston, MA.

Landry, C. (2000) *The Creative City: A Toolkit for Urban Innovators*. Earthscan Publications, Leicester.

Lash, S. and Urry, J. (1994) *Economies of Signs and Space*. Sage, London.

Leadbeater, C. (2000) *Living on Thin Air: The New Economy*. Penguin, Harmondsworth.

Leadbeater, C. and Oakey, K. (1999) *The Independents: Britain's New Cultural Entrepreneurs*. Demos, London.

Leemhuis, J. P. (1985) Using scenarios to develop strategies. *Long Range Planning* 18 (2), pp. 30–7.

Lenneberg, H. (1983) The myth of the unappreciated genius. In R. S. Albert (ed.), *Genius and Eminence: The Social Psychology of Creativity and Exceptional Achievement*. Pergamon Press, Oxford, pp. 40–3.

Lessig, L. (2001) *The Future of Ideas: The Fate of the Commons in a Connected World*. Random House, New York.

Lessig, L. (2004) *Free Culture: How Big Media Uses Technology and the Law to Lock Down Culture and Control Creativity*. Penguin, New York.

Levitt, T. (2002) Creativity is not enough. *Harvard Business Review* 80 (8), pp. 137–44 [1963].

Lewin, R. (1993) *Complexity: Life at the Edge of Chaos*. Collier Books, New York.

Leys, C. (2001) *Market-Driven Politics: Neoliberal Democracy and the Public Interest*. Verso, London.

Liebes, T. and Katz, E. (1990) *The Export of Meaning: Cross Cultural Readings of Dallas*. Oxford University Press, New York.

MacDonald, J. and Tobin, J. (1998) Customer empowerment in the digital age. In D. Tapscott, A. Lowy and D. Ticoll (eds.), *Blueprint to the Digital Economy: Creating Wealth in the Era of e-Business*. McGraw-Hill, New York, pp. 202–20.

Maslow, A. (1968) *Towards a Psychology of Being*. Van Nostrand Reinhold, New York.

Matthews, R. and Wacker, W. (2002) *The Deviant's Advantage: How Fringe Ideas Create Mass Markets*. Crown Business, New York.

McCrimmon, M. (1995) Teams without roles: Empowering teams for greater creativity. *Journal of Management Development* 14 (6), pp. 35–41.

McGee, J., Thomas, H. and Wilson, D. (2005) *Strategy: Analysis and Practice*. McGraw Hill, Maidenhead.

McGregor, D. (1960) *The Human Side of Enterprise*. McGraw Hill, New York.

McGuigan, J. (1992) *Cultural Populism*. Routledge, London.

McGuigan, J. (2004) *Rethinking Cultural Policy*. Open University Press, Buckingham.

McGuigan, J. (2005) Neoliberalism, culture and policy. *International Journal of Cultural Policy* 11 (3), pp. 229–41.

McLuhan, M. (1968) *Understanding Media: The Extensions of Man*. Routledge & Kegan Paul, London.

Meyer, J. W. and Rowan, B. (1977) Institutionalized organizations: Formal structure as myth and ceremony. *American Journal of Sociology* 83 (2), pp. 340–67.

Miller, D. (1993) The architecture of simplicity. *Academy of Management Review* 18 (1), pp. 116–38.

Miller, P. and Hopwood, A. G. (eds.) (1994) *Accounting as Social and Institutional Practice*. Cambridge University Press, Cambridge.

Miller, T., Govil, N., McMurria, J. and Maxwell, R. (2001) *Global Hollywood*. British Film Institute, London.

Mintzberg, H. (1987) The Strategy Concept I: Five Ps for strategy. *California Management Review* (Fall), pp. 11–23.

Mintzberg, H. (1994) *The Rise and Fall of Strategic Planning*. Prentice Hall, Hemel Hempstead.

Mintzberg, H., Lampel, J. and Ahlstrand, B. (1998) *The Strategy Safari: A Guided Tour through the Jungles of Strategic Management.* Prentice Hall, Englewood Cliffs, NJ.

Mintzberg, H. and McHugh, A. (1985) Strategy formation in an adhocracy. *Administrative Science Quarterly* 30, pp. 160–97.

Mintzberg, H. and Quinn, J. B. (1996) The Sony case. In H. Mintzberg and J. B. Quinn, *The Strategy Process.* Prentice-Hall, Englewood Cliffs, NJ, pp. 781–804.

Mintzberg, H. and Waters, J. (1985) Of strategies, deliberate and emergent. *Strategic Management Journal* 6, pp. 257–62.

Montuori, A. (2003) The complexity of improvisation and the improvisation of complexity: Social science, art and creativity. *Human Relations* 56 (2), pp. 237–55.

Morgan, A. (1999) *Eating the Big Fish: How Challenger Brands Can Compete against Brand Leaders.* John Wiley, New York/Chichester.

Morley, D. (1989) Changing paradigms in audience studies. In E. Seiter, H. Borchers, G. Kreutzner and E.-M. Warth (eds.), *Remote Control: Television, Audiences, and Cultural Power.* Routledge, London, pp. 16–43.

Mumford, M. D. and Gustafson, S. B. (1988) Creativity syndrome: Integration, application, and innovation. *Psychological Bulletin* 103, pp. 27–43.

National Advisory Committee on Creative and Cultural Education (1999) *All Our Futures: Creativity, Culture and Education,* May.

Negroponte, N. (1995) *Being Digital.* Hodder and Stoughton, London.

Negus, K. (1992) *Producing Pop: Culture and Conflict in the Popular Music Industry.* Edward Arnold, London.

Negus, K. (1999) *Music Genres and Corporate Cultures.* Routledge, London.

Negus, K. (2000) Music divisions: The recording industry and the social mediation of cultural production. In J. Curran (ed.), *Media Organisations in Society.* Arnold, London, pp. 240–54.

Nicholls, J. G. (1972) Creativity in the person who will never produce anything original and useful: The concept of creativity as a normally distributed trait. *American Psychologist* (August), pp. 717–27.

Nonaka, I. and Takeuchi, H. (1995) *The Knowledge-creating Company: How Japanese Companies Create the Dynamics of Innovation.* Oxford University Press, New York/Oxford.

Novitz, D. (1999) Creativity and constraint. *Australasian Journal of Philosophy* 77 (1), pp. 67–82.

Orwell, G. (1946) Benefit of clergy: Some notes on Salvador Dali. In G. Orwell, *Critical Essays.* Secker and Warburg, London [1944].

Orwell, G. (1954) *1984.* Penguin, Harmondsworth.

Osborn, A. F. (1957) *Applied Imagination: Principles and Procedures of Creative Thinking.* Scribner, New York.

Pascale, R. T. (1984) Perspectives on strategy: The real story behind Honda's success. *California Management Review* 26 (3), pp. 47–72.

Perkins, D. N. (1994) Creativity: Beyond the Darwinian paradigm. In M. A. Boden (ed.), *Dimensions of Creativity.* MIT Press/Bradford Books, Cambridge, MA/London, pp. 119–42.

Perry-Smith, J. E. and Shalley, C. E. (2003) The social side of creativity: A static and dynamic social network perspective. *Academy of Management Review* 28 (1), pp. 89–106.

Peters, T. J. (1988) *Thriving on Chaos: Handbook for a Management Revolution.* Macmillan, Basingstoke.

Peters, T. J. and Waterman, R. H. (1982) *In Search of Excellence: Lessons from America's Best Run Companies.* Harper and Row, London.

Peterson, R. (1990) Cycles in symbol production: The case of popular music. In S. Frith and A. Goodwin (eds.), *On Record: Rock, Pop and the Written Word.* Routledge, London, pp. 140–59 [1975].

Pine, B. J. and Gilmour, J. H. (1999) *The Experience Economy: Work Is Theatre and Every Business a Stage*. Harvard Business School, Boston, MA.

Piore, M. J. and Sabel, C. F. (1984) *The Second Industrial Divide: Possibilities for Prosperity*. Basic Books, New York.

Plato (1987) The ion. In T. J. Saunders (ed.), *Early Socratic Dialogues*. Penguin, Harmondsworth, pp. 47–65.

Poincaré, H. (1982) *The Foundations of Science*. University Press of America, Washington DC [1908].

Porter, M. E. (1985) *Competitive Advantage: Creating and Sustaining Superior Performance*. Free Press, New York/London.

Porter, M. E. (1996) What is strategy? *Harvard Business Review* (November–December), pp. 61–78.

Porter, M. E. (1998) Clusters and the new economics of competition. *Harvard Business Review* 76 (6), pp. 77–90.

Porter, M. E. (2001) Strategy and the Internet. *Harvard Business Review* 79 (3), pp. 62–78.

Powell, W. W. and Friedkin, R. J. (1986) Organisational factors in public television decision making. In P. J. DiMaggio (ed.), *Non-Profit Enterprise in the Arts: Studies in Mission and Constraint*, Oxford University Press, New York, pp. 245–69.

Prahalad, C. K. (1990) The role of core competencies in the corporation. *Research Technology Management* 36 (6), pp. 40–7.

Pratt, A. C. (2000) New media, the new economy and new spaces. *Geoforum* 31 (4), pp. 425–36.

Pratt, A. and Jeffcutt, P. (2002) Managing creativity in the cultural industries. *Creativity and Innovation Management* 11 (4), pp. 225–32.

Prichard, C. (2002) Creative selves? Critically reading 'creativity' in management discourse. *Creativity and Innovation Management* 11 (4), pp. 265–76.

Quinn, J. B. (1978) Strategic change: 'Logical incrementalism'. *Sloan Management Review* 20 (1), pp. 7–21.

Reed, M. and Hughes, M. (eds.) (1992) *Rethinking Organization: New Directions in Organization Theory and Analysis*. Sage, London.

Reich, R. B. (1992) *The Work of Nations: Preparing Ourselves for 21st Century Capitalism*. Vintage Books, New York.

Robbins, H. and Finley, M. (1998) *Transcompetition*. McGraw-Hill, New York/London.

Rifkin, J. (2000) *The Age of Access: The New Culture of Hypercapitalism Where All of Life Is a Paid-for Experience*. Tarcher Putnam, New York.

Robinson, K. (2001) *Out of Our Minds: Learning to Be Creative*. Capstone, London.

Roos, J. and von Krogh, G. with Brønn, P. S. (1996) *Managing Strategy Processes in Emergent Industries: The Case of Media Firms*. Macmillan Business, Basingstoke.

Rothenberg, A. and Hausman, C. R. (1976) *The Creativity Question*. Duke University Press, Durham, NC.

Rowan, J. (1989) *Sub-Personalities: The People Inside Us*. Routledge, London.

Runco, M. A. and Albert, R. S. (eds.) (1990) *Theories of Creativity*. Sage, Newbury Park/London.

Sandblom, P. (1992) *Creativity and Disease: How Illness Affects Literature, Art and Music*, 7th edn. Marion Boyars, New York/London.

Schiller, H. (1989) *Culture Inc. – The Corporate Takeover of Public Expression*. Oxford University Press, New York.

Scott, A. J. (1999) The cultural economy: Geography and the creative field. *Media, Culture and Society* 21, pp. 807–17.

Scott, A. J. (2000) *The Cultural Economy of Cities: Essays on the Geography of Image-producing Industries*. Sage, London.

Senge, P. (1990) *The Fifth Discipline.* Doubleday, New York.

Stacey, R. D. (1995) The science of complexity: An alternative perspective for the strategic change process. *Strategic Management Journal* 16, pp. 477–95.

Stacey, R. D. (1996a) *Complexity and Creativity in Organisations.* Berrett-Kohler, San Francisco.

Stacey, R. D. (1996b) *Strategic Management and Organizational Dynamics*, 2nd edn. Pitman, London.

Sternberg, R. J. (1988a) A three-facet model of creativity. In R. J. Sternberg (ed.), *The Nature of Creativity: Contemporary Psychological Perspectives.* Cambridge University Press, Cambridge, pp. 125–47.

Sternberg, R. J. (ed.) (1988b) *The Nature of Creativity: Contemporary Psychological Perspectives.* Cambridge University Press, Cambridge.

Sternberg, R. J. (ed.) (1999) *Handbook of Creativity.* Cambridge University Press, Cambridge.

Sternberg, R. J., O'Hara, L. A. and Lubart, T. I. (1997) Creativity as investment. *California Management Review* 40 (1), pp. 8–21.

Stevenson, H. (1989) A perspective on entrepreneurship. In J. J. Kao (ed.), *Entrepreneurship, Creativity and Organization: Text, Cases and Readings.* Prentice Hall, Englewood Cliffs, NJ, pp. 166–77 [1983].

Stewart, T. A. (1997) *Intellectual Capital: The New Wealth of Nations.* Nicholas Brealey, London.

Storey, D. (1994) *Understanding the Small Business Sector.* International Thomson Business Press, London.

Storper, M. (1994) The transition to flexible specialisation in the US film industry: External economies, the division of labour and the crossing of industrial divides. In A. Amin (ed.), *Postfordism: A Reader.* Oxford University Press, Oxford, pp. 195–225.

Storr, A. (1972) *The Dynamics of Creation.* Secker and Warburg, London.

Stout, D. (1998) Uses and abuse of scenarios. *Business Strategy Review* 9 (2), pp. 27–36.

Sutton, R. I. and Hargadon, A. (1996) Brainstorming groups in context: Effectiveness in a product design firm. *Administrative Science Quarterly* 41, pp. 685–718.

Sweeney, J. J. (1948) Joan Miró: Comment and Interview. *Partisan Review* (February), p. 212.

Sykes, N. (2003) *Envisioning, Enacting, Enabling: Metamorphosing the Enterprise.* Working Paper, Centre for Small and Medium Enterprises, Warwick Business School.

Tapscott, D., Lowy, A. and Ticoll, D. (eds.) (1998) *Blueprint to the Digital Economy: Creating Wealth in the Era of e-Business.* McGraw-Hill, New York.

Taylor, F. W. (1947) *The Principles of Scientific Management.* Harper, New York [1911].

Thierer, A. and Crews, C. W. Jr (eds.) (2002) *Copyfights: The Future of Intellectual Property in the Information Age.* Cato Institute, Washington, DC.

Thompson, L. (2003) Improving the creativity of organizational work groups. *Academy of Management Executive* 17 (1), pp. 96–109.

Toffler, A. (1970) *Future Shock.* Bodley Head, London.

Tomlinson, A. (ed.) (1990) *Consumption, Identity, and Style: Marketing, Meanings, and the Packaging of Pleasure.* Routledge, London.

Torrance, E. P. (1988) The nature of creativity as manifest in its testing. In R. J. Sternberg (ed.), *The Nature of Creativity: Contemporary Psychological Perspectives.* Cambridge University Press, Cambridge, pp. 43–75.

Tusa, J. (2003) *On Creativity: Interviews Exploring the Process.* Methuen, London.

Vaidhyanathan, S. (2001) *Copyrights and Copywrongs: The Rise of Intellectual Property and How it Threatens Creativity*, New York Press, New York.

Wack, P. (1985a) Scenarios: Uncharted waters ahead. *Harvard Business Review* 63 (5), pp. 73–90.

Wack, P. (1985b) Scenarios: Shooting the rapids. *Harvard Business Review* 63 (6), pp. 139–50.

Wallas, G. (1926) *The Art of Thought*. Harcourt Brace, New York.

Webster, F. (1995) *Theories of the Information Society*. Routledge, London.

Weisberg, R. W. (1986) *Creativity: Genius and Other Myths*. W. H. Freeman, New York.

Weisberg, R. W. (1993) *Creativity: Beyond the Myth of genius*. W. H. Freeman, New York.

Willis, P. (1990) *Common Culture: Symbolic Work at Play in the Everyday Cultures of the Young*. Open University Press, Milton Keynes.

Wolff, J. (1993) *The Social Production of Art*. Macmillan, Basingstoke.

Wolff, M. (1999) *The Entertainment Economy: How Mega-Media Forces Are Transforming Our Lives*. Penguin, Harmondsworth.

INDEX

Note: 'n' after a page number refers to a note on that page.

Actors in Industry, 107

adhocracy, 92, 94–5, 100–5, 113

advertising, 30–3, 141, 153
    push vs. pull, 154, 157

Adorno, Theodor and Horkheimer, Max, 129–32, 165

Amazon, 140, 158n

Amis, Martin, 16

Ansoff, H. Igor, 113

Apple Computers, 94, 120–1, 155

Archimedes, 8–9

artistic integrity, 126–9

arts marketing, 142–4, 158

Amabile, Teresa, 73

Aristotle, 14

attention economy, 141, 150, 157

audience development, 142

audience theory, 145–6, 157

Baylis, Trevor, 4–5

Belbin, R. Murray, 25, 43n

Bennett, Tony, 141

'Big Brother', 66

Big Brother, 147

Birt, John, 67–9

'bisociation' *see* Koestler

Blair Witch Project, 99

Boden, Margaret, 3, 5, 21–2, 66, 77, 89, 112, 126, 127, 136
    'boundary tweaking', 5, 125, 126
    'bounded conceptual space', 77, 89

Bolton, Roger, 2, 78–9, 86

Boorsma, Miranda, 143–4

Bourdieu, Pierre
    symbolic goods, xv
    field of cultural production, 64, 127
    sociology of taste, 64, 143

brainstorming, 7, 35, 74, 110–11, 122

brands, 138–9, 153–6
    affinity branding, 140
    brand-based economy, 161
    consumer-led branding, 152–4
    genius as brand, 16
    non-branding, 141
    pioneer brand, 120

British Airways, 126

Brown, Stephen, 156–7

'buffering', 74–6, 82, 86–7

Bukowski, Charles, 73–4

Cantona, Eric, 18–19

Carey, Mariah, 16

Cashmore, Bill, 107

club culture, 152–3

Coleridge, Samuel Taylor, 10–11
competitive advantage, 91, 93–4
    collaboration versus competition, 102
complexity theory, 58, 62–4, 96–102, 114,
    156
creative class, xvi, 162
creative economy, xvi–xviii, 159–64
    definitions, 160
creative industries, xiv–xv, 19–21
    branding of, 161
    cultural geography, 46–7
    and 'cultural' industries, 164–6
    definition of, xiv, 22
    employment in, xvii, 50–2, 83, 161–2,
        170
    'mapping' of, 49, 61
    majors and independents, 54–6
    specialization and multi-tasking, 26–30
    statistics, 161
    structure of, 83–4
    substitute for manufacturing, xvi–xvii,
        160–1, 170
    in UK, 169–71
    unpredictability, 49
'creative listening', 106–8
'creatives and suits', 12–13, 66–7, 143, 156,
    172, 174
creativity see also creative economy,
        creative industries
    boundaries and constraints in, 76–80,
        85–8
    branding of, 160–2
    and childhood, 72–3, 81–2
    and complexity, 47–9
    contradiction, xii
    consumer creativity, 138–58
    criteria for, 3–4
    definition of, xii, 2–6
    and management, 171–4
    motivation and, 72–4
    networks and, 47–9
    organizational creativity, 49
    personality, 23
    systems theory of, 45–65
    tensions, 39–41, 130–1

'thinking outside the box', 5, 77, 89,
    124–5
CRM (Customer Relationship
    Management), 140, 153–5
Crossman, Mike, 31
cultural democracy, 165
cultural industries, 164–6; see also creative
    industries
cultural policy, 15, 59–62, 142, 160–71;
        see also subsidy, neo-liberalism
    in China, 169
    European models, 165–8
    'exception culturelle', 164, 169
    globalization and, 168–9
    in Korea, 169
    national development approach, 167
    neo-liberalism and, 164–6, 170–1
    systems approach, 167–8
    talent-based approach, 167
    urban regeneration, 162

Dali, Salvador, 17
Dallas, 148
De Bono, Edward
    blocks on creativity, 76–7
    lateral thinking, 6, 80, 89
    Six Thinking Hats, 28–9
'deadline magic', 86
decision-making, 108–11; see also
    strategy
Department of Culture, Media and Sport,
    xiv, 14
Deschamps, Didier, 18–19
Dewey, John, 147
disintermediation, 52–4, 147
divergent and convergent thinking, 6, 20,
    42, 93, 95–6, 105, 112, 125
dot.com businesses, 120–1
downsizing, 36
Dyke, Greg, 40, 67–9

education, 12–14; see also training
ego strength, 22, 28, 173
e-mail, 58, 65n
Enron, xvii

entrepreneurship, 101, 119–20
'evidence-based policy', 161

Fanning, Shawn, 54, 57
Fenichell, Susan, 50–2
'fitness for purpose', 4, 7, 42, 121
Ferrie, Frank, 76
Florida, Richard, 64
   'no-collar workplace', 84
Freud, Sigmund, 21–2
   'Creative Writers and Daydreaming', 72,
     89

genius, myth of, 14–19, 160
   branding of, 16
   portrayal of, 81–2, 90
Gore, Al, xvii
Granovetter, Mark, 47
growth, models of
   cyclical/revolutionary change, 118–21
   incremental/evolutionary change, 121–6
   individual and collective, 129–32

Handy, Charles, xiii
   shamrock organization, 83
   Davy's Bar, 136
Hardisty, Matt, 156
Heartfield, James, xxi, 22
Hesmondhalgh, Dave, 22, 175
Hirst, Damien, 12
Honda, 95–6
Horkheimer, Max; *see* Adorno
Howkins, John, xx, 159, 174, 175n
human resources, 38–9; *see also*
   recruitment, training

IBM, 81
improvisation, 86–7, 106–8
innovation
   aesthetics of, 129–30, 135
   and constraints, 89
   and creativity, 2–6, 21, 122–5
   and entrepreneurship, 101, 119–20
   limitations of, 7, 130, 135–6, 172
   and strategy, 103–4, 111–12
   and teams, 24–6

intellectual property, xiv, 3–4, 19, 160–1
intellectual property rights, 61–2, 165
interactivity, 147–51
investment, 101, 120
   in the creative industries, 49, 61

Johnston, Chris, 86–7

Katz, Elihu, 148
Kirton, Michael, 24
knowledge management, 56–9
Koestler, Arthur, 1, 36, 40
   bisociation, 24, 43–4, 95

Lash, Scott and Urry, John, xv, xxi
Lee, Ang, 5
leadership, 94, 96, 108–9, 112
   entrepreneurial leadership, 119
   transactional and transformational,
     71
Levitt, Theodor, 7
Leigh, Mike, 75
Liebes, Tamara, 148
Lockwood, Ben, 106

management; *see also* 'new management
     style', knowledge management,
     strategy
   change management, 102–5, 133–5
   and complexity, 56–9
   'cool' management, 66–7, 81
   and creativity, 86, 171–4
   release and control, 87–8, 134
   'trade-offs', 93
market failure, 142, 167
marketing, 138–58; *see also* brands
   arts marketing, 142–4, 158
   experience marketing, 141, 143–6, 148
   film marketing, 99–100
   four Ps, 142–3
   postmodern marketing, 139–42, 144–5,
     156–7
   product led vs. customer led, 142
   product surround, 141–2
   viral marketing, 54
Marks and Spencer, 122–5

Maslow, Abraham, 20
   theories of motivation, 70–1
   hierarchy of needs, 139, 141
Mendes, Sam, 50, 75
Metcalfe's Law, 47, 65n
Microsoft, 120, 127–8
Miller, Danny, 136
Mintzberg, Henry, xiii, 91, 92, 94, 113–14;
   see also adhocracy
Morris, William, 72
motivation, theories of, 70–4
Mullarkey, Neil, 107–8
multi-tasking, 27, 28–9
Myers-Briggs, 43

Naked Communications, 31, 156
Napster, 54
neo-liberalism, 15, 66, 80, 84, 86–7, 164,
   172
Negroponte, Nicholas, 138, 146, 157
networks
   strong and weak ties, 47–9
   horizontal and vertical, 46–7
   managing networks, 52–9
   in the creative industries, 50–2
'new management style', 66–71, 80–5
   empowerment, 71, 80–1
   freedom, 66–7, 84–5
   personality cult, 81
New Zealand, 163–4
Nike, 138, 141, 154, 156, 157
novelty, 7, 130, 135–36

open source, 54, 102, 148
organizational change, 33–9, 116–37
   aesthetics of, 126–9
   alignment with individual change,
     129–33
   change cycle, 118–21
   incremental change, 116–18, 121–6
   managing change, 133–5
   'virtual' change, 128–9
organizational structure
   matrix, 25–6
   networks, 47–9, 102
   'petal', 69

project-based, 27–8
   'shamrock', 83
   'virtual', 128
Orwell, George, 17
Osborn, Alex, 7

peer-to-peer, 54, 146
Peters, Tom, xix, 117, 121
Pixar Studios, 37
Plato, 14
Poincaré, Henri, 8–11, 22, 24, 95
'policy-based evidence'; *see* 'evidence-based
   policy'
Porter, Michael
   on strategy, 93–4, 113–14
   value chain concept, 53–4, 64
   strategy and the internet, 120–1
post-Fordism, xvi, 24, 53, 64, 158, 171
'posthocracy', 108–11
postmodern marketing, 139–45, 155–7
postmodern theory, 109–10, 137

recruitment, 35–6, 38
risk, 101, 171–2
Rivett, Alan, 35–6
role-play, 29

St Luke's, 31–2
Schiller, Herbert, xvii
scenario planning, 104–5
second mover advantage, 120
Shakespeare, William, xi, 174
Sims, Mike, 30–3
'social products', 153–4
'soft control', 66
Stanislavski, Konstantin, 29
Stacey, Ralph D., 114
statistics, limitations of, 161–2
storytelling, 127, 141, 154
strategy, 91–115
   and adhocracy, 100–5
   and complexity, 96–102
   and creativity, 92–6, 111–13
   in creative industries, 97–100
   definitions, 91–2
   hierarchy of objectives, 93

strategy (*cont'd*)
  improvisation, 106–8
  and organizational culture, 102–3
  and 'posthocracy', 108–11
  'strategic conversations', 103
subcultures, 145, 152–3, 157
subsidy, 59–60
Sykes, Nigel, 137
'symbolic goods', xv, 138–9, 153
systems theory; *see* creativity, systems
    theory of *and* complexity theory

Taylor, Frederick W., 11
teams, 23–44
  in creative industries, 26–8, 30–3
  limitations of, 24–6
  management of, 34–9
  multitasking and, 28–9

over-specialization and
    over-familiarization in, 33–4
  specialization, 27, 39
theatre, 29, 41, 50–2, 86–7
Theory X and Theory Y, 70
training, 38; *see also* education
trust, 41–2

value chain, 9–11, 52–6, 147–8, 151, 155,
  158

Warhol, Andy, 12
Weisberg, Robert, 7, 14–15, 21, 77, 89, 126,
  136
Williams, Robbie, 16
Wright, Tim, 148–51

XPT, *see* Tim Wright